Rethinking the Informal City

Remapping Cultural History

General Editor: **Jo Labanyi**, Director, King Juan Carlos I of Spain Center and Professor in the Department of Spanish and Portuguese, New York University

Editorial Board: **John Foot**, University College, London; **Panivong Norindr**, University of Southern California; **Ellen Sapega**, University of Wisconsin-Madison; **Svetlana Slapšak**, Institutum Studiorum Humanitatis, Ljubljana

This series aims to challenge theoretical paradigms by exploring areas of culture that have previously received little attention. Preference will be given to volumes that discuss parts of the world that do not easily fit within dominant northern European or North American theoretical models, or that make a significant contribution to rethinking the ways in which cultural history is theorised and narrated.

Volume 1
Cultural Encounters: European Travel Writing in the 1930s
Edited by Charles Burdett and Derek Duncan

Volume 2
Images of Power: Iconography, Culture and the State in Latin America
Edited by Jens Andermann and William Rowe

Volume 3
The Art of the Project: Projects and Experiments in Modern French Culture
Edited by Johnnie Gratton and Michael Sheringham

Volume 4
Locating Memory: Photographic Acts
Edited by Annette Kuhn and Kirsten McAllister

Volume 5
Intersecting Identities: Strategies of Visualisation in Nineteenth- and Twentieth-Century Mexican Culture
Erica Segre

Volume 6
Fetishes and Monuments: Afro-Brazilian Art and Culture in the Twentieth Century
Roger Sansi

Volume 7
Journeys Through Fascism: Italian Travel-Writing between the Wars
Charles Burdett

Volume 8
Border Interrogations: Questioning Spanish Frontiers
Edited by Benita Sampedro and Simon Doubleday

Volume 9
Love and the Idea of Europe
Edited by Luisa Passerini

Volume 10
Indispensable Eyesores: an Anthropology of Undesired Buildings
Mélanie van der Hoorn

Volume 11
Rethinking the Informal City: Critical Perspectives from Latin America
Edited by Felipe Hernández, Peter Kellett and Lea K. Allen

Rethinking the Informal City

Critical Perspectives from Latin America

Edited by
Felipe Hernández, Peter Kellett
and Lea K. Allen

Berghahn Books
New York • Oxford

First published in 2010 by

Berghahn Books

www.berghahnbooks.com

©2010, 2012 Felipe Hernández, Peter Kellett and Lea K. Allen
First paperback edition published in 2012

Library of Congress Cataloging-in-Publication Data
Rethinking the informal city : critical perspectives from Latin America/
edited by Felipe Hernández, Peter Kellett and Lea K. Allen.
 p. cm. -- (Re-mapping cultural history ; v. 11)
 Includes bibliographical references and index.
 ISBN 978-1-84545-582-8 (hbk.) -- ISBN 978-0-85745-607-6 (pbk.)
 1. Sociology, Urban--Latin America. 2. Cities and towns--Latin
America. 3. Architecture--Social aspects--Latin America. I.
Hernández, Felipe, 1971- II. Kellett, Peter. III. Allen, Lea K.
 HT127.5.R48 2009
 307.76098--dc22

2009047792

British Library Cataloguing in Publication Data
A catalogue record for this book is available from the British Library

Printed in the United States on acid-free paper.

ISBN: 978-0-85745-607-6 (paperback)
ISBN: 978-0-85745-608-3 (ebook)

Contents

List of Figures

Acknowledgements

This volume has been a collaborative effort between numerous people in multiple locations around the world. Although some of us have not even had the opportunity to meet personally, and in spite of the geographical distance that separates us, communication between all the contributors, the editors and the publisher was made possible by our shared interest in studying the development and contemporary conditions of informal settlements in Latin America. The process has been long and eventful. Hence we first want to thank each of the authors who kindly contributed their essays because the project would have never materialised without their support and extraordinary patience. We are also indebted to Marion Berghahn of Berghahn Books and Jo Labanyi, editor of the Remapping Cultural History series, for supporting the project since the beginning and for not losing hope despite the many deadlines that we missed. We are also grateful to Lea Allen for injecting a full breath of fresh air that allowed the completion of the volume when editing had fallen out of our hands. Finally, we would like to thank numerous other people who were involved indirectly in the process of producing the final manuscript, particularly Angela Uribe de Kellett for her translations and the technical staff at the School of Architecture of the University of Liverpool whose help proved to be vital at various stages and when the computers refused to work.

Foreword

Rahul Mehrotra

Today, in most cities around the world, several forms of urbanism coexist in the same space. These varied concepts of urbanism (whether everyday urbanism, new urbanism, post-urbanism or the several forms of indigenous urbanism) actually collapse into a simultaneous – often kaleidoscopic – manifestation which generates a variety of urban conditions. The collapse of varying conceptions of urbanism into a singular but multifaceted entity takes on a bizarre form in the cities of Latin America, Asia and Africa where disparate levels of economic development complicate the already schizophrenic landscape of the contemporary city. In these urban conditions, the physical manifestation of the city is reversed and, here, the 'static' or formal city is most often situated in the temporal landscape of the 'kinetic' or informal city.

It is in these urban landscapes of Latin America, Asia and Africa that the informal or kinetic city can be seen as the symbolic image and metaphor for the physical state of the contemporary city. In fact, it is from the kinetic city that these cities derive their image today. The processions, festivals, street vendors and dwellers, all result in an ever-transforming streetscape – a city in constant motion whose very physical fabric is characterised by this kinetic quality. Furthermore, the kinetic city is incomprehensible as a two-dimensional entity and is instead perceived as a city in motion – a three-dimensional construct of incremental development. It is temporary in nature and often built with recycled materials: plastic sheets, scrap metal, canvas and waste wood – it constantly modifies and reinvents itself.

In contrast, the static city is built of more permanent materials – such as concrete, steel and brick – and is comprehended as a two-dimensional entity on conventional city maps and is monumental in its presence. Architecture is clearly the spectacle of the static city. And while the static city depends on architecture for its representation, it is no longer the single image by which the city is read. On the other hand, the kinetic city is not perceived through its architecture, but through spaces, which hold associative values and support lives. Patterns of occupation determine its form and perception. It is an indigenous urbanism that has its particular 'local' logic. It is not necessarily only the city of the poor, as most images and discussions of the informal city might suggest; rather it is a temporal articulation and occupation of space which not only creates a richer sensibility of spatial occupation, but also suggests how spatial limits are expanded to include formally unimagined uses in dense urban conditions.

The informal or kinetic city carries local wisdom into the contemporary world without fear of the modern, while the static city aspires to erase the local and recodify it in a written formal order. The issue of housing (slums, shanty towns, etc.) most vividly demonstrates the reordering process of the kinetic city by the static city. Flow, instability and indeterminacy are basic to the kinetic city. Regular demolitions exacerbate the tenuous occupation of land by the inhabitants of the informal city. Demolitions inhibit any investment the occupants might make in their physical living conditions. Thus the kinetic city is a fluid and dynamic city that is mobile and temporal (often as a strategy to defeat eviction) and leaves no ruins. It constantly recycles its resources, leveraging great effect and presence with very little means.

Clearly, static and kinetic cities go beyond their obvious differences to establish a much richer relationship both spatially and metaphorically than their physical manifestations would suggest. Here affinity and rejection are simultaneously played out and are in a state of equilibrium maintained by a seemingly irresolvable tension. The informal economy of the city vividly illustrates the collapsed and intertwined existence of the static and kinetic cities. In fact, the kinetic city presents a compelling vision that potentially allows us to understand more clearly the blurred lines of contemporary urbanism in Latin America, Asia or Africa and the changing roles of people and spaces in urban society. The increasing concentrations of global flows in these contexts have exacerbated the inequalities and spatial divisions of social classes. In this context, an architecture or urbanism of equality in increasingly inequitable economic conditions requires that one looks deeper to find a wide range of places to mark and commemorate the cultures of those excluded from the spaces of global flows. These do not necessarily lie in the formal production of architecture, but often challenge it. Here the idea of a city is an elastic urban condition, not a grand vision, but a 'grand adjustment'.

Thus it is critical that any discussion about the informal city takes as its starting point a broadening of the definition of the 'informal' to go beyond the normal understanding of this phenomenon as the city of the poor and marginalised. That is, to expand the original definition where the informal stems from the essential conditions of correcting or compensating for the unequal distribution of resources in an urban condition. These are resources that extend all the way from access to social and physical infrastructure to city culture in the broadest sense. But, the limits of informal urbanism are hard to define or outline clearly. It seems to be a notion that extends beyond the mere provision of the non-regulated, non-official or governmental system. Instead, it seems to be about the tactics and innovations which the urban poor and marginalised people have to offer. That is, their ability to absorb, recycle, provide services, establish networks, celebrate, play and essentially extend the margins of the urban system to new levels of robustness. In short, informal urbanism or the kinetic city is about invention within strong constraints with indigenous resources with the purpose of turning odds into a survival strategy – often a sustainable strategy.

The 'kinetic' quality of informal urbanism does not allow most governmental or formal systems to keep pace with or respond meaningfully to the spontaneity inherent in the nature of informal action. This creates a great gulf disallowing accurate identification or analysis of the condition, resulting in mistrust and opening up questions about citizenship and legality. Ironically, often it is the informal city that is the site of meaningful production in the city and, as Saskia Sassen has pointed out, the informal city is often the strategic component of advanced urban economies.

With this as the ground, the essays in this book add an insightful dimension to the understanding of the process of what makes up informal urbanism in the Latin American context. The discussions in the book make us look again at this urban condition from the perspective of economy, legality, activism, governance and collaboration. In addition, questions of representation – or how to map and register the temporal, transient and flexible – are shown to be lacunas in the debate about informality. And most importantly, the authors in this book argue that the question of simultaneity and coexistence will need increasing attention from the perspective of new challenges in the design and constant redesign of cities: can the spatial configuration for how this simultaneity occurs actually be formally imagined? The kinetic city obviously cannot be seen as a design tool but rather a demand that conceptions of urbanism create and facilitate environments that are versatile and flexible, robust and ambiguous enough to allow this kinetic quality of the city to flourish. Perhaps the kinetic city might be the tactical approach to take when dealing with the urbanism of the temporary, or of high densities and intensities.

Rethinking the Informal City: Critical Perspectives from Latin America will, hopefully, move the discussion on informal urbanism beyond the humanitarian dimension (of empathising with the city of the poor) to look at its value as a crucible of innovation. Adaptability, flexibility, resistance and several other aspects that would inform the broader discourse on urbanism in general are obvious pointers for design. However, in order to make a more substantial connection to understand and inform contemporary urbanism, it is critical that the binaries that have come to define the terms for this debate (rich and poor, formal and informal, centre and periphery, third and first worlds) be dissolved. Instead, as the majority of the essays in this collection assert, the discussion should be positioned in different terms and include questions about the hybrid, simultaneity, notions of coexistence and other ways of framing the issue. That is, to reframe the debate about the informal would sustain this innovative form of urbanism and its seamless integration into the discussion of contemporary urbanism. It is with this shift that the informal city would perhaps be seen not as a condition that needs to be remade but rather as a contagious phenomenon that actually remakes and humanises cities.

Chapter 1

Introduction: Reimagining the Informal in Latin America

Felipe Hernández and Peter Kellett

According to traditional architectural histories, Latin American cities have been characterised by a tension between their formal and informal dimensions. These two terms have been used in order to describe and theorise not only the physical aspect of cities but also their entire socio-political fabric. In theory, the term 'formal' is taken to represent the ordered city – in terms of its urban and architectural shape as well as its cultural, economic, political and social organisation – while the 'informal' is understood as the opposite: the shapeless areas of the city where economic and socio-political structures are particularly unstable and in which culture is characterised by its apparent incoherence. However, in practice, the enormous critical capacity assigned to the terms formal and informal casts a shadow of scepticism over their ability to embody the complex conditions that they attempt to represent. The terms are either used in order to encompass too much – as occurs in disciplines such as geography and urban planning – or they are reduced to illustrate too little. In the former situation, the terms formal and informal never achieve political specificity due to the vast scales in which they are made to operate. In the latter, the terms are reduced to their mere semantic connotations, thus losing their critical efficacy. Architecture belongs to the second category. Architects and architectural historians have appropriated the terms formal and informal in order to theorise what they are mainly concerned with: the form of buildings and, by extension, cities. In architectural speech, the formal stands for the buildings that have been designed by architects and the parts of cities that have been planned. The 'informal', on the other hand, is all the rest: the buildings and parts of cities that have developed without the participation of architects. In architecture, then, informal is a derogatory term used to dismiss anything that escapes the realm and control of the architect. Therefore, it can be affirmed that the term formal represents a spatial abstraction created in order to disavow other forms of space conceived within or outside it. As a result, so-called formal space aims at the elimination of differences, even its own internal differences and the historical conditions that gave rise to them, in an attempt to present itself as homogeneous and confirm its legitimacy.

Although the current usage of the terms formal and informal is relatively new – in architecture as well as in other disciplines within the social sciences – the conflict that they attempt to represent is not.[1] Historical evidence demonstrates that such a conflict existed in Latin America even before colonisation, but became more acute with the arrival of Europeans and has remained an escalating characteristic of the continent's cities ever since. In order briefly to demonstrate this point, we will explore two historical moments when the superimposition of different urban logics and power structures exacerbated the collision between what is described in architecture as formal and informal. These moments are: the foundation of colonial cities in the early sixteenth century and the 'developmentalist' period of the mid twentieth century.[2] The analysis of these two moments exposes multiple processes of transculturation which affected dramatically the formation and development of Latin American cities.[3] In turn, the complexity of such processes renders the terms formal and informal insufficient for taking into account all the factors that have given shape to Latin American cityscapes. It is argued pointedly that the complexity of sustained processes of transculturation requires us to depart from such a reductive approach – as represented by the formal–informal dichotomy – for in order to tell the story of Latin American cities one must engage with a great variety of factors beyond their physical form. Together, these factors determine their historical and current, non-dichotomous condition.

Brief Historical Background: Formality and Informality in Colonial and Modern Latin American Cities

The foundation of cities was a fundamental part of the Spanish and, to a lesser extent the Portuguese, colonising strategy. New urban settlements were founded throughout their new territories in the Americas on a scale with few historical parallels. According to historical registers, between 1492 and 1700 more than 440 new cities were established in Spanish and Portuguese territories. It thus becomes clear that conquering new lands was synonymous with the founding of cities, particularly considering that 'the colonial city was the centre of power and domination' (Hardoy 1982: 23). Cities served as a means for the colonisers to impose their own socio-political and economic structures, thereby establishing themselves in a position of authority. Hence, cities had to be planned in order to materialise such a hierarchical structure, and this was achieved through the use of a perfect orthogonal grid. The order imposed by this highly rationalised urban space constituted a violent act of appropriation and denial – appropriation in the sense that it marked the seizure of the conquered territory, and denial because pre-existing, or consequent, structures that did not comply with the newly imposed system were utterly rejected.

Orthogonal planning has a long history dating back to pre-Roman times. The present form of many Latin American cities can be traced back directly to the founding of the Spanish colonial settlements which after 1573 followed the *Ordenanzas* of Philip II (Law of the Indies), and which owe much to the Classical treatise of Vitrivius (Kostoff 1991: 114). However there was also a long experience with formal layouts in the Americas prior to the arrival of Europeans. Several pre-Columbian cultures employed grid plans for ceremonial and military settlements (e.g., Aztec Tenochtitlan; pre-Inca Chanchan; Inca Cuzco and Ollantaytambo). Some authors suggest that knowledge of these cities combined with the experience of founding the early cities may have influenced the *Ordenanzas* (Kostof 1991: 115; García Fernández 1989: 217). In contrast, Portuguese colonial cities lacked overarching planning principles. Even though there are a few examples of regular town planning, most Portuguese cities were mostly irregular in an attempt to respond to the topographical features of their location.

In spite of their similar layouts, the imposition of an urban grid in places where Spanish foundations coincided with pre-existing indigenous settlements –such as Cuzco or Tenochtitlán – was particularly dramatic.

The violence of the colonial (Spanish) city as an act of simultaneous appropriation and denial is seen in the fact that while the physical layouts of indigenous and colonial cities (particularly Spanish ones) shared multiple formal features, the socio-political implications attached to such forms did not correspond. The *Ordenanzas* of Philip II were the official means used in order to endow the Spanish orthogonal city plan with authority to undermine the architecture and layout of indigenous settlements. The clash between indigenous and colonial cities was reinforced by the subsequent physical segregation of indigenous people who were not allowed to live inside the formal city but were pushed to its perimeter.[4] Despite the fact that on the periphery indigenous settlements continued to develop – initiating the contrast between the ordered centre and the so-called 'informal periphery' which still persists in many cities – the imposed hierarchy meant that their architectures were not fully recorded and, consequently, never historicised. It is important to note here that the ambiguity of the colonialist strategy of simultaneously appropriating and denying renders the authority entrusted to the planned city, as expressed in the *Ordenanzas* of Philip II, highly questionable.

But if the architectures of indigenous groups in the period of the first colonial foundations have been poorly historicised, the contribution of other groups has received even less attention, or none. Commonly, traditional accounts about the formation of early colonial cities overlook the fact that the indigenes and Spanish were not the only groups that participated in the processes: black African people who were brought as slaves represented a third significant group that contributed actively to the consolidation of colonial cities.

Unlike indigenes, black slaves lived both inside the perimeter of the Spanish city as servants and in the country as mining and agricultural labourers. Despite their captivity, slaves surreptitiously appropriated areas of the city, and made subtle spatial alterations in order to perform occasional collective activities. In time, slaves found ways to escape from their owners and settled on the periphery of cities alongside the indigenous population, although their social and cultural traditions did not mix completely. The forms of slaves' settlements and their architectures differed greatly from those of indigenous groups and from the Spanish. However, the subtle alterations carried out by black slaves inside the city, and the architectures of their peripheral settlements have never been studied from an architectural perspective.[5]

Nonetheless, it is clear that there were not only two, but a multiplicity of architectures and urban logics coexisting inside and outside the

Spanish and Portuguese colonial city. Given the circumstances of the groups involved, such coexistence was rarely harmonious. On the contrary, in most cases their coexistence was antagonistic. Considering also that each of these groups underwent historical processes of transculturation, prior to and during colonisation, each of them contained internal differences.[6] At this point, we can conclude that the complex coexistence of the three heterogeneous groups challenges the clean dichotomy between formal and informal because the so-called formal centre was already inhabited by a degree of informality and the informal periphery included multiple elements: indigenes and black slaves of different origins. There were also significant geographic variations throughout the vast continent, which inevitably led to variations from the diagrammatic plan, especially in the Portuguese territories.

With some deviation – particularly in socio-political terms – the urban conditions described so far were maintained for over three hundred years as the cities gradually expanded. However, towards the middle of the twentieth century, predominantly between the 1940s and 1960s, the ambiguous relationship between the formal and the informal was exacerbated by the emergence of a precarious industrialisation. This caused the colonial centre to become obsolete, as it was no longer able to satisfy the demands of the modern city, either in scale or in typology. New urban models were applied in order to 'modernise' the city. The urban grid was expanded and its scale enlarged to cope with new forms of transport, production and commercialisation. Moreover, new and larger architectural typologies were developed which dwarfed pre-existing buildings. Thus, the colonial city was increasingly displaced by the emergence of alternative centres which, in turn, replaced its dominant functions (social, cultural, political and symbolic).

Industrialisation and changes in rural practices also caused an accelerating mass migration of labourers from rural areas to major cities, which gave rise to numerous informal settlements on the perimeter of the newly expanded modern city. Like the peripheral settlements around the colonial city, these settlements – known today as *favelas*, *invasiones* and *barrios* among other terms – were not homogeneous. On the contrary, they were, and still are, comprised of people from different rural origins, races and socio-cultural groups who lived on the periphery but worked in the city centre or new industrial areas. In the periphery some migrants tried to replicate the rural environments where they used to live while others attempted to reproduce the forms of the affluent classes. In the city, they carried out aggressive spatial alterations and introduced new activities which transformed the order of the former city centre.[7]

Although most of the capitals and major Latin American cities were founded early in the colonial period, there is one obvious exception: Brasilia, which is a paradigmatic example of Latin American architecture and planning during this industrialisation period. It is a fascinating case because it echoes in several ways the processes by which the early colonial cities were planned. The formal orthogonal planning of the colonial city was substituted in Brasilia by the modernist planning principles of the hugely influential Congrès International de l'Architecture Moderne, or CIAM,[8] in an attempt to embody the modernist and nationalist aspirations of the Brazilian state. In both cases an 'ideal' social order was imposed through rigid planning which made tangible in built form and space the power and value system of those in authority. Despite the radical credentials of Lucio Costa and Oscar Niemeyer, the planning and design of Brasilia demonstrates the exclusionary and narrow nature of this vision for the new capital. In the colonial city there was no place for the indigenes; in Brasilia there was no place for the manual workers who had literally built the city. In both cases these people had to make their own cities beyond the boundaries (physical as well as social) of the formal cities which were intended only for the affluent and powerful.

The above-mentioned examples illustrate complex processes of urban and architectural transculturation that have never been fully studied from an architectural perspective. As with the case of indigenous and slave settlements, twentieth-century informal cities and settlements have been dismissed for not corresponding with the idea of the modern city, which, as Rahul Mehrotra points out in his Foreword to this volume, offered a new paradigm of 'formality'. However, the present study shows how, at this moment, the formal and the informal have become not only inseparable and interdependent but also indefinable.

Theoretical Background

One of the most interesting aspects of this volume is that it shows the ways in which Latin American architects – practitioners as well as theorists and academics – employ, successfully and with great ability, complex theoretical models in order to illustrate the convoluted situation of contemporary Latin American cities while at the same time going beyond the dualistic approach represented in the terms formal and informal. The book includes essays that are purely theoretical as well as others that combine theoretical discussion with the analysis of specific case studies. Contributors are at pains to highlight the dynamism found in contemporary cities, the speed at which changes occur, the transitory nature of many of the buildings produced by common people and the way such buildings obliterate the orderly ways architects and planners have traditionally conceived of the city.[9] Instead of subscribing to a single methodology or a given terminology, authors adopt multiple methods of analysis and use a rich terminology which in many cases is borrowed from other disciplines such as philosophy and cultural studies. Thus, it becomes clear that many Latin American architectural theorists and practitioners are at the front of architectural debates although their practices do not conform to the parameters established by Euro-American academia. Instead, the success of their work rests heavily on the fact that it focuses on specific socio-cultural groups in contained geographical contexts with a particular set of political and economic conditions. This is the case of the Caracas Think Tank led by Alfredo Brillembourg and Hubert Klumpner, the Favela-Bairro programmes in Rio de Janeiro in which Jorge Jáuregui has played a leading role and, finally, the various workshops organised in Havana which are analysed by Ronaldo Ramírez. Equally, the Latin American scholars included in this volume are less interested in generating a narrative of universal applicability – or in joining one – than they are in examining individual cases in order to unveil their distinct characteristics. That is the case of Zeuler Lima and Vera Pallamin, Fernando Luiz Lara and Paola Jirón, among other authors in the volume. It is notable that many of the key theorists and commentators are also directly involved in practice. Their commitment to improving conditions for the majority goes beyond reflection and analysis and frequently leads to active engagement in informal settlements.

This preoccupation with socio-cultural, geographical and political specificity, along with an interest in broadening the discussion about informal settlements in Latin America beyond the limitations set by the formal–informal dichotomy, were among the main motivations behind this volume. Various other thinkers have presented alternative models in order to illustrate the tensions which the terms formal and informal fail to represent fully and, also, in order to incorporate a much wider set of social and political circumstances.

In his book *The Production of Space*, for example, Henry Lefebvre differentiates between abstract space and social space, two forms of space that are considered to be antagonistic. The former, abstract space, is understood as a tool of domination, a form of space 'which destroys the historical conditions that gave rise to it, its own (internal) differences, and any such differences that show signs of developing, in order to impose an abstract homogeneity' (Lefebvre 2003: 370). As in the case of the colonial city given above, abstract space is instrumental for the authorities – be they political, religious or military – not only to impose but to maintain their authority. Social space, on the other hand, is intrinsically connected to the people who produce it. According to Lefebvre, social space 'incorporates social actions, the actions of subjects both individual and collective who are born and who die, who suffer and who act. From the point of view of these subjects, the behaviour of their space is at once vital and mortal; within it they develop, give expression to themselves, and encounter prohibitions; then they perish and that same space contains their graves' (Lefebvre 2003: 33–4). For that reason, Lefebvre argues, social space works as a tool for the analysis of society. Here, Lefebvre contrasts the concept of space as conceived by the elites against the actual space produced by the people.

More recently, the postcolonial theorist Homi Bhabha has developed a different terminology in order to describe a similar set of circumstances. While Bhabha is not directly concerned with the concept of space itself, he is interested in studying the coexistence of multiple temporalities inside each (modern) nation, and his terminology coincides with the issues brought up by Lefebvre. The terms employed by Bhabha are the 'pedagogical' and the 'performative'. The former corresponds with the official project of the nation as historicity and self-generation, whereas the latter brings to the fore the people as agents of a process of national signification which renders the homogenising intent of the nation's narrative both inappropriate and unrealisable. Thus, the performative temporality can be understood as the anti-official or, as Bhabha puts it, 'a counter-narrative of the nation that continually evokes and erases its totalising boundaries – both actual and conceptual – disturbs those ideological *manoeuvres* through which "imagined communities" are given essentialist identities' (Bhabha 1994: 149). This is because the political unity of the nation resides on the permanent negation of its plurality, or, again in Bhabha's words, 'the continual displacement of the anxiety of its irredeemably plural modern space' (Bhabha 1994: 149). In spite of the different terminology, both Lefebvre and Bhabha unveil the perennial struggle between projects that always attempt to impose order and control – generally led by institutions such as the government, the military, the church or a combination of them at any given time – and their unrealisability due, primarily, to the agency of the people.

Other well-known thinkers who engage theoretically with this ongoing conflict are Gilles Deleuze and Felix Guattari (2002). Like

Lefebvre, Deleuze and Guattari are directly concerned with the concept of space. For this reason, architects have shown great interest in their theory and have appropriated it in order to illustrate and to analyse the current situation of contemporary cities, architectural practices as well as the use of advanced digital technologies. What concerns us here is how architects approach the two kinds of space discussed by Deleuze and Guattari: smooth and striated space.

Deleuze and Guattari explain that smooth and striated spaces are different in nature. The former is representative of nomadic organisations while the latter is characteristic of sedentary groups. However, Deleuze and Guattari underline the fact that in spite of their intrinsic differences, the two spaces 'exist only in mixture: smooth space is constantly being translated, transversed, returned into a striated space; striated space is constantly being reversed, returned to smooth space' (Deleuze and Giattari 2002: 474). Such a proposition is of interest for us because the essays in this volume will demonstrate, through examples from different Latin American cities, how the inherent interdependence between these two forms of space operates. Another aspect of great interest to us is the fact that, according to Deleuze and Guattari, shanty towns – or informal settlements – are the places where, as well as through which, the two different kinds of space are reversed into one another.

> In contrast to the sea, the city is the striated space *par excellence*; the sea is a smooth space fundamentally open to striation, and the city is a force of striation that reimparts smooth space, puts it back into operation everywhere, on earth and in the other elements, outside but also inside itself. The smooth spaces arising from the city are not only those of worldwide organisation, but also of a counterattack combining the smooth and holey and turning back against the town: sprawling, temporary, shifting shantytowns of nomads and cave dwellers, scrap metal and fabric patch-work, to which the striation of money, work or housing are no longer even relevant. (Deleuze and Guattari 2002: 481)

In this passage, not only do Deleuze and Guattari establish the irreducible correlation between the two forms of space but they also make a direct link between cities as forces of striation – represented in its abstract form as imposed by the state apparatus as well as by architects – and shanty towns, or informal settlements, as examples of smooth space which emerges within the striated space of the city but refuses to conform to the rules it attempts to enforce. It is not that money, work or housing are no longer important, as Deleuze and Guattari metaphorically write. On the contrary, the point is that economic and spatial informality gain so much momentum – smooth space – in the development of contemporary cities, that attempts at formalisation or striation (represented economically, for example, in registration with social security departments for the purpose of taxation or, spatially, in the arrangement of houses numbered along linear streets) appear to be no longer relevant for these inhabitants.

These issues were brought up by Rahul Mehrotra in his Foreword. Mehrotra, an architect and theorist who has worked extensively on the question of informal settlements in India, introduced the terms static and kinetic. As with the previous three sets of terms, Mehrotra is at pains to denote the tension between the city conceived as a still and unchanging construct and its dynamic character. Such a dynamism arises from the innumerable and unpredictable activities carried out by people in cities around the world – primarily the developing world – in order to respond to the exigencies of the world's economy, or as Mehrotra puts it bluntly, in order to survive. Ultimately, such activities have an effect on the fabric of cities, yet the question is not exclusively architectural. That is why Mehrotra, and nearly every contributor to this volume, emphasises the political aspects necessary for architecture to respond successfully to the circumstances that affect the development of Latin American cities. One thing is clear: no word, or pair of words, seems to be able individually to represent the intricate conflict between what has been termed formal and informal. Precisely for that reason, there is a proliferation of concepts and the contributors to this volume tend to resort to various terms simultaneously in order to make their own cases.

Rethinking Informal Cities in Latin America

The present volume provides a wide panorama of the work that is currently being carried out by scholars, practitioners and governmental institutions in Latin America on the question of architectural and urban informality. It comes at a moment when such questions are receiving more attention, and the isolated groups which work to improve the conditions of life in informal settlements around the world are gaining greater recognition. The United Nations, for example, is active in seeking solutions to the housing, and other related problems, of those inhabiting informal settlements. The UN is also increasingly recognising that such dwellers must play an active role in improving their own living conditions. This was confirmed in the UN Habitat II conference in Istanbul in 1996 where the ideas developed in the Global Shelter Strategy were combined with Agenda 21 to promote increased participation, local control and in situ settlement upgrading within the umbrella of greater sustainability. These ideas are reinforced in the recent publication of the Global Reports on Human Settlements (UN-Habitat 2003), which argues that policies to address slum conditions must go beyond the mere assessment and improvement of the physical condition of dwellings and infrastructure in order to deal with underlying causes such as poverty. There is now an acknowledgement of housing as a basic human right and, hence, of the need for policies and programmes to support the livelihoods of the urban poor by enabling informal sector activities to flourish as well as to link low-income housing development to income generation. This is encouraging given the long history of negative and destructive responses to informality.

As some of the essays in this volume point out, until the mid 1970s informal, illegal and unplanned settlements were generally regarded as health hazards, a threat to social order and a challenge to authority and, consequently, were subject either to benign neglect or actively repressive policies of eradication and forced removal. Such negative responses to the actions of the poor were sometimes paralleled by attempts to build 'low-income' housing projects which were generally sponsored by state organisations.

The Habitat I conference in Vancouver in 1976 provided a platform for those who offered a radical reinterpretation of housing, arguing that the actions of the poor to provide their own shelter should be supported. It was also argued that attempts to provide social housing for the poor through large-scale social housing projects were doomed to failure. This effectively marked a change from the 'provider' to the 'enabler' paradigm, and led to the promotion of 'aided self-help' through settlement upgrading projects and site and service schemes. The most articulate proponent of this approach was the British architect John Turner who believed that housing should be understood as a process, 'housing as a verb'. Through his work in Perú, Turner was one of the first to document how, in positive circumstances, informal settlements are gradually consolidated by their owner–dwellers who replace temporary shacks with solidly built houses and collectively organise themselves in order to install infrastructure networks. In some cases these consolidated settlements can eventually become indistinguishable from formal settlements, especially where tenure regularisation and upgrading programmes are implemented (Kellett 2005). It is this emphasis on process which is such a significant aspect of informal housing. Informal settlements are by definition unfinished projects in which the agency and creativity of the occupant–builders is central, in contrast to architect-produced architecture which emphasises the physical form of the buildings often at the expense of users. This recognition of the aspects of informal construction which are deeply rooted in local contexts has led some theorists to identify many similarities with vernacular design processes (Oliver 2006) and to argue that such urban settlements should be reinterpreted as new urban vernaculars (Rapoport 1988).

On the other hand, the recognition of such dynamism has led many theorists to argue that informal architectural practices do not conform to the principles of other popular architectures and exceed the parameters set by mainstream architectural discourses (mainly modernism) which require a great degree of stillness and homogeneity – spatial but also social, cultural and political – for their full realisation. The contributors to this volume seem to subscribe to this latter position, arguing that new and more dynamic methods of analysis and intervention need to be developed in order to deal with the conditions of informality that exists in Latin American cities, conditions which vary between countries and cities and, in some cases, even within the same city.

To assist developing policy responses, UN-Habitat has recently readopted the pejorative term 'slum' as a collective category to identify the broad range of substandard housing and introduced a multi-point measure to define slums: inadequate access to safe water and sanitation; poor structural quality and dangerous location; overcrowding; and insecure residential status. This means of course that many informal settlements, especially those older ones which have been improved and regularised, can no longer be classified as slums. This makes defining the scale of informal housing a little more complex.

Irrespective of definitions, what is indisputable is that the scale of informal activity is both massive and increasing. In 2001, over 128 million (32 per cent) of Latin America's urban population were estimated to be living in housing conditions defined as slums (UN-Habitat 2003), and that globally 85 per cent of new housing is produced in an extra-legal manner (Berner 2001). In most large Latin American cities informality of housing production as well as informal sector employment is the experience for the majority. In Lima, 70 per cent of the city can be defined as informal; in Caracas per cent of new housing is self-built. Squatters, *favelados* and ordinary citizens are the real city builders and, therefore, it is vital that we deepen our understanding of the phenomenon and its multiple manifestations.

The rapid development of informal cities – slums, favelas, squatter settlements and so forth – was also the theme of an exhibition at the 2006 Venice Biennale, entitled *Cities: Architecture and Society*. The exhibition focused on fourteen cities and presented not only alarming statistics and eye-catching images but, also the work carried out by numerous governmental as well as non-governmental groups in various cities around the globe. Interestingly, the exhibition highlighted the fact that urban and architectural informality do not only affect the developing world but also cities in Europe, North America and other areas in the so-called developed world. Amongst the work highlighted at the Biennale exhibition was that of Alfredo Brillembourg and Hubert Klumpner, with their work as leaders of the Caracas Think Tank; Rahul Mehrotra, with his ongoing work in Mumbai; and projects carried out in Rio de Janeiro, Brazil, where Jorge Jáuregui has been a key player in the Favela-Bairro Programme.

In addition to these entries, there were outstanding exhibits showing the current urban conditions in cities such as Bogotá, Cairo, Istanbul, Mexico City, New York and Shanghai among others. The main aim of the exhibition was to develop awareness about the conditions of life in certain areas of the world, its fragility and its interconnected character, irrespective of whether those areas are part of the developed or the underdeveloped world. While many aspects of the exhibition may be criticised,[10] its main success lies in the fact that it put together, and brought to the fore, the work of groups and individuals who usually work in isolation and receive little recognition outside their own contexts. This is the case particularly in Latin America where numerous people in different countries have worked extensively on the topic – both theoretically and in practice – but have had little international exposure. This volume constitutes one such opportunity. It comprises the work of academics, architectural and urban practitioners, and governmental institutions in various countries throughout Latin America. Its aim is to broaden the discussion, bring new questions to the fore and, eventually, promote the creation of an international research network to facilitate ongoing interaction between different participants.[11] We recognise the fact that many countries are not represented in this volume and, hence, it fails fully to accomplish the ambition of its title. Yet, we take this as an opportunity to highlight the lack of literature on countries like Bolivia, Ecuador or Guatemala – amongst others in South and Central America – and the Caribbean, places whose architectures and cities – either mainstream or not, formal or informal – are rarely discussed. This is an aspiration we expect to fulfil in future publications, hopefully with the support of the authors who have kindly contributed to this volume.

Considering the growing interest in issues regarding informal settlements around the world, and the pressures these issues place on the development of cities throughout Latin America, this volume offers a wide panorama of positions, interpretations and actual projects currently taking place in the continent. The book is divided into two sections: the first is broadly theoretical-historical while the second examines practical interventions and projects in various Latin American cities.

The essays included in the first section, entitled 'Critical Perspectives', study a number of issues relating to the processes involved in the formation of informal settlements as well as to the architectures that arise in such settlements. Some essays are fiercely critical of top-down interventions led primarily by governmental institutions while others advocate the benefits of state intervention. An important aspect of this section is the way it brings to the fore the agency of people in the production and construction of cities. Together, these essays highlight the way in which people transform both the city and the way it is built.

In Chapter 2, Fernando Luiz Lara looks at the way in which popular builders in Brazil have subverted a building technique and a typology developed by modernist architects in the process of making it into a common practice. This essay adds to the weight of literature which confirms that many informal settlements contain housing not only of high quality construction but considerable ingenuity and creativity, frequently achieved through complex processes of hybridity which draw on ideas and designs from divergent sources and which have complex political connotations beyond architecture.

Chapter 3 focuses on how people, through the collective appropriation of spaces, introduce new meanings and generate alternative significances to areas of downtown São Paulo. Zeuler Lima and Vera Pallamin argue that such processes thereby destabilise spaces normally considered to be part of the formal city. In Chapter 4, Annalisa Spencer uses postcolonial discourse to explore in depth the complex interrelationship between the modernist city of Brasilia, designed by Costa around the motor car, and the self-built satellite cities which surround it. Continuing the historical perspective, in Chapter 5 Paola Jirón analyses the different ways in which the government of Chile has responded to the challenges presented by the accelerated growth of squatter and illegal settlements in the country. Jirón also advances an acute critique of contemporary programmes which are presented as an alternative to the 1970s policies of slum eradication but which, ultimately, generate social tensions.

The final chapter in this section, another case study from Chile, takes a rather different view on urban rehabilitation programmes. Margarita Greene and Eduardo Rojas argue that with sensitive approaches it is possible to balance the competing needs of low-income residents, the pressure to bring new investment, and the need to protect deteriorating heritage buildings. They illustrate how, through using participatory design approaches, it is possible to achieve significant improvements and emphasise that incremental solutions can be understood as forms of architectural design that develop, rather than seek to erase, informal building activities.

The second section, 'Critical Practices', contains six essays which look at specific projects in Venezuela, Cuba, Brazil and Argentina. Each project is the result of extensive studies and innovative conceptualisations of urban conditions as well as the socio-cultural, economic and political realities of Latin American cities today. The principal architects of each case study reflect on their own practices and on the contribution that architecture can make to improving the quality of life of the urban poor in their countries. In addition, three experts analyse the historical conditions in which the Favela-Barrio programme evolved and the effects it has had on recent developments in Rio de Janeiro.

In the first chapter this section, Alfredo Brillembourg and Hubert Klumpner from the Urban Think Tank Caracas offer an incisive and inspirational analysis of how we can reimagine the informal city. In their essay they offer fresh alternatives for understanding the process and formation of such settlements and explain how, in their office, they work 'with pencil and hammer' to initiate change through direct intervention. In Chapter 8, Ronaldo Ramírez also examines innovative practice through an analysis of informal community projects which have developed in the strongly state-controlled context of Havana, Cuba. His essay raises fascinating questions about the role of informal activities and the relationship between civil society and the state in socialist systems.

In Chapter 9, Roberto Segre provides a detailed analysis of the internationally renowned Favela-Bairro project in Brazil. He places it in a firm historical context and the theoretical arguments are augmented with several detailed examples from the programme. In particular he stresses the role of sensitive urban design projects in identifying and strengthening formal–informal articulations. Following this, in Chapter 10 Jorge Fiori and Zeca Brandão offer a strong critique of conventional upgrading projects which follow the introverted logic of urban engineering in the context of the favelas of Rio de Janeiro. In their essay, Fiori and Brandão contrast these projects with interventions that draw on creative urban design approaches to strengthen the connectivity of settlements to their immediate surroundings and the city as whole. They believe that the Favela-Bairro programme represents a new generation of urban social policies which valorise spatial strategies and design as intrinsic components of a multi-sectoral and integrated approach to slum upgrading and poverty reduction.

The Favela-Bairro programme is further studies in Chapter 11 where Jorge Mário Júaregui, a lead architect in the project, uses his experience with radical settlement upgrading projects to illustrate his argument about the differing and shared characteristics of different forms of urban production. His exploration of the complexity of urban praxis concludes with the need to articulate the three dimensions of the social sphere: the symbolic, the imaginary and the real. Chapter 12, the final essay of the volume, engages with similar issues but from the perspective of public interest. In it, Claudio Vekstein identifies the multiple ways in which the formal city is informed by informal practices and illustrates the argument with examples from his work in Argentina.

In sum, the essays included in this volume give a thorough indication of the different ways in which architectural scholars and practitioners, as well as some governmental organisations, approach the question of urban informality in Latin America. As a whole, this collection reveals the magnitude of the numerous challenges presented by the continuous and incessant development of informal settlements in cities across Latin America. Significantly, most of the contributors to the book display an extraordinary optimism and believe that architecture can not only respond to such challenges but can also contribute greatly to improving the living conditions of the urban poor in the continent. Considering the scale of the challenge(s) and the fact that it represents an ever-changing set of situations which eludes resolution, we trust that this book will make a valuable contribution to the continued study of Latin American cities, their architectures and their inhabitants.

Notes

1. The terms 'formal' and 'informal' became popular among Latin and North American social theorists in the 1970s. Initially these terms were not concerned with architecture. They were useful to illustrate the development of alternative economies blooming in developing countries since the 1950s. In the 1980s, Juan Pablo Pérez Sáins used the expression *informalidad urbana* ('urban informality') in order to describe the way informal economies operated in Central American nations. Soon after, the notions of formality and informality were appropriated by architects in order to describe squatter settlements developing around Latin American cities. In the introduction to their book on 'uban informality', Roy and AlSayyad (2001) comment extensively on the evolution of these two terms.

2. These two historical periods have been chosen as examples. We are by no means suggesting that the clash between the formal and the informal ceased to affect the evolution of the continent's cities in the intervening four hundred years or so. On the contrary, we are indicating that the conflict between these two conditions has had an effect on the entire history of Latin American cities from before the arrival of the European coloniser through to the present.

3. The term 'transculturation' was coined by the Cuban anthropologist Fernando Ortiz in the book *Contrapunteo cubano del tabaco y del azúcar* (1995), translated into English as *Cuban Counterpoint*. Ortiz coined the term in order to explore the cultural dynamics in operation between Cuban and other cultures. Other theorists have used transculturation in order to study a wide range of artistic, cultural and social manifestations throughout Latin America. More recently, transculturation has been used as a generic term in order to examine issues relating to the cultural economy between peripheries and centres in general; a development that shows some benefits but also presents multiple theoretical shortcomings. For further information see Hernández, Millington and Borden (2005).

4. In some regions there were also separate settlements designed specifically to assist in the evangelisation of the indigenous population, *pueblos de indios* and missions. These also followed orthogonal design principles centred on large religious spaces and buildings (CEHOPU 1989: 134).

5. There is little archaeological and architectural evidence of the interventions carried out by black Africans inside colonial cities. Their interventions were, generally, temporary. The most significant evidence is found in written archives which document daily activities such as fairs, festivals and markets where black Africans had the opportunity to perform their activities, in most cases surreptitiously. The fact that the majority of activities carried out by African slaves were considered to be pagan contributed to the fact that they were not fully recorded or maintained. Other sources of evidence come from black African settlements founded by slaves who escaped their owners on the periphery of main cities during the sixteenth, seventeenth and eighteenth centuries and which still remain. See for example the case of Palenque near Cartagena de Indias, Colombia.

6. Spain, for instance, was not yet a unified kingdom and was still heavily influenced by Moorish culture and architecture.

7. The term 'periphery' is used here to represent a great majority of cases. However, the essays in this volume refer to multiple cases of so-called 'informal settlements' located inside the main cores of cities. See, for example, the cases described by Alfredo Brillembourg and Hubert Klumpner in Caracas (Chapter 7) and by Jorge Fiori and Zeca Brandão in Brazil (Chapter 10).

8. CIAM was founded in 1928 by a select group of 28 European architects who believed strongly in the principles of modern architecture as formulated by Le Corbusier, the organiser and leader. The congress met eleven times in different European cities until it was finally disbanded in 1959.

9. Here we refer primarily to the fact that the kind of architectural practices we refer to in this book do not coincide fully with traditional methods of historicisation and theorisation developed by academics in Europe and North America. Nor can the practitioners who work in slums afford – economically but also in terms of

time – to carry out the laborious documentation that Euro-American academic methods demand because of the speed at which solutions have to be produced and unstable conditions of employment, amongst many other reasons.

10. For example, the fact that the exhibition was organised at a biennial in a time when biennials have lost a great deal of their credibility due to the enormous proliferation of such events around the world. There is also the fact that Venice, both as a city and as the most prestigious of the biennials, represents an elite that is largely exempt from the problems generated by informal settlements, a fact which raises questions as to whether the theme was chosen in order to rebuild the subversive character that the event has lost or, simply, for its power to attract a large number of visitors. One final aspect that deserves severe scrutiny is the homogenisation of the visual material presented at the exhibition. The presentation transformed a problem that has different characteristics in each country into a harmonious experience of similar photographs, models and videos that emphasise sameness and homogeneity.

11. Other initiatives include the CYTED-D (El Programa Iberoamericano de Ciencia y Tecnología para el Desarrollo-V Centenario) which included a sub-programme, Technology for Social Housing. This programme broadened its remit to go beyond technological aspects of housing in order to engage with conceptual issues of informality (see Kellett and Franco 1993), and has spawned a number of continent-wide networks.

References

Berner, E. 2001. 'Learning from Informal Markets: Innovative Approaches to Land and Housing Provision', *Development in Practice* 11(2–3): 292–307.

Bhabha, H. 1994. *The Location of Culture*. London: Routledge.

Burdett, R. (ed.) 2006. *Cities: Architecture and Society*. Venice: Marsilio.

CEHOPU (ed.) 1989. *La Ciudad Hispanoamericana: El Sueño de un Orden*. Madrid: Centro de Estudios Históricos de Obras Públicas y Urbanismo (CEHOPU), Ministerio de Obras Públicas y Urbanismo.

Deleuze, G. and F. Guattari. 2002[1992]. *A Thousand Plateaus: Capitalism and Schizophrenia*. London: Continuum.

García Fernández, J.L. 1989. 'Trazas Urbanas Hispanoamericanas y sus Antecedentes', in CEHOPU (ed.) *La Ciudad Hispanoamericana: El Sueño de un Orden*. Madrid: Centro de Estudios Históricos de Obras Públicas y Urbanismo (CEHOPU), Ministerio de Obras Públicas y Urbanismo, 213–21.

Hardoy, J.E. 1982. 'The Building of Latin American Cities', in A. Gilbert (ed.) *Urbanization in Contemporary Latin America: Critical Approaches to the Analysis of Urban Issues*. London: Wiley, 19–33.

Hernández, F., M. Millington and I. Borden (eds). 2005. *Transculturation: Cities, Space and Architecture in Latin America*. New York: Rodopi.

Kellett, P. 2005. 'The Construction of Home in the Informal City', in F. Hernández, M. Millington, and I. Borden (eds), *Transculturation: Cities, Space and Architecture in Latin America*. New York: Rodopi, 22–42.

Kellett, P. and F. Franco. 1993. 'Technology for Social Housing in Latin America: An Evaluation of the CYTED Research and Development Programme', *Habitat International* 17(4): 47–57.

Kostof, S. 1991. *The City Shaped: Urban Patterns and Meanings through History.* London: Thames and Hudson.

Lefebvre, H. 2003[1991]. *The Production of Space.* Oxford: Blackwell.

Oliver, P. 2006. *Built to Meet Needs: Cultural Issues in Vernacular Architecture.* Oxford: Elselvier.

Rapoport, A. 1988. 'Spontaneous Settlements as Vernacular Design', in C.V. Patton (ed.) *Spontaneous Shelter: International Perspectives and Prospects.* Philadelphia: Temple University Press, 51–77.

Roy, A. and N. AlSayyad (eds). 2001. *Urban Informality: Transnational Perspectives from the Middle East, Latin America and South East Asia.* Westport, CT: Praeger.

UN-Habitat. 2003. *The Challenge of Slums: Global Report on Human Settlements.* London: Earthscan.

Part I:

Critical Perspectives

Chapter 2

The Form of the Informal: Investigating Brazilian Self-Built Housing Solutions

Fernando Luiz Lara

Formal
1a: belonging to or constituting the form or essence of a thing **b:** relating to or involving the outward form, structure, relationships, or arrangement of elements rather than content **2a:** following or according with established form, custom, or rule **b:** done in due or lawful form **3a:** characterised by punctilious respect for form **b:** rigidly ceremonious **4:** having the appearance without the substance

Informal
1: marked by the absence of formality or ceremony **2:** characteristic of or appropriate to ordinary, casual, or familiar use

—*Webster Dictionary*, 10th edition

Definitions of the terms 'formal' and 'informal' appear to be challenging to architecture due to the prevailing assumption that the formal is something that has 'appearance without substance' while the informal has no 'outward form' whatsoever. This situation poses difficulties for us, considering that the goal of this chapter is to examine, precisely, the substance behind the appearance (the form) of the informal city. Contrary to the above dictionary definition of the term 'informal', this chapter argues that informal settlements have a formal architectural structure.

Anyone who arrives in a large city in Latin America notices how the apparently formless city sprawls over the entire landscape as an ocean of different roof materials that changes from country to country. From the distance it seems organic and as informal as the economy of the busy streets. It looks familiar, casual, ordinary. As in any working-class housing environment in most places on this planet, the degree of informality seems to have a directly inverse relationship to per capita GDP or development indices: the poorer the population, the more informal the settlement. However, upon closer inspection, the logic behind the accumulation of volumes – housing units – occupying the space begins to emerge. Although most buildings have not been designed by an architect, or had the input of an engineer – in the strict sense of the term – they are no less logical than those which have been designed by professionals; they simply follow a different logic.

This chapter investigates the so-called informal neighbourhoods that comprise a large part of the fabric of Brazilian cities. Its goal is to understand the logic – urban and architectural – behind those settlements. In other words, this chapter attempts to unveil the form of the informal.

Figure 2.1 The Famous Informality of Brazilian Favelas

The Brazilian Case

Aqui tudo parece que ainda é construção e já é ruína
[Here everything seems still under construction and already a ruin]
—Caetano Veloso, 'Fora da ordem' (1991).

Brazil is a rich but socio-economically unbalanced country: it has the tenth largest economy in the world in terms of GDP Purchasing Power Parity (CIA 2006). Brazil has inscribed itself in the history of twentieth-century architecture for its innumerable elegant buildings designed by an outstanding generation of architects that includes Lúcio Costa, Oscar Niemeyer, Affonso Eduardo Reidy, Henrique Mindlin and João Batista Vilanova Artigas amongst many others. Its urban planning, on the other hand, has not been quite as successful (a point which could be argued for modernism in general), although Brasilia and Curitiba are commonly included in most books about twentieth-century architecture, urbanism and urban planning. Inequality, which has been the subject of almost every governmental urban policy during the last century (although most often only rhetorically), is evident in the spatial organisation of its cities, an organisation which reflects the fact that 10 per cent of the population (the rich elite) has an income twenty-eight times that of 40 per cent of the population (Barros 2001: 12). Thus, inequality is part of the daily routine of most Brazilians, whether you are amongst the majority who live in informal settlements or amongst the wealthier minority who drive past the poor areas every day. For the foreign visitor the situation is even more acute. Inequality strikes their eye even before their arrival in the city itself, due to the fact that from any major airport one can see an endless fabric of naked red brick walls covered by shabby slabs or tin roofs, attesting to the degree of informality that characterises Brazil's built environment.

Degrees of Informality

In order to investigate the formal characteristics of these settlements it is important to expound some definitions and differentiations that will help us understand the logic behind their spatial organisation. Brazilian cities are organised in many layers, not all of them informal. All buildings are supposed to comply with building regulations and follow the municipal code, according to which, buildings need to have a registered architect or engineer responsible for their design and construction and the builders need to have proper employment documents and social security. In turn, the city authorities – such as the council of architects and engineers as well as the Ministry of Labour – try to enforce building regulations and planning codes. In fact, there are heavy fines for not complying with such requirements. However, regulations are applied with rigour in the wealthier areas of the city where the real-estate market may suffer if legal irregularities emerge, whereas in the deprived areas regulations are applied much more casually. In deprived areas, the production of legal documents such as property titles and the issuing of sales and rent agreements are rare. The majority of transactions are not properly registered or notarised and, as with the informal labour market, there is little incentive for people to follow the official procedure and to pay taxes or other legal fees. In fact, the majority of the population is not aware of the procedure for registering property. Such a situation appears not to be problematic amongst the working-class who rarely question ownership rights while tenants live and/or take care of the property they occupy. Yet, it can be problematic when disputes emerge and cases are taken to a court of law. The most common cases are the transference of inherited property and the partition of ownership rights after divorce or separation. In order to properly register a building one has inherited after the death of a relative, for example, the average Brazilian worker would have to pay numerous high fees, a cost which many people cannot afford. Divorce is an even more complex situation, particularly when none of the parties holds a property title. To make matters worse, due to inadequate education, most working-class women have a limited knowledge of legal procedures as well as less access to legal documentation regarding the family's assets, whether a house or an apartment. In many divorce cases, women are simply unaware of their rights, putting them in a disadvantageous social situation. The point to be made is, nonetheless, that with such a degree of informality in the entire legal system – and the lack of education on how the system works – most of the population are discouraged from complying with planning codes and building regulations. In fact, most people do not even know about the existence of such norms.

More alarmingly, when laws are enforced by the authorities in order to correct planning irregularities, they seem not to affect the value of the property in the real-estate market because transactions are equally informal and generally under-documented. Indeed, compliance with codes and regulations varies from city to city or even neighbourhood to neighbourhood. One fully documented example is cited by Amorin and Loureiro (2002). They have analysed cases in the periphery of Recife where owners of apartments in housing blocks have built fences between the columns around their parking plots, or have built stairs and balconies which directly connect their first or second-floor apartments to the street. Thus, it can be argued that the degree of informality is associated either with the degree of social vulnerability or with the extent to which the resident population is marginalised and 'informalised' in all dimensions of their lives, or both.

The Informal Climax: Favelas and *Loteamentos*

Born from a process of illegal occupation of land in the immediate vicinity of formal neighbourhoods, favelas have the highest degree of informality among all the different layers that comprise a large Brazilian city. Favelas tend to be built on land that has been deemed by city officials not worthy of developing for a number of reasons, including legal ownership disputes, problems associated with building on abandoned farmland and dangerous inclines beyond those permitted by city's building codes (gradients often exceed 30 per cent). Because of their topographic characteristics, the occupied land of the favelas gradually becomes divided in an organic manner, sometimes following steep pathways in the case of favelas in the hills, or the elevated walkways in the case of swamp areas, that function as access routes.

Other neighbourhoods, not called favelas but *loteamentos* because the inhabitants do own the land, are born of a slightly more planned process in which the land is divided into plots and sold, usually being paid for in small monthly instalments that conceal an excruciatingly high interest rate. In order for a *loteamento* to be sold legally the development has to be approved by the municipality and registered in the property title office. Most often, however, the legality stops here. Water and sewage, which should be installed by the developer, are often not supplied and remain unbuilt for many years. The problem is complicated by the fact that once the plots are occupied, the pressure is on the city to provide the infrastructure rather than on the developer.

In terms of infrastructure and amenities there is little difference between the occupied favelas and the legally owned plots of the lower class. The main difference might be the straight line of the unpaved streets of the *loteamentos* in contrast with the meandering stairways of the favelas. But while the street grid does make some poor neighbourhoods seem less informal than the organicism of the favelas, this difference does not translate into a better built environment. In addition to similarities in terms of available infrastructure, the use of building materials is almost the same in both favelas and *loteamentos*: exposed brick, concrete slabs, metallic or asbestos-based roofs. In terms of occupation, inhabitants of both types of housing settlement perform similar jobs: they work as housemaids, unskilled construction workers, supermarket clerks and janitors. The typical income for these labourers is between U.S.$200 and U.S.$300 a month. Their educational level is also very similar: the poor and lower class, which make up 40 per cent of the population of Brazil, have an average of only five years of formal schooling. As this quick outline of demographic characteristics reveals, there is a clear pattern, or formal vocabulary, that permeates the apparently chaotic environment of the informal.

Formal Sources

This formal vocabulary is even more apparent when we consider the structures that provide the formal organisation of informal buildings. Two very important factors that shape the form of buildings in favelas and *loteamentos* are the lack of attention given to the design process and the predominance of decisions made during the construction phase. The majority of houses built are based on very sketchy and undetailed plans, and almost always the plans are nothing more than a simple drawing used to calculate the costs of labour and materials. After an initial agreement between the owners and the construction crew, led by a more experienced worker, this very rudimentary plan with basic measurements is used as a guideline for the foundations. From this point on, every construction step follows the dimensions of what is already built, allowing for so much flexibility that it seems as if no design is actually necessary. Design decisions are reduced to simple divisions of space into rooms and later decisions about window and door placement. Given the standardisation of cheap metallic windows (around 100 x 120 cm) and doors (around 70 x 210 cm), the main design decisions become where to place such openings. Little or no consideration is given to solar orientation and/or ventilation strategies. Furniture layout is also rarely considered before it is too late and it is typical to find a dining room, for instance, with such irregular placement of doors that a table cannot be properly placed despite the area being sufficient.

In the absence of design prior to breaking ground, the main generator of form is the chosen structural system: foundations are normally made of reinforced concrete blocks, columns and beams are made of reinforced concrete cast in situ and a slab roof (also made of concrete cast in situ) tops everything. The similarity with the Le Corbusier Domino system is not a coincidence (Le Corbusier, 1986 [1923]). The process of laying foundation blocks, building a formwork out of wood, placing the steel reinforcement and pouring concrete is known to every construction worker in Brazil. The dissemination of this knowledge will be addressed later in this chapter. For now, let us consider the form induced by this system: usually columns are between three and four metres apart, giving a certain rhythm to the volumes. Data from the United Nations shows that the average house size in Brazilian cities like Rio de Janeiro is sixty-seven square metres, roughly coinciding with the 9 x 8 metre average plot in which a grid of 3 x 4 bays would be the most common. However, there is so much variation with smaller bays where bathrooms and stairs are located that it is very hard to see any logic besides the limits imposed by the equation structure/economy. What is visually perceived is the cubic shape of these volumes, highlighted by the walls of exposed hollow clay blocks, almost always following the planes of the structural grid despite carrying no load. Although the walls are not load bearing, they are built before the upper beams which are poured on top of the last row of brick. Such a practice makes for a more economic and more quickly built structure but joins walls and beams inexorably and thus reduces the options and advantages of an independent structural system. Another limitation of this structural

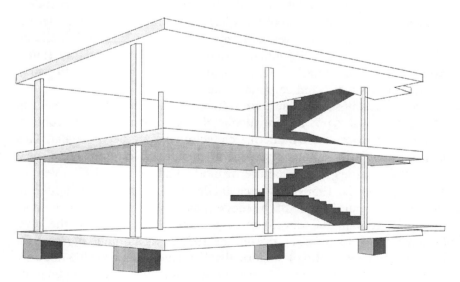

Figure 2.2 Domino scheme by Le Corbusier

system is the overwhelmingly predominant choice of small windows that, again, do not take advantage of the reinforced concrete structure.

The construction follows what is known as a wet process, in which the materials are mixed on site and very little prefabrication is used. The industrial processes responsible for standard materials like bricks, cement, steel, aggregate stone and wood are not carried any further. Local stores deliver the materials on site and from then on the construction crew is responsible for mixing, cutting, bending, welding and connecting everything. The only opportunity for prefabrication is the use (more common in recent years) of small prefabricated beams for the floor slabs. Those beams have an inverted T-shaped section of about 10 x 10 cm and span over 3 to 5 metres. Spaced every 25 cm, they support a row of shallow clay blocks especially shaped for these slabs. A 3cm coat of concrete is poured on top of the system of beams and clay blocks, making it more affordable and easier to build than the older poured concrete slabs.

The question that emerges is: how did the Domino scheme become so prevalent in Brazil and much of the developing world? Reinforced concrete transformed the construction industry in Brazil after its introduction in the late nineteenth century but it was only after the unique success and dissemination of the modern movement that it became a household solution. The majority of houses built before the 1950s had solid load-bearing walls and wooden trusses supporting clay-tile roofs. The dissemination of the waterproof slab, the independent structural system and thin columns has to be credited to the modernist avant-garde of the early twentieth century (Lara 2002: 213). Initially an elite venture, modern vocabulary (first) and modern spatiality (later) eventually permeated all social strata and became the form with which informal cities were, and continue to be, built.

One of the most singular characteristics of the built environment in contemporary Brazil is the prevalence of modernism. This is in contrast to many countries where modern architecture has not been popular. This lack of popularity among the general population is among the most publicised reasons for the failure of modernism (Brolin 1976; Venturi 1966). During the 1950s, however, modernism became very popular in Brazil as it lay at the core of the modern national identity and played an important role in the development of Brazilian culture of the time (Segawa 1994; Lara 2004). In fact, the 1950s was a unique moment for the development of Brazil's national self-image. This was due not only to the international success of its modern architecture, but also due to its optimism, relative political and economic stability and the acceleration of the model of national development, especially in the second half of the decade.

The country had grown fast and urbanised even faster between the 1930s and the 1980s, a period which coincides with the hegemony of modern architecture in Brazil. Brazil had something close to two million urban household units in 1940, the year considered to be the turning point towards modernism.[1] In 2005, census data estimates something close to forty million urban households. Given the fact that it is hard to imagine urban construction in Brazil that does not use modernist technology – an independent structure in reinforced concrete – or that is not influenced by modern spatiality, we can say that 90 percent of the country's built environment is, to some extent, modern. After 1980, coinciding with a sharp decrease in birth rates, the pace of urban growth diminished. Yet, the penetration of modern architectural vocabulary and spatiality has endured, influencing even the few public buildings built during the 1980s and labelled 'postmodern'. Largely due to the success of the DOCOMOMO[2] seminars (beginning in the early 1990s, and held every three years), the fact that Brazil's main architectural heritage is modernism has been widely discussed and recognised in recent years. It is also not a coincidence that the Brazilian DOCOMOMO chapter is the largest worldwide, both in the number of meetings and of its members, because this heritage is both outstanding in terms of quality and quantity.

But the historiography of twentieth-century Brazilian architecture has barely included buildings not designed by architects. While sociologists, anthropologists, economists and demographers have scrutinised the favela's social and economical foundations, architects have either ignored it or attempted to 'solve' the issues with formal solutions that are foreign to the inhabitants. Exceptions are the work of architect Joao Filgueiras Lima with pre-fabricated elements and scholar Paola Berenstein (2003) on the peculiar aesthetic of the favelas. Research by Angelo Arruda (2003) and Juliana Nery (2003), in addition to my own research (Lara 2006), has tried to document and analyse this built environment, one which is not designed by architects but constitutes a large majority of Brazil's urban landscape. Aside from these few cases, the study of this architecture has not yet received the attention it deserves, neither from fellow Brazilians nor from foreign Brazilianists.

My own research on vernacular modernism in the informal sectors of Brazilian cities is prompted by the question: how and to what extent is architectural vocabulary disseminated? If we are going to ask ourselves how the Domino scheme became the prevailing spatial structure of Brazil's informal cities and most of the developing world, we should try to trace the path of this information. As much as it seems an impossible task, there is much knowledge to be gained from trying to dissect architectural dissemination. As we say in Brazil, good architecture is contagious; the problem is that bad architecture can also be virulent.

The Dissemination of Modernist Vocabulary without Architects

Walking around the residential neighbourhoods of major Brazilian cities, one cannot avoid noticing a repetition of certain architectural elements employed on many facades. The rooflines are often sloping inward. Innumerable concrete slabs float above entrances supported by thin metal columns. Ceramic tiles in pastel colours cover most of the front surfaces of the houses. Shadow and ventilation are very often provided by *brise-soleils* or hollow blocks cast in clay or concrete. It is no coincidence that many high-rise buildings in the city centre use the same tiles, *brise-soleils* and canopies.

The insistent repetition of these elements was what first drew my attention to the wider acceptance and use of modernism in Brazil. As the historiography states, in Latin America in general and in Brazil in particular, modern architecture achieved a distinct level of identity (Fraser 2000: 8). It is also common knowledge that modern architecture in Brazil had been strongly influenced by Le Corbusier and the Bauhaus ideals, but somehow achieved a broader and deeper dissemination. The outstanding examples of the 1940s and 1950s, labelled 'anti-rationalist pioneers' by Nikolaus Pevsner (1961), which combined the modernist avant-garde with traditional heritage, can be considered a modernist success in terms of popular acceptance. Such acceptance can be perceived in the innumerable elements of modern architecture adopted and applied to middle-class houses in many Brazilian cities during the 1950s and 1960s.

Though they presented modernist elements reused and redesigned, the vast majority of these Brazilian houses were not designed by architects. Built by the owners themselves, with help of a contractor and unskilled workers, the houses show an ingenious adaptation and application of a modernist vocabulary. Most of the houses that I analysed were built in *loteamentos* of 12 x 30 metres, with a facade of usually only 9 or 8 metres. Despite the narrow plots, these houses present complex facade compositions, usually with one or two major volumes defined by different roof slopes and other minor elements that complete the facade. As mentioned above, thousands of middle-class houses manifest other formal characteristics of modernism, such as inverted roofs and concrete canopies accompanied by smaller elements such as thin steel columns, ceramic tiles and *brise-soleils*, which are even more common. Used to indicate modernity, this popular modernism (as I call it) became fashionable during the 1950s (Lara 2006).

From Upper to Middle to Lower Classes: The Path of Dissemination

It has been reiterated that modernist architecture was disseminated in Brazilian cities in the form of complex facades and elements such as canopies and thin steel columns. While such elements and even building techniques are evident in buildings across all social strata, the precise manifestation of these differ due to the availability of materials or to socio-cultural preferences. In tracing the various manifestations of 'popular modernism', I will briefly discuss the following elements: windows, canopies and *brise-soleils*. I will then move to an analysis of interior spaces. This progression from modern vocabulary to modern spatiality, it turns out, follows the actual dissemination route of architectural forms in informal settlements.

Although the modern buildings designed by famous architects use large glazing panels, middle-class housing usually includes smaller windows which become even smaller the lower we get in the social strata. Proximity of neighbours (due to the narrowness of lots) and a conservative attitude towards family privacy explain the absence of larger glazing on the facades.

The issue of privacy is also related to the use of the canopy or the veranda. The veranda is normally transitional space from public to private space, used in Brazilian architecture to enlarge the area of shading, protecting the facade from the sun and rain. On these modernist houses, the canopy plays the role of the veranda, either enclosed or not. Inclined in many different slopes, and taking many different shapes, the canopy, which is usually supported by very thin steel columns, is taken directly from buildings designed by architects. The thin steel columns reinforce the lightness of the inclined canopies and help to define the space under it as a transition. One very interesting pattern that I was able to discern is that almost every time a flat roof occurs, the canopy is inclined and the reverse is also true, for an inclined roof is often accompanied by a flat canopy. This level of compositional ingenuity is what prompted me to investigate the design dissemination further. The precariousness of favela settlements, unfortunately, does not allow for any money to be spared on formal articulations and what is manifested in their houses is simply an overhang extension of the slab that serves as transition between inside and outside.

Brise-soleils are used in many different shapes, materials and positions, as well as to protect the facades from the sun and to increase privacy. Some *brise-soleils* are placed directly on the facade plane, protecting the window, while others are detached from the facade plane, advancing over the verandas or facing the edge of the roof. While detached shading elements almost disappeared from houses not designed by architects after the 1970s, another kind of *brise-soleil* survived the end of modernism as a style: the hollow clay elements, or *cobogos* as they are usually called. Used as a fixed panel defining the veranda or to ventilate garages or roofs, these hollow elements control sun exposure while allowing for ventilation and increased privacy. Often referred to as a modern version of the wooden trellises (*muxarabis*) of Portuguese colonial architecture, the use of hollow clay elements has been transfigured in the favelas into a strategy of using the very same bricks rotated ninety degrees to allow for ventilation with privacy.

Once we move inside, the plans of these houses (retrieved from city archives) indicate that, despite a very modern facade, the families' lifestyles changed at a much slower pace. The first impression when entering some of the houses is that modernity is kept outside. In general, the interiors of the houses display very little difference between modern and traditional houses. Instead, the layout merges into one predominant organisational pattern. Only in a small number of the houses studied did the interior features match the modernism displayed on the facades.

In a previous analysis I was able to demonstrate that in the 1950s only the wealthiest houses had a modern spatial configuration in which private bedrooms and bathroom(s) are separated from the semi-public domain of kitchen, dining and living rooms (Lara 2006: 106). The majority of the houses built in the 1950s presented a very traditional plan with bedrooms opening directly into the dining room and the wet areas of the bathroom and kitchen located at the back of the building, reminiscent of nineteenth-century Brazilian building traditions. However, such traditional plans often had a very modernist facade, adding a very interesting layer of complexity to the phenomena of vernacular modernism.

Additional data later revealed that the dissemination of facade elements occurred first (primarily in the 1950s) while modernist spatial arrangements were disseminated later in the 1960s (Lara 2002). Plans from the 1960s show that the middle-class spatial configuration moves gradually towards the plans designed by architects. This shift can be perceived by the increasing privacy assigned to bedrooms that now connect to a small corridor and, therefore, no longer open directly onto social areas. Parallel to this removal or retreat of the bedroom, the kitchen is no longer located in the back but instead comes to the front and is connected to the dining and living rooms. The integration of the kitchen indicates that cooking and housework is now part of family life instead of the removed and invisible task of servants and/or women. While the new spatial arrangement does not indicate that suddenly the work of the house became shared equally, these spatial relations surely suggest a gradual transformation in the domestic arrangements of the household that are a move in this direction.

But when we look at the buildings of the favelas, there seems to be no pattern of spatial organisation other than the very pragmatic solutions that result from constructing with restricted means. Therefore, the location of a kitchen and bathroom is due to the fact that a water pipe runs over this side of the building, or the placement of bedrooms follows the history of additions every time some money was available. In the houses of the favelas, thus, modernist spatial arrangements are not typically found, even if the materials and building techniques are similar.

Conclusion: Exchanges between the Formal and the Informal

If I am correct in arguing that the dissemination of architectural knowledge provides the form behind the informal, we must consider how and under what conditions this slow but steady exchange of information and technology between architects, engineers, construction crews and lay people took place. How, we should ask, did a revolutionary scheme like Le Corbusier's Domino house become the basic spatial configuration of low-income communities across the globe? If the simplicity of the scheme and the ways in which reinforced concrete became widely and easily available provide ready answers to the question of under what conditions did the spread of modernism take place, then it remains to look at the means of dissemination itself.

In 1999, I interviewed twenty-one elderly people who had built houses with modernist elements by themselves in the 1950s. In the course of the interviews, I was struck by the variety of ways in which architectural information reached them. If I had hypothesised previously that magazines and newspapers would have been the main avenues of architectural dissemination, the interviews showed me a completely different path. I discovered that people carry information much better and longer than any written or visual media. The construction of a *brise-soleil* addition or a veranda slab was often motivated by a relative or a friend who had been in contact with modern architecture through their jobs or through a third party. Significantly, the house owners recalled this fact more than five decades later.

Figure 2.3 An Expensive House under Construction with Precisely the Same Technology as the Favelas

In the case of favelas or other informal Brazilian neighbourhoods, dissemination occurs through the construction workers themselves who carry the Domino scheme from the architect's drawings to their own households. Once Warchavchik[3] and other pioneers of modern architecture started building formwork for placing steel rods and pouring concrete, the method started to be absorbed by every worker involved in the process. Today, every construction worker in Brazil, no matter how unskilled and unprepared, knows how to build wooden formwork, fold and place steel, mix, pour and vibrate concrete. And when building their very own as well as their neighbours' houses, those men (very few women work in construction in Brazil, even today) adopt and adapt the techniques they learn when building wealthier peoples' houses. Significantly, the houses of the elite and the poorest favela *Barraco* look exactly alike before external treatment is applied to the buildings of the rich. If there is a form to the endless informal fabric of Brazilian cities, it is the form derived from a simplified Domino frame in concrete filled with red clay brick.

Notes

1. In 1940, Oscar Niemeyer designed the Ouro Preto Hotel which is now perceived as the coup de grace of modernism in Brazil. By building a modern structure blended with elements of traditional architecture in the heart of the main colonial buildings in Ouro Preto, the modernist group dismantled the arguments of their opponents about modernism not being Brazilian and, simultaneously, established for themselves an authority over both the future and the past.
2. DOCOMOMO International, also written DoCoMoMo, is a non-profit organisation whose full name is the International Working Party for the Documentation and Conservation of Buildings, Sites and Neighbourhoods of the Modern Movement. DOCOMOMO has chapters in various countries, including Brazil, although its International Secretariat is currently located in Paris.
3. Gregori Warchavchik was a Russian-born architect who studied in Italy before migrating to Brazil 1923 where he became a prolific and very influential modernist architect after working briefly for Lúcio Costa.

References

Amorin, L and C. Loureiro, C. 2002. 'Uma figueira pode dar rosas', *Vitrivius*. Retrieved 7 November 2006 from www.vitruvius.com.br/arquitextos/ arq000/esp053.asp
Arruda, Â. 2003. 'A popularização dos elementos de arquitetura da casa moderna em Campo Grande', Proceedings of V *Seminário Nacional DOCOMOMO*, São Carlos, Brazil, October 2003, [CD-Rom].
Barros, R. et al. 2001. *A estabilidade inaceitável, desigualdade e pobreza no Brasil.* Rio de Janeiro: IPEA, texto para discussão #800.
Berenstein, J.P. 2003. *Esthétique des favelas.* Paris: L'Harmattan.
Brolin, B. 1976. *Failure of Modern Architecture.* New York: Van Nostrand.
CIA. 2006. *World Factbook*, retrieved 7 November 2006 from https://www.cia.gov/ cia/publications/factbook/rankorder/2001rank.html
Fraser, V. 2000. *Building the New World: Studies in Modern Architecture in Latin America, 1930–1960.* London: Verso.
Lara, F. 2002. 'One Step Back, Two Steps Forward: The Maneuvering of Brazilian Avant-Garde', *Journal of Architectural Education* 55(4): 211–19.
———— 2004. 'Designed Memories, the Roots of Brazilian Modernism', in E. Bastea (ed.)

Memory and Architecture. Albuquerque: University of New Mexico Press, 79–98.

———— 2006. 'Brazilian Popular Modernism: Analysing the Dissemination of Architectural Vocabulary', *Journal of Architectural and Planning Research* 23(2): 91–112.

Le Corbusier. 1986 [1923]. *Towards a New Architecture*. New York: Dover Publishers.

Nery, J. 2003. 'Registros: as residências modernistas em Aracaju nas décadas de 50 e 60' in Proceedings of V *Seminário Nacional DOCOMOMO*, São Carlos, Brazil, October 2003, [CD-Rom].

Pevsner, N. 1961. 'Modern Architecture and the Historian, or the Return of Historicism', *RIBA Journal* 68(6): 230–40.

Segawa, H. 1994. 'The essentials of Brazilian Modernism', *Design Book Review* 32(33): 64–68.

Venturi, R. 1966 *Complexity and Contradiction in Architecture*. New York: Museum of Modern Art.

Chapter 3

Informal Practices in the Formal City: Housing, Disagreement and Recognition in Downtown São Paulo

Zeuler R. Lima and Vera M. Pallamin

At first sight, São Paulo is as hard to understand as a mosaic of misplaced pieces. Informal practices of urbanisation and urban life coexist with regulated urban development in a vast territory of contrasting physical, social and legal conditions. The metropolitan region of São Paulo is made up of the city of São Paulo itself and thirty-eight other adjacent cities with a population of around sixteen million residents occupying an area of more than 900 square kilometres (370 square miles). The occupation of two large river valleys and an irregular topography, the accumulation of cultural and economic capital and massive waves of migration into the city produced both considerable wealth and substantial poverty.

Historically, the regular development and urban amenities of the city have been concentrated in the areas southwest of the historic centre, areas which stand in contrast to irregular settlements that have developed throughout the metropolis in conditions of extreme poverty. This metropolitan reality is the result of a process of modernisation that took place in a discontinuous way both in time and space. São Paulo offers no recognisable plan or preconceived layout, even though there are legible patterns of urban development. There are not many visible traces of historic continuity, even though there is plenty evidence of how the city grew from a small town at the turn of the twentieth century into one of the largest metropolitan areas in the world at the turn of the twenty-first.

These oppositions are not new. The Swiss poet Blaise Cendrars described with enthusiasm contrasts in the modernisation of São Paulo during his visits to Brazil in the 1920s, as did the French anthropologist Claude Lévi-Strauss in the 1930s in a melancholic social tone. Later in the 1950s, the massive industrialisation of the city coincided both with its transformation into a cosmopolitan cultural laboratory and with the emergence of organised labour unions. The 1970s marked a strong division between central areas of real-estate investment and the growth of peripheral shanty towns and illegal settlements. Since the late 1980s, with the ending of more than two decades of military dictatorship and the subsequent adoption of neoliberal economic policies, the city has grown more slowly, but wealth has been kept in concentrated areas and poverty has become more dispersed, highlighting the city's pervasive social segregation.

One can no longer identify the sharp divisions between the city's centre and its periphery, which, respectively, marked regular and irregular occupation a few decades ago. São Paulo became more complex and more socially complicated and so did its physical form. A closer look at the historic centre of the city presents an interesting case for understanding this phenomenon and how formal and informal practices are intertwined in the production of the urban spaces of this large metropolis. Although some parts of the downtown area have physically deteriorated, the region has a rather vital urban life. It is still a strong symbolic centre as well as an important commercial and service destination for business and professional people, public workers and a large low-income population living in dormitory neighbourhoods and engaged in formal and informal commercial activities.

The central area is served by excellent mass transportation such as buses, suburban trains and subway lines. It also concentrates a large and valuable stock of empty real-estate property, infrastructure and public services, which have been the target of a remarkable struggle between different social agents in the city in the last two decades. Despite the fact that the stock exchange and main banks are still in the historic centre, the area has gradually lost its permanent population and many commercial and financial institutions have moved to the south-western regions of the city and beyond. Land values have decreased in the old downtown, and consequently the number of tenements and informal economic activities have increased. On the one hand, public and private initiatives have tried to reverse this devaluation process by investing in the construction of cultural institutions and new urban projects in order to embellish and gentrify the area. On the other hand, a growing number of social movements have intensified their claim to create alternatives for the inclusion of low-income housing in the city centre, some of them employing more drastic actions such as the squatting of empty buildings.

Urban Space, Disagreement and Recognition

Figure 3.1 Homeless Protest Group Camping in Front of the City Hall in São Paulo, May 2006 (drawing by Zeuler Lima)

São Paulo, like other cities, is defined by the image and layout of its buildings, open spaces and infrastructure as much as it is defined by the formal and informal social life that shapes and reshapes its physical spaces. The effect of urban modernisation in Brazil – either planned by the state or left in the hands of real-estate developers – has often been accompanied by inequity and by demonstrations against the unbalanced distribution of material and social benefits. Contemporary social practices have expanded different forms of symbolic and political representation in urban spaces, and São Paulo is no exception, especially in the dispute over housing alternatives in the historic city centre. The presence of social movements in public spaces since the 1980s and the competition for specific urban areas have revealed how social and physical coexistence in a metropolis like São Paulo is often based on values that are mutually incompatible. Informal practices have transformed democratic urban life and the space of the city based on two simultaneous political premises: the ability to introduce new voices into existing public social and political discourses, and the increasing need to recognise and to value these voices and the social groups they represent. In other words, the productive practice of disagreement and the claim for social and moral recognition have increasingly had a strong impact on the way the city is used, imagined and produced.

These two political premises have important conceptual and practical implications. The notion of disagreement, or dissent,[1] comes from Jacques Rancière's use of the term to rethink the constructive potential of political conflicts (Rancière 1996a). He suggests that the term enhances difference as an alternate possibility for working out social antagonism and cultural specificities. It mediates the definition of urban public and private spaces, as well as the varying interests of individuals and groups included in and excluded from them. Disagreement entails conflict between different voices, but not necessarily a belligerent opposition. As Rancière puts it, 'disagreement is not a war of all against all' (Rancière 1996a: 374). Instead, its purpose is to foster ordered situations of conflict. Above all, it has the potential to define the mode through which social and public argumentation takes place and, therefore, to reshape the way in which new public subjects and public spaces are created.

The practice of disagreement operates according to what Rancière defines as 'alternating acts of emancipation' (Rancière 1996a: 374). This notion critically goes beyond the Marxist revolutionary paradigm by proposing the examination of the logic of inequality that is inherent in social relationships. This examination, or dissent itself, implies a polemical, discontinuous and precarious – and not universal – process challenging the status quo based on the confrontation between proper and improper values, needs and chattels. Disagreement has the potential to transform this imbalance by expanding the discussion beyond an existing circle of social actors and by releasing new voices into the argument. These acts of emancipation call into question the difference between formal, recognisable enunciation and informal, unrecognisable background noise. They challenge how the status quo defines who and what may or may not be represented in the public sphere. Disagreement is part of a political process that destabilises existing realities by opening up their established framework of perception, action and thought. It presents the simultaneous possibility for establishing a debate and for changing the sensitive field in which different social experiences exist. This change depends on how the debate promotes and affects values, practices and cultural and social forms that are kept invisible and recognises them in the transformation of a common, collective realm.

The notion of recognition comes from the work of Honneth (2003), Fraser and Honneth (2003) and Benhabib (2003) on the organisation of demonstrations against social and moral discrimination. These movements have defined a paradigmatic form of political and cultural conflict in the last few decades. Their purpose is to change the status of otherness, moving its perception away from the circle of prejudice, disrespect, domination and inequality. In due course, their goal is to modify patterns of social representation and interpretation that sustain social injustice. The struggle for recognition involves the transformation of social and cultural urban life in order to promote coexistence and tolerance. It fosters symbolic and political changes and has a great impact on the restructuring of the public realm and urban spaces. These changes require a difficult but necessary rethinking of how the common public sphere of cities serves collective participation and how social subjects position themselves within it. For this reason, they also call into question existing physical boundaries, interests and values attributed to places in order to remake – and, in the best case, to even out – the topography of interdictions that control access to and enjoyment of social benefits and esteem.

Movements for recognition take place through the productive practice of disagreement. Together, they motivate many contemporary demonstrations occupying symbolic and highly visible urban spaces in large metropolitan areas like São Paulo. These interventions have advanced considerable change in social values in Western societies. They have also served to maintain what, in the recent history of Latin America, has become a particularly strong tradition: the occupation of urban spaces as an important arena for political debate. These processes generate new discursive abilities for negotiation as they reveal existing social tensions, introduce new voices into the public realm and make visible repressed needs. They define the democratic public space as a space of confrontation between social projects and goals in constant transformation. By doing so, they promote constructive disagreement as an important part of social and political life and not as an obstacle to be avoided. They call social justice and responsibility into question and increasingly expose and absorb the struggle for individual and collective moral recognition. The historic centre of São Paulo is a good example of this situation, since it has been the stage for several housing movements in the last couple of decades which have amplified the meaning and practice of citizenship. They have increased the social and legal recognition of lower-income citizens who informally live and work in the area by promoting formal rights and mechanisms for them to continue to live in the city.

Living in the Centre, Living on the Edge

Figure 3.2 Families Meet with the Leadership of Movimento Sem Teto Centro (MSTC) in a Squatted Building on Prestes Maia Street, downtown São Paulo, 2002 (drawing by Zeuler Lima)

Housing remains one of the central problems of urbanisation in Brazil and in São Paulo in particular. This significant problem comprises a complex and fast process of urbanisation framed by the reality of poverty and the myth of state intervention. Political rhetoric and administrative decisions have often treated the housing problem in Brazil with fragile promises and weak results. In the latter part of the twentieth century, the historic centre of São Paulo suffered the effects of profound transformation in the economic life of the metropolis brought about by decreasing investment in economic activities, urban infrastructure and social programmes. The deep recession of the 1980s, which affected the world in general and Brazil in particular, accelerated the impoverishment of São Paolo's historic downtown as well as other areas of the city. The changes associated with deindustrialisation and the expansion of business and services had a great impact on the urban structure and life of São Paulo as well as on the models used to understand its dynamics. For example, the centre–periphery model previously used to describe socio-spatial inequity in the city has progressively become insufficient to describe the complexity of the spatial distribution of population and material resources.

The metropolitan region presents a high demand for housing and also a very aggressive pattern of urban occupation, while most areas suffer from a lack of investment in urban development. In the last couple of decades, illegal occupation by squatters in some metropolitan areas has increased by 223 per cent, and today around 20 per cent of São Paulo's inhabitants live in shanty towns. Informal growth rates are also notably high in areas of environmental protection, which constitutes a major problem for the preservation of river sources in the region. The general growth rate of the city has decreased from 5 per cent per annum to 0.5 percent over the last three decades. Since the 1980s, the central districts of São Paulo, described by urban historians as the 'expanded centre', have lost population while urban growth has occurred in peripheral regions within an area of influence of up to 100 km from the city centre. This inversion presents a striking paradox: regular, urbanised areas of the city lose population while areas which are not urbanised, or have a lack of basic infrastructure, gain population in an expanding movement of poverty (Bonduki 2001: 8).

The historic downtown has lost 11 per cent of its permanent population in the last few decades and, because of real-estate devaluation, the rate of under-occupation and vacancy in the area is estimated at around 30 per cent (Piccini 1999: 66). Yet, there are about 185,000 people living in tenements in the central area of São Paulo. It is very common to find rental contracts that are not regulated. This informal and mostly illegal practice, which is overlooked by corrupt city inspectors, favours the imposition of conditions determined by landlords, leaving tenants with no rights or security of tenure or even rent negotiation guaranteed by the legal system. Although a large number of these informal tenants have often little or no access to the same rights that protect landlords, they actively participate in the formal labour market. Tenement residents subject themselves to such a situation because it is often the only means of living close to their jobs, since there are no housing policies, or projects, or even mortgage and financing mechanisms available to low-income residents in the country and in the city.

One of the factors maintaining this inversion and imbalance in downtown São Paulo is the combination of unequal historic distribution of public investment in the city and the recent positioning of São Paulo on the margins of the urban globalisation network. The country adopted neoliberal policies in the early 1990s shortly after the approval of a new Federal Constitution in 1988. A few important legal changes were introduced which recognised rights of property and settlement regulating urban and rural areas, but the practical results have been proportionately meagre in this recent economic context. As São Paulo adopted economic practices that favour transnational market connectivity, these complicated existing spatial inequalities in the city.

Recent Housing Movements in Downtown São Paulo

Figure 3.3 Protest Group Movimento dos Trabalhadores Sem Teto da Região Central (MTSTRC) Camping in Front of the State Government Building on Boa Vista Street, downtown São Paulo, June 2006 (drawing by Zeuler Lima)

Housing movements started in São Paulo in the 1970s and gained political power in a complex and contrasting situation. The struggle for access to land rights and public housing has been strongly supported by entities such as Comunidades Eclesiais de Base (Church Community Groups), which represents progressive sectors of the Catholic Church, and the Partido dos Trabalhadores (Worker's Party), among other political institutions engaged in the struggle for human rights (Maleronka 2001: 8). Many of these groups merged into the União dos Movimentos de Moradia (United Housing Movement), or UMM, created in 1987 to advocate and act in favour of better housing conditions for low-income residents in São Paulo. Similar coalitions have been formed since then, such as the Unificação das Lutas dos Cortiços (United Tenement Struggle) in 1993, and the Fórum de Cortiços e Sem Tetos de São Paulo (Forum for Tenement Residents and Homeless in São Paulo) in 1995, which has over 5,000 individual members. These coalitions have participated in negotiations with the state government of São Paulo in order to develop policies and programmes favouring dispossessed urban populations (Maleronka 2001: 10). Other broader social movements have also included issues of land use and housing, such as the creation of Assembléia Nacional Popular e da Esquerda (National Popular Assembly of the Left) in 2005.

Social housing movements have achieved a few significant results since the late 1970s. Improvement came with the provision of urban infrastructure in the urbanisation of shanty towns, which originated with the work of Carlos Nelson Pereira do Santos in Rio de Janeiro, and with the approval of legal instruments expanding and socialising the meaning of land and property rights. An important progressive step occurred in 1988 when the National Congress approved a new Federal Constitution after the end of the military regime, including amendments specifically regarding the problem of low-income housing and social inclusion. The 1988 legislation defined the principle of social purpose of urban property, which was adjusted in 2001 with the approval of a federal law titled City Statute. This recent legislation revokes the long-lasting Land Law of 1850 that kept several generations of rural and urban populations from having access to legal rights of land ownership (Maricato 1996: 35). These laws have dominated many recent struggles over the use and ownership of land – both urban and rural – in Brazil.

Nonetheless, not all events have taken the same direction in the struggle over urban space in the central areas of São Paulo. In a different line of action, since the 1970s the city has promoted consecutive attempts at urban revitalisation and gentrification. The creation of the Associação Viva o Centro (Live Downtown Association), a non-profit organisation established in the early 1990s, has been the largest among these ventures so far, and boosted the drive to redevelop the historic centre of the city. Representatives of the real-estate market, civil society and prestigious financial and business institutions are among the founders of this public–private coalition. Several of the private partners have significant national and international presence and financial power, most notably the Bank of Boston, which has played a leading role in the programmes developed by Viva o Centro.

The association looked to the experience of Barcelona in the 1980s as a model for its urban revitalisation projects. The Catalan model helped articulate an apparent consensus based on the premise that underused and undervalued strategic spaces of the historic centre should be preserved for more noble purposes, meaning economic uses. This is the same discourse that supports current practices of strategic planning and urban development in different centres of global modernisation. In the derivative and less resourceful case of São Paulo, the different members of Viva o Centro legitimised their intentions and activities by announcing that the historic downtown was semi-defunct, violent and physically deteriorated, an idea that was largely absorbed and broadcast by the press. To counter this urban decay, the association advocated the need to transform São Paulo into a world city with a strong and well-articulated centre with large investments in projects for capital accumulation.

Despite the initial interest in promoting social policies, in concrete terms this public–private coalition prioritised public investment in symbolic projects to raise real-estate value in the area. For example, the investment of public resources has been predominantly directed at the recovery and conversion of historic buildings for cultural institutions catering to the middle and upper classes, which access these places through security systems that effectively segregate the population. The implementation of cultural activities in the city centre is certainly a good cause. However, what underlines this monoculture of urban projects is the shift in intended use and also in the target population. As these institutions increasingly try to attract high-income users to the city, they tend to exclude low-income citizens who have traditionally occupied downtown areas. So far, this strategy has had little success since new occupation in the historic centre is proportionally small by comparison to the whole urban area. As a result, this situation has made the gap between different social groups in the city even more visible.

Housing Movements and New Political Subjects in São Paulo

Given this controversial and contentious condition, one can see that the strong presence of social movements lobbying for better housing policies in the historic centre of the city is not a mere coincidence. Current housing and land movements in São Paulo constitute a basic element in the extension of rights to the city to a larger population. By incorporating a large number of individuals kept in a situation of semi-citizenship, these grassroots movements have reorganised the struggle

Figure 3.4 Homeless Individuals and Families Occupying the Lobby of an Empty Building on Prestes Maia Street in Downtown São Paulo, Movimento Sem Teto Centro (MSTC), 2002 (drawing by Zeuler Lima)

over urban spaces and contributed to their social and physical improvement. They represent the emergence of new political subjects within the public sphere, operating through practices of dissent and claiming social recognition.

The historic centre of São Paulo has been an important stage for political conflicts among different sectors of the city's society since the end of the military regime in the 1980s. Even though the historic downtown area has traditionally been a place of residence for a large population, the novelty in this process has to do with the nature of the political conflict. Housing movements have organised tactics with the technical support of social workers, architects and urban designers for forcing legal and political authorities to respond to their claim for better housing. One of the most controversial acts of dissent among these groups was the occupation of vacant buildings. The scale of this radical takeover is unprecedented in São Paulo, showing that the exclusion of certain social groups from democratic representation can lead to an even more complicated scenario. In the first few years of the 2000s, seventeen buildings that were vacant for more than ten years were taken over by 1,300 families in the central areas of the city.

Despite the fact that the real-estate market sees this kind of appropriation as negative and problematic, some people are more optimistic about its political role. According to architect and former city councillor Nabil Bonduki, the illegal occupation of vacant buildings sets an important political precedent (Bonduki 2001: 4). Because of the political pressure caused by squatting and the existence of a considerable stock of vacant buildings in the downtown area, it has become more and more difficult to ignore the problem presented by informal tenements and by the lack of low-income housing. This confrontation potentially contributes to the debate about the rights to housing financed by government agencies, and to the design of units that avoid the old bureaucratic model of minimal-cost housing on the outskirts of the city.   Instead, this situation offers the possibility to explore public housing policies and practices in a larger sense. In addition to providing housing units, these policies and practices should also ensure access to the rights to the city – and to be in the city – as well as to the infrastructure, and economic and cultural opportunities that the formal city has to offer (Bonduki 2001: 4).

The number of activist groups has increased since the creation of Viva o Centro (Feldman 2001: 21). This reaction responds to the fact that the programmes coordinated by the coalition present a higher threat of eviction to low-income groups in areas of increased real-estate value. Fórum Centro Vivo (Live Downtown Forum) is one of the most recent examples of this phenomenon. It includes many of the institutions that have traditionally coordinated housing movements, such as labour and student unions, NGOs, the Catholic Church, technical consultants and cultural and human rights groups. This large group was created in 2000 primarily to propose low-income housing policies for the central districts that would avoid displacing social groups victimised by real-estate development. [2]

The examples of recent housing movements and redevelopment projects in the historic centre of São Paulo illustrate a complex urban scenario of dissent and also an important step towards social recognition. In this situation, not only is there opposition among different groups, there is also dialogue about the symbolic and material ways of producing and inhabiting urban spaces. These movements have produced positive results such as the creation of public credit lines for financing low-income housing as well as changes in legislation to allow the social use of existing building stock in the city. Housing movements are based on the need to transform both the discourses and the conditions under which social debate and negotiation for the right to the city occur. They ultimately reveal different meanings about what the city is and what it should be.

As one sees the fast-changing dynamics of capital transfer and formal urban models and practices around the globe, new housing movements contribute toward the consolidation of democratic practices at the local scale of the city. They create possibilities for enlarging the exercise of citizenship beyond the realm of the nation-state and traditional politics. They alone do not solve historic problems, but they help create new forms of presence in the public sphere and in the spaces of the city. They are evidence of the need for recognition and access by different social groups to economic, civil and cultural rights that must be represented in the public sphere. Conflicts over the production of urban space and the representation of social differences in the urban territory are elements necessary to the advancement of democratic life. To investigate alternatives in such a situation seems a Herculean task, but it is also an invitation to understand the changing social, cultural and political facts that frame the reality in which architectural design and political and social life operate.

Notes

1. The term *mésentente* from the original French was translated into English as 'disagreement'. In this text, the term 'dissent' appears as an alternative translation that appropriately reflects a political and social connotation opposed to the term consensus, which has often been used in contemporary neoliberal economic and urban discourses. See Rancière (1996a, 1996b).
2. By the time of the final version of this chapter, conflicts over invasion and property rights had increased in São Paulo. Hundreds of families have been removed from squatted buildings with legal warrants, and the city has offered neither support nor housing alternatives to this population.

References

Benhabib, S. 2003. *The Claims of Culture: Equality and Diversity in the Global Era.* Princeton, NJ: Princeton University Press.
Bonduki, N. 2001. 'Habitação na área central de São Paulo', *Comissão de Estudos sobre Habitação na área central. Relatório final.* São Paulo: Câmara Municipal de São Paulo.
Feldman, S. 2001. 'Tendências recentes de intervenção em centros metropolitanos', in *Comissão de Estudos sobre Habitação na área central. Relatório final.* São Paulo: Câmara Municipal de São Paulo.

Fraser, N. and A. Honneth. 2003. *Redistribution or Recognition? A Political-Philosophical Exchange*, trans. J. Golb, J. Ingram and C. Wilke. London: Verso.

Honneth, A. 2003[1992]. *Luta por Reconhecimento – a gramática moral dos conflitos sociais*, trans. L. Repa. São Paulo: Editora 34.

Maleronka, C. 2001. *Por uma casa digna no centro da cidade: cortiço e movimento organizado em São Paulo. O caso do edifício 9 de julho*. São Paulo: FAUUSP – TFG.

Maricato, E. 1996. *Metrópole na periferia do capitalismo*. São Paulo: Hucitec.

Piccini, A. 1999. *Cortiços na cidade: conceito e preconceito na reestruturação do centro urbano de São Paulo*. São Paulo: Annablume.

Rancière, J. 1996a[1995]. *O Desentendimento. Política e Filosofia*, trans. Â. Leite Lopes. São Paulo: Editora 34.

——— 1996b. 'O Dissenso', in A. Novaes (ed.) *A Crise da Razão*. São Paulo: Companhia das Letras, 367–382.

Chapter 4

The Informal Architecture of Brasilia: An Analysis of the Contemporary Urban Role of its Satellite Settlements

Annalisa Spencer

Informal settlements are a fundamental part of Brazilian society, culture and economy. This is evident in all major Brazilian cities where significant unplanned growth has occurred, expanding out from historic centres. However, Brasilia, the country's capital, is a unique case due to the fact that it did not grow by radiating outwards from its own historic centre but, instead, grew inwards from its outskirts which latterly became its periphery. Thus, Brasilia offers a particularly stark example of how informal settlements are unavoidably and intrinsically embedded in Brazil's society, culture and politics.

As is well known, the city was planned following a specific architectural ideology and the whole set of principles established by modern architecture. To some extent, Brasilia can be considered as the culmination of the theories and ideas of modernism. However, on the other hand, Brasilia can also be seen as a traditional Latin American city which, in spite of the particularities of its conception, does not escape the predicaments faced by other major cities both in Brazil as well as in the rest of the continent. Notwithstanding the government's intention to prevent the appearance of peripheral informal settlements typical of most Brazilian cities, these had appeared even before Brasilia's grand inauguration in 1960. Unplanned peripheral settlements around Brasilia have subverted the city's distinctive *Plano Piloto*[1] – and the larger Federal District of Brasilia – requiring a remapping of the city not only architecturally but also socially, culturally and politically.

Far from advancing a traditional critique of its modernist architecture, this chapter[2] approaches Brasilia as a city that was never finished and which remains in a permanent state of evolution, rather than decline. Brasilia's development will be analysed in the light of postcolonial discourse as a means to engage critically with issues regarding Brazilian identities, and to bring to the fore some political questions that are intrinsically connected with the built environment but which have been usually overlooked.

To this end, Brasilia is taken as the ultimate embodiment of the planning principles set out by the Congrès International d'Architecture Moderne (CIAM). Placing Brasilia within the context of CIAM sets up a situation where Brasilia can be seen as an attempt to impose homogeneity on the rich and heterogeneous set of cultures that is Brazil. This allows us to approach Brasilia as a case study that exemplifies the historical struggle among the formal and the informal experienced in all other major cities in Brazil and the rest of Latin America.

Postcolonial Discourse and the Principles of the CIAM

The postcolonial theorist Homi Bhabha has drawn attention to the inherent complexities, which are often glossed over, of the modern nation, its identity (and indentities), its culture(s) and its people(s). Bhahba emphasises the temporal nature of the nation as locality and opposes the notion of 'one-ness' suggested by historicism. On the contrary, Bhabha calls for the recognition of the 'cultural differences that span the imagined community of the nation-people' (Bhabha 1994: 140), implying that the nation is not singular or unified but, on the contrary, plural and broken.

Any attempt to narrate the nation is thus fraught with the tension Bhahba highlights between the pedagogical and the performative. The performative temporality of the nation can easily be recognised in the heterogeneity of the population of the Federal District of Brasilia who constantly, and by various means, challenge the authority invested in the city as Brazil's capital. Thus, Brasilia can be likened to the liminal signifying space which Bhahba describes as 'internally marked by the discourse of minorities, the heterogeneous histories of contending peoples, antagonistic authorities and tense locations of cultural difference' (Bhabha 1994: 160). The pedagogical, on the other hand, can be recognised in the CIAM's principles of rationalised urban planning and functional order, which, undeniably, influenced Brasilia's Master Plan and its architecture. Eric Mumford points out that Brasilia is one of the few built examples of the CIAM's 'Functional City' – a zoned city based on a 'collective and methodical land policy' devised in order to abolish the 'chaotic division of land' typical of most prewar European cities. In fact, all seven finalists in the 1957 competition submitted designs proposing the capital as a model of the Functional City, 'each showing a rigid separation of functions [dwelling, recreation, work and transportation] and the use of express highway systems as the primary means of circulation' (Mumford 2000: 268). Lucio Costa's Master Plan for Brasilia, in other words, adheres to the rules of modernism laid out by the architects who drafted the Athens Charter.

Designed as an 'ideal' modernist city, Brasilia demonstrates an attempt to impose a pedagogical narrative associated with homogeneity and an erasure of social, cultural and economic differences. This pedagogical impulse comes not only from the Master Plan but also from the desire of political authorities to create a 'new Brazil'. In his winning scheme for Brasilia, Lucio Costa aimed to create an independent identity for Brazil; he did not want his design to be associated with a legacy of European colonisation or with the United States and its ideology. However, despite Costa's intentions, historical distance allows us to recognise Euro-American architectural and economic influence in Latin America, particularly in the years immediately after the Second World War when Brazil's higher classes championed what may be called a 'Brazilianisation' of the American dream represented by the ideals of progress, order and modernity; looking towards the United States, they hoped to be no longer dependent on Europe. Such a set of ideals served as a vehicle used by the elites in order to mobilise popular support for the development of a new Brazil. In order to realise this modernisation of Brazil, vast unbuilt areas of the country were identified as strategic planning opportunities for the materialisation of Brasilia.

The construction of the new capital had precedents in the many North American-based planning initiatives for various Latin American cities – Cidade dos Motores (Brazilian Motor City) in Brazil, Chimbote in Peru, Havana in Cuba, Ciudad Pilar in Venezuela and Bogotá in Colombia, to mention just a few – although none of them ever materialised fully. Nonetheless, such projects, the majority of which were designed by the

New York-based firm Town Planning Associates,[3] helped to solidify the CIAM principles for the design of cities that led, eventually, to the construction of Brasilia. The design of Cidade dos Motores (1943), for example, was entrusted to Town Planning Associates by the chief of the Brazilian Airplane Factory Commission which wanted to develop a new town on the site of its aeroplane engineering factory. The project was part of Brazil's postwar development initiative, encouraged and supported by the United States. Indeed, Mumford describes the project as 'part of a capitalist strategy of modernisation backed by a foreign power with strategic interests in the region' (Mumford 2000: 50).

Given the political complexity and significance of their projects in Latin America, the architects of Town Planning Associates adopted an ambiguous position in trying to satisfy a number of antagonistic agendas. On the one hand, there was the economic expansionist agenda of the United States; yet, on the other hand, there were the developmentalist aspirations of the Brazilian government, the interests of private investors and, also, the firm's own modernist architectural ideology. That is why, despite attempts to observe the original CIAM principles, as outlined in the 'Town Planning Chart' (published later as the Athens Charter), the architects of Town Planning Associates needed to modify their approach in order to incorporate new issues and to satisfy the complex demands of their multiple commissioners. One such modification was the creation of what they called the 'Fifth Function', the civic core, in Ciudade dos Motores which recognised the importance of the town square in Latin American cities. The plans for Bogotá, Cali and Medellin, developed by Town Planning Associates, are also indicative of the resulting shift of emphasis away from using the international style of modernism – which is evident in Le Corbusier's proposal for Bogotá – while at the same time maintaining the basic principles of CIAM.

Critics have since suggested that the inclusion of Latin American vernacular architectures had an effect on modernism (instigating a major change in the CIAM principles). However, Brasilia's current reality and its modernist and modernising aspirations draw attention to the fact that the principles of CIAM were particularly inappropriate considering the diversity of Brazilian society. It is thus necessary to analyse this reality in order to reasses the values and effects that the so-called informal elements have had on the planned city.

Active Users: The Reproduction of Brasilia

The notions of functionalism that are synonymous with modern architecture suppose humans to be a component of a machine (Hill 2003: 12). By implication, the 'user' is taken to be a passive receiver. Jonathan Hill has called for a reconsideration of the role that the user plays in architecture, arguing that the user is a creative, hence, active participant in the production of architecture. Despite the negative connotations associated with the term 'user',[4] we will use it in the context of Hill's argument: 'it is a better term than occupant, occupier or inhabitant because it suggests positive action and a potential for *misuse*' (Hill 2003: 40, emphasis added). It is this misuse, allegedly carried out by the 'creative user',[5] which can be identified in the Latin American city today. It is important to note that the term must be treated as an abstraction and not as an indication of a unification of the disparate and often conflicting parties indicated by the singular user. In the current context, the term 'user' refers to the inhabitants of today's Federal District of Brasilia. It alludes to the 'Other' that was not anticipated or provided for in the original plans. It speaks of Bhabha's 'nation-people', located in performative time, actively redefining the space of the city and the boundaries that have been imposed upon them.

This way of defining the user has important implications for recognising the character and individuality of Brazilian people and socio-cultural groups in the shaping of Brasilia. Acknowledging creative users marks a departure from functionalism and the specific zoning of uses demonstrated in the original planning of Brasilia. It also dispels any notion of the informal urban development being subconscious or haphazard. The developments discussed here are not just a response to random opportunities and chances. Latin American cities with their informal urban settlements can be seen to demonstrate how this creative use of space is engrained in the culture, history and contemporaneous development of people in relation to the city.

Informal settlements have become an inevitable part of the development of all major Latin American cities, due in part to urban patterns initiated during colonialism and in part due to contemporary economic and social policies. As Alfredo Brillembourg argues in relation to Caracas, Venezuela – another Latin American city with a turbulent political and social history heavily influenced by the aspirations of modernisation that also affected Brazil[6] – its urban settlements of 'resistance and despair' can be identified as a response to the colonial era (Brillembourg 2004: 81). In Brillembourg's analysis, the public square and the urban grid represent Spanish Catholicism and the control of the state while the informal housing system is linked to 'Devil-worship', as well as the anti-state in 'an attempt to achieve some kind of justice' for the years of oppression (Brillembourg 2004: 80). Following attempts in the latter half of the twentieth century to modernise Caracas, rebellion against the state emerged in the form of 'self-built slum urbanism' (or illegal squatter housing).[7] Whilst being unavoidable due to poverty and circumstance at the level of the individual, as a collective, 'slum urbanism' can be seen as a reaction against the ruling classes and those urban forms perceived to represent the control of the state. Thus we may see these settlements as deliberate reactions to the colonial era and the era of modernisation, as well as the current disparity of wealth and lack of social mobility which act as mechanisms of control and oppression in the city.[8]

According to this logic, Caracas demonstrates not only a peripheral settlement condition found in many Latin American cities but also the proactive resistance of the people as users within them. In other words, Brillembourg asserts that it is incorrect to describe such settlements as informal. On the contrary, he describes them as a distinctly formal response to historical and current economic and social conditions: 'The balance between the marginal and the centre was broken, and the marginal jumped into the centre, in politics, in culture, and of course in the city' (Brillembourg 2004: 79).[9] This breakdown between 'marginal' and 'centre' alludes to a transcendence of boundaries which affects the formation and shape of the city, as suggested by Bhahba. Moreover, this breakdown reveals that although there is essentially an antagonistic relationship between the state and settlements representative of the 'anti-state', there is also a symbiotic element to it.

Brasilia's significance as the capital exacerbates the disparity that is usually identified between the inner and outer city, between the state and anti-state in Brillembourg's terms. The disproportionate population of the satellite communities compared to that of the *Plano Piloto*, reveals the fact that the production of forms and patterns within today's Latin American city is linked to the complex and shifting relationship between the state and the people. In the case of Brasilia, the entire Master Plan represents the state and its pedagogical principles. The notion that the new capital could be created from an 'empty' site indicates that Brasilia was founded on the basis that its location had no culture, no unwanted past. Given Brasilia's conception and location on an 'empty' site, one might expect that it would have escaped the conflict between colonial urban typologies and North American-influenced transformations that many Latin American cities underwent in the twentieth century. But in fact this conflict – which should be referred to as antagonistic coexistence to avoid the negative connotations that 'conflict' suggests – was ingrained from the point of conception. The colonial legacy could be eradicated from the soil but not from the collective memory of the people. Another way of stating this would be to say that Brasilia is an extreme case of a recurring spatial clash between historical urban patterns and ideological typologies associated with modernisation.

The emergence of the Federal District and the development of the informal settlements within it demonstrate this spatial clash. The original exclusion of the *candangos* or labourers who built the city followed a precedent for exclusion established in the colonial era. In the face of such rejection, the *candangos* set a pattern of resistance that has intensified and hardened over time. Upon realising they were the excluded, the marginal, the labourers seized land outside the formal planned city. In an era when peripheral squatter settlements were seen as an undesirable reminder of a colonial past, a sort of infliction of the un-modern city, these land seizures were met by further expulsions from the centre, in the hope that the settlements and their inhabitants would be kept at bay. The growth of the Federal District, today a mixture of illegal, semi-legal and legal settlements, can be seen as a backlash to that original expulsion. Even within these settlements of resistance, however, the pedagogical imperative of the state to impose uniformity can be seen in the architecture of the satellite settlements with its varied stages of formality.[10] This coexistence, catalysed by officialisation, articulates a disjunctive architecture.

It is perhaps ironic that, despite the attempt to create a new identity for Brazil independent of colonial influence, the city echoes the very forms of its colonial past that it was trying to erase. Spanish and Portuguese colonial strategies often inform the spatial characteristics of different Latin American cities; and Brasilia, despite its overtly modernist Master Plan, manifests a lingering urban form of Brazil's colonial past. Portuguese Brazil was originally intended as a strategic commercial foothold, a base for exploration and the exploitation of natural resources. Portuguese-Brazilian cities, from the beginning, were preoccupied with defence and not expansion, as was the tendency of Spanish New World cities. Natural obstacles often supplied constraints (most famously articulated in the case of Rio de Janeiro), which facilitated easier control and protection.[11] It is interesting but not surprising, then, that Brasilia was allocated 'natural' borders since the city was to be sited where there were no geographical features to constrain its development. Thus a green belt was imposed upon the area, as well as an artificial lake. These physical parameters are demonstrative of the intention to control and impose order on the new capital. In this way they can be seen as imitative of the strategies of early Portuguese explorers just as much as they are indicative of the 'Functional City' with its rigid separation of spaces.

As postcolonial discourse reminds us, however, just as to separate modernday Brazil from its colonial past is to over-simplify the complex nature of its national identity, attempts to identify a 'Brazilian Architecture' are equally misleading for they imply the false scenario of a homogeneous national identity. As Sophie Trelcat (2005) argues, the term 'Brazilian Architecture' is not really sufficient to explain the diversity and complexity of the architectural production of the country. To establish a 'Brazilian Identity' is to ignore the socio-cultural diversity and heterogeneity that exists in Brazil. Thus, while Trelcat identifies 'several remarkable and recurring components of Brazilian architectural practice' (Trelcat 2005: 44),[12] she warns us not to attach too much significance to them as demonstrative of a 'national spirit' or identity. She suggests, rather, that it is necessary to refer to demographic movements in order to establish how these trends emerge and where they occur.

Frederico de Holanda's spatial syntax diagrams of the Federal District explore such demographic movements, particularly what he calls urban or architectural 'compactness',[13] and demonstrate that informal settlements are inevitably embedded in Brazil's society. In order to analyse compactness he uses a map of axial lines, attempting to identify successive developments. The maps begin by depicting Brasilia in 1960, still under construction, alongside the first three satellite towns and the Nucleo Bandeirante (the provisional pioneer settlement, originally called Cidade Livre, 'Free Town') which would eventually become a satellite town. His work continues to map the evolving compactness of the *Plano Piloto* and its satellite settlements over each decade up to the present. Successive axial line diagrams demonstrate a pattern of emerging new settlements, increasing density of peripheral settlements and the relative decrease in the compactness of the *Plano Piloto* despite an intensifying 'metropolitan' area.[14]

De Holanda identifies a decreasing 'compactness' in Brasilia's central core up until the 1970s. At that time it became apparent that the green belt would have to be compromised. Despite the intended function of the green belt being to preserve the 'purity' of the *Plano Piloto*'s character by separating it from the intended commuter towns, the settlements were – and still are – expanding inward. That is to say, the highest population density in the Federal District currently belongs to the areas on the periphery of the *Plano Piloto* and they are growing towards the monumental centre of Brasilia, into its vast open spaces, and encroaching on the low-density areas of the *Plano Piloto*. Whilst the first satellite nuclei were located between 25 km and 40 km away from the centre of the *Plano Piloto*, it eventually became unjustifiable that its workforce should be banished so far away. To prevent further squatter settlements, a new set of social accommodation was planned between the *Plano Piloto* and Taguatinga, one of the original satellite towns.[15]

The location of this planned settlement, Guará,[16] is of particular interest as it suggests a reshaping of 'metropolitan' Brasilia. For with the admission that the green belt would have to be compromised, and with the new 'social housing super blocks' built in order to facilitate expansion towards Taguatinga, de Holanda demonstrates a reversal in patterns of development, particularly in the area on the periphery of the *Plano Piloto*.[17] The recognition of the importance of these settlements, not previously anticipated, was conducive to the gradual spatial redesign of the city and required its remapping. This remapping, which has already started, is an ongoing process and will continue to reshape the city in the future. De Holanda goes so far as to indicate a diminishing importance of the Monumental Axis.[18] However, this indication is contrary to the assertions we are making. In fact, an increase in activity within the *Plano Piloto* results from the increasing proximity of the satellite settlements. Nonetheless, de Holanda's methods of analysis help to indicate developmental patterns which are otherwise very difficult to establish. This demographical data highlights the role and the agency of people, the user, in the constant reshaping of Brasilia. Thus, the importance of the spontaneous developments, the informal settlements, in successfully subverting the authority of the pedagogically imposed formal city as represented in the *Plano Piloto*. More significantly, de Holanda's spatial syntax diagrams clearly indicate Brasilia's particular growth pattern, from the outside inwards. Brasilia's evolution thus reveals that informal settlements are inevitably embedded in Brazil's society.

Human Scale

The reshaping of Brasilia by the informal developments discussed above can also be seen at a human scale. Within the *Plano Piloto* specific architectural and infrastructural elements – particularly the streets and squares – can be identified in order to demonstrate how the people as creative 'users', as part of the nation's performative temporality, actively redesign the city.

Streets and Corners

The architect and anthropologist James Holston claims that Brasilia lacks the street life traditional of other Brazilian cities due to the 'absence not only of corners but also of curbs, sidewalks edged with continuous facades of shops and residences, squares, and streets themselves' (Holston 1989: 68). In Holston's analysis, the corner is a 'metonym for the street system of exchange between people, residence, commerce, and traffic' (Holston 1989: 68). Although Holston is accurate in his assertion that Brasilia lacks the traditional element of 'the street corner', it is naïve to assume that people cannot recreate similar systems of exchange within the physical structures of Brasilia.

What Holston fails to acknowledge are the vital processes of reappropriation carried out by users who have modified a master plan that was a contradiction of their traditional social practices. For example, he argues that the first dwellers of the Master Plan reproduced 'the street' when they 'refused the intended garden entrances of the commercial units and converted the service backs into storefronts' (Holston 1989: 139). Rather than seeing this as creative use, however, Holston sees this as signs of old habits refusing to die: 'Not surprisingly, the signs of the popular street reappeared: mixed-up functions (cars and people), uncoordinated signs, colours and displays, window-shopping, sidewalk socialising, loitering, and even littering. The riot of urban codes reasserted itself in spite of the best attempts yet devised to prevent it' (Holston 1989: 140). Holston suggests that this misuse is representative of an architectural failure and thus he diminishes its benefits. However, what Holston refers to as misuse and a 'riot of urban codes' could be reinterpreted as subversive acts of appropriation by non-passive, creative users. One might, therefore, see the recurrence of certain behavioural patterns within an imposed architecture as a hybridisation of the commercial units.

Although he does not use the term hybridisation, de Holanda also documents at length the ways in which the city's users have redesigned the street element. Thus he notes, for example, the transformation of the W3 Avenue from a service road supporting wholesale firms into 'something which, in Brasilia, most closely looks like an urban street' (de Holanda 2001: 6). According to de Holanda, this transformation was as much due to the unexpected proximity of residential areas created by the last-minute inclusion of the '700s' (affordable housing blocks) along the W3 Avenue – an inclusion which had already began to contradict CIAM intentions of separation of functions – as it was to the activities of the users. In this way, de Holanda appears to endorse the people not only as occupiers of abstract space, but as reproducers of lived space.

The Square: The Space of the People

It is not sufficient to measure the success of Brasilia merely by assessing its reality in relation to its original intentions as a CIAM city. If we are to view Brasilia in terms of the division of functions advocated by CIAM, then, as Holston suggests, the traditional marketplace should be seen as a 'commercial sector' and the market street a 'motorised service way'.[19] However, if one is to consider the effect that people as creative users have on the city, then it is inappropriate to reduce these institutions to elements of a *Plano Piloto*. In Brasilia today, the functions of the market place and the street have not been eliminated but rather displaced; they have been established away from the designated commercial sector and the motorised service way. Such is the case of the *rodoviária*, Brasilia's Interurban Bus Terminal, which can not only be taken to replace the functions of the traditional town square, but also of the market place. Although Holston recognises that the *rodoviária* seems to have taken on the functions of the traditional town square, he also maintains that the *rodoviária* is simply an exchange related to its function and, therefore, it cannot be a satisfactory imitation of the square. From a functional perspective, Holston's argument is accurate; however, his critique suggests that no other type of social activity could exist or develop in spaces whose function has been specified by the *Plano Piloto*.[20] What Holston thus misses is the radical potential of users to transform the city: the *rodoviária* is not an imitation of the square but represents an adaptation of the typical square to suit the city's users.

There is no deliberate attempt to create a typical square in Brasilia. Nonetheless, the *rodoviária* is the point of entry and exit to Brasilia for all commuters from the satellite cities. 90 per cent of the Federal District's population lives in satellite cities and peripheral settlements, and many of these are not in a position to afford a car. It is also the main point of embarkation and disembarkation for any bus journey within the city.[21] Thus, the *rodoviária* is the principal element in the legibility of the city for the majority of migrants, workers and visitors; it is the first point of information for anyone without a car in Brasilia.

It is clear that the *rodoviária* can, therefore, be seen as a reinterpretation of the square, but one in which the element of control has shifted. The square, in this case, is not produced as a result of the street's interaction with the city's principal buildings but by the interaction of people in the available spaces. The constant flux of workers through the *rodoviária* is what gives the space its meaning and socio-cultural significance, not the function pedagogically assigned to it. In this way, the controlling element is somewhat reversed. It is thus interesting to observe how the elevated pedestrian circulation places people in a higher position from where they look down towards the Monumental Axis and the parliamentary complex, as opposed to the traditional square in which people are looked upon from the buildings that surround it.

Street Vendors

The interconnecting commercial spaces that have developed between the *rodoviária* and the central market which developed spontaneously at the base of the television tower,[22] also demonstrate how users adapt and change the formal city to meet their needs. Not only have these interconnecting spaces increased in number but also in their significance within the city, for an informal sales network of vendors has been established between the two crowded areas. As a result, pedestrian activity has also increased and multiple 'desire lines'– circulation routes – have become pathways, engrained in the earth, cutting through the city's Monumental Axis. This kind of appropriation of space in a city that was conceived mainly for the traffic of automobiles, adds a new layer of complexity beyond the simplistic intersection of roads as presented by Holston.

Although this is only a small-scale development, the presence of street vendors is an example of informal commerce typical to Latin American city centres. Additional factors, such as the spatial layout of this central axis and the climatic conditions, facilitate the necessity of such commercial enterprises, in particular numerous water and refreshment vendors. Other such opportunistic, entrepreneurial ventures include youths offering car-park watching and car-washing services. Such small-scale enterprises can be seen as the beginnings of the market square. Further facilitation and accommodation could result from the formalisation and development of this space. Incremental architectural opportunities could begin to infiltrate this vast open space, in response to the informal commercial activity already being carried out here.[23] De Holanda, for his part, highlights that this 'intense' use of space occurs despite an inadequacy in user facilities.

I have discussed these three examples – the street, the market/square and street vendors – to demonstrate on a human scale the symbiotic relationship between the state and the user that has been suggested at the macro level of the Federal District. These popular and spontaneous appropriations have a strong effect on the city's management which might, eventually, be forced to 'formalise' the area as a commercial sector and to upgrade the physical facilities provided in order to accommodated new functions and users.[24] It is clear that these developments are the result of the constant traffic of people who commute between the informal satellite settlements and the Monumental Axis daily. At this point, Brasilia can no longer be taken to operate independently from its satellite towns. The peripheral informal settlements have altered dramatically, tangibly and intangibly, the principles of the *Plano Piloto* and subverted the urban significance of its Monumental Axis. The people have enforced their needs and priorities, thereby changing the city's form. Brasilia is no longer a static piece of architecture, with an untouchable Monumental Axis at its core. Brasilia is, instead, a city in progress.

Conclusion

Brasilia is frequently referred to as an inappropriate case study in the context of Brazilian culture and history, as an exception to the rule. It is often used as an example of the failures of modernism, or as a utopian planning experiment. In this chapter, however, I have demonstrated that the Federal District today is a successful and thriving Brazilian city; a case in which the performative has outgrown and overpowered the pedagogical even while both continue to coexist. By focusing on the antagonistic coexistence of formal and informal elements that make Brasilia a city, I have tried to exceed the boundaries of a merely aesthetic analysis and to engage with issues beyond the field of architecture. In this way, this essay highlights the emergence of an architecture of resistance; an architecture which challenges the significance of the Monumental Axis and the totality of the original *Plano Piloto*.

As a student of architecture and as a visitor to the city, I was surprised to find such a reality in a city that is often perceived to have no other architectural and urban interest beyond the original buildings of the Master Plan attributed to Lucio Costa and Oscar Niemeyer. Today, nearly fifty years after its foundation, there is a wealth of architectures and urbanisms, most of which have developed spontaneously and which have been denied value. It is not enough begrudgingly to accept that informal developments exist; the importance of informal architectures and their effect on the city need to be recognised.

Brasilia is significant as the representation of the state as well as being a physical embodiment of CIAM theories; both aimed to create a new Brazilian identity. Thus, Brasilia is a perfect case study of the coexistence of antagonistic elements. This can be described, using postcolonial discourse, as the adding together but not the summing up. The encroachment of the Federal District and the appropriation of the architecture itself by the people serve to articulate this tension. The users of the city are (re)asserting their way of life in this transforming environment. The development of informal architecture in Brasilia is not passive. It is deliberate and proactive.

In this way, Brasilia must be acknowledged as a true representation of a Latin American condition. The impact of informal architecture on the Federal District can only be realised incrementally over time, yet there is an urgency within it which observes the instinct for survival that this form of development symbolises. Thus the architecture of these peripheral urban settlements is found to be in a continuous state of flux. As Bhahba might say, it signifies the performative time of the nation; that is, the continuous process of establishing its own hybrid identity.

Notes

1. This is the name used for the initial Master Plan of the distinctive airplane shaped area of the Federal District associated with Lucio Costa's original design.
2. This essay is an abbreviated version of a dissertation supervised by Felipe Hernández at the School of Architecture, University of Liverpool, and submitted in 2006. The completed dissertation was nominated to represent the school at the RIBA President's Medals Awards that year. The present version was edited for inclusion in this volume by Lea K. Allen.
3. The firm Town Planning Associates was founded in 1942 by Joseph Luis Sert (1902–1983) and Paul Lester Wiener (1895–1967). Sert, a disciple of Le Corbusier, was involved in the establishment of the 'Town Planning Chart', developed at CIAM 4 in 1933. A later a version of this document was published by Le Corbusier as his Athens Charter (1943) and in Sert (1942). Between 1947 and 1959, Sert was president of CIAM. Wiener was a German-born architect based in New York. He was appointed guest lecturer at the University of Brazil in 1942 and was also linked to the U.S. State department through his father-in-law, Henry Morgenthau Jr., Secretary of the Treasury under President Roosevelt.
4. As Hill points out, the term is associated with modernist discourse and it often reduces architecture to a question of practicality. Here Hill refers to Lefebvre's (1991) opinion that the term 'user' implies something 'vague – and vaguely suspect' – and is an attempt in itself to turn the 'inhabitants of space into abstractions'.

5. Hill identifies three types of use: passive, reactive and creative. Whereas the passive user is 'unable to transform use, space and meaning' and the reactive user can only modify space slightly, the 'creative user either creates a new space or gives an existing one new meanings and uses' (Hill 2003: 21).

6. An interesting comparison between Brasilia and Caracas can be made, although these two cities appear to be in complete contrast with one another. Many argue that the modern movement in Caracas took into account the existing culture of the characteristics of the locale, whilst Brasilia was founded on the basis that its location had no culture as the site was 'empty'. However, both cities have experienced similar patterns of urban and architectural resistance.

7. These are identified by Brillembourg as 'inter-urban ranchos', meaning illegal squatter settlements. He claims that half the population of Caracas are housed in precarious settlements that climb the hillsides surrounding the city.

8. Despite the programmes of the current socialist government, Venezuela remains a highly segregated society. Thus, in Caracas there is a tendency for the poor to aggressively appropriate spaces 'inside' the city, as opposed to on its periphery, in order to contest the traditional and hierarchical centrifugal distribution of space.

9. Architect and writer Federico Vegas, quoted from a letter to Brillembourg.

10. The process of formalisation of these settlements in Brasilia is comparable to those in Lima, Peru, such as the 'peripheral urbanisation' of Vila El Salvador, one of Lima's satellite settlements (Golda-Pongratz 2004: 39). Lima is characterised by waves of rural to urban migration which have seen the city change shape to the point where 40 per cent of the city live in what can be described as a 'consolidated informal city' (Golda-Pongratz 2004: 39). The invasion of public territory is tolerated as it is 'responsible for the majority of city and housing development in Peru' (Golda-Pongratz 2004: 40). Golda-Pongratz attributes the success of the *barriada* or informal settlement to a combination of industrial and artisanal development. Thus the *barriadas* continue to grow, 'surrounding, conquering, and *overtaking* the old city' (Golda-Pongratz 2004: 45, emphasis added). The transition of these settlements is a gradual process, according to Golda-Pongratz, and is closely related to the aspiration for an official recognition of property entitlement.

11. These differences are further articulated by Ruth Verde Zein (2004) under the heading 'Settlers Versus Explorers', a clear reference to the differing traits of Spanish and Portuguese colonisation of the Americas.

12. It is beyond the scope of this study to elaborate at length on the characteristics identified by Trelcat. They are, however, interesting and indicative of certain developmental trends. See Trelcat (2005).

13. Compactness is shown as 'a relation between the number of lines and the area of the polygon' (de Holanda 2001: 1–9). De Holanda argues that basic transformations in the spatial dynamics of Brasilia are a response to the city's original problems and partly the result of the dynamics of the city's growth (de Holanda 2001).

14. This term is used by de Holanda to define Brasilia's central core. De Holanda argues that it does not just mean the originally designated *Plano Piloto*, and instead refers to the 'actual economic centre of the metropolis'. He indicates in

his spatial syntax diagram that the metropolitan core of the city is being pulled away from the *Plano Piloto* and towards Taguatinga (de Holanda 2001).

15. Taguatinga was the second of the original designated satellite settlements to be populated. It currently has a population of 243.575 inhabitants. .

16. New social housing built between Taguatinga and the *Plano Piloto*. Current population 2538.1inhabitants..

17. These 'super blocks' refer to the settlement of Guará. This was a result of Costa himself admitting to the necessity of low-income housing closer to the *Plano Piloto* (de Holanda 2001).

18. His assumptions are the result of his spatial syntax analysis which prove that the 'compactness' of the Monumental Axis is significantly lower than many of the other settlements.

19. It is suggested that 'the Master Plan transforms the age-old institutions of the market place and the market street into a "commercial sector" and a "motorised service way"' (Holston 1989: 138).

20. He implies that the only reason for going to the *rodoviária* is to take a bus or to sell something to people taking a bus. He states that Brasilia consists only of 'house and work' and is missing a 'third term', which he describes as 'the outdoor public life of the city, a public sphere of encounters based on *movimento*, conversation, play, ceremony, ritual, pageantry, as well as political congregation' (Holston 1989: 163). In other words, Holston does not recognise the potential for the 'public life of the city' to take place in such spaces as the *rodoviária*.

21. So far, the metro has proved redundant. However, there are plans to connect the satellite cities with the *Plano Piloto*. The recognition of this need is, in itself, a sign of influence exercised by the satellite cities. There are actually six non-operational or 'ghost' stations in the Federal District. The metro officially opened in 2001. Source: Kevin Harris.www.personal.psu.edu/users (retrieved January 2006). During my visit in August 2005, I saw no evidence of this metro system. Yet, according to Harris, it is believed that the stations could promote social mix, providing a cheap and socially acceptable way of travelling in the Federal District, without the stigma of the informal bus network or other methods of commuting to and from the satellite settlements. Presumably, the metro would go through the *rodoviária* thus further increasing its significance as the entry point to the *Plano Piloto*.

22. This market began as an illegal street hawking spot, responding to the TV tower as a visitors' attraction and a central location within the city. The market has now become legalised and mainly sells handicrafts and tourist items. This is not an isolated case where an informal enterprise has been formalised. As opposed to the *rodoviária*, the central market does not function on a daily basis; it is mainly aimed at tourists yet it also attracts local workers.

23. An example of this type of architectural opportunity can be seen in Rocinha Market, an open market at the foot of Rio de Janeiro's largest favela, Rocinha. The market is 'designed like a commercial street under cover ... the project arranges all the various activities under one roof while maintaining the free flow of people and goods as well as visual permeability' (AAA-Azevedo Arquitetos Associados, 2004). The project is a response to the legalisation of 166 street

hawkers in recognition of their vital role in the local economy (AAA- Azevedo Arquitetos Associados, 2004).
24. Further proof of the purpose of formalising the informal market can be observed with the 'Feira do Paraguai'. This began as an informal market selling illegal electrical goods in the car park of Brasilia's football stadium. In 1997 a 7000 sq.m. retail area was allocated within the *Plano Piloto*'s commercial sector, in response to the market's popularity. Other informal markets from Guará have joined it in this central retail space of 2000 licensed pitches. Now named the Feira dos importados, it boasts the biggest commercial market in Brazil, with the highest diversity of electrical goods. It is significant that the license and the space are now provided by the government, yet the items on sale are recognised to be illegally purchased. This also has a link to the whole of Latin America's informal economy, stemming from Ciudade de l'Este, Paraguay, on Brazil's border.

References

Bhahba, H. 1994. *The Location of Culture*. London: Routledge.
Brillembourg, A. 2004. 'The New Slum Urbanism', Architectural Design 74(2): 77–81.
de Holanda, F. 2001a. 'The Morphology of Brasilia', Brasilia: Universidade de Brasilia. Retrieved 10 Novemeber 2005 from: http://www.tba.com.br/pages/fredrosa.
de Holanda, F. 2001b. 'Eccentric Brasilia', 3rd International Space Syntax Symposium, Atlanta, GA. Retrieved 10 November 2005 from: http://www.undertow.arch.gatech.edu/homepages/3555/ papers_pdf/53_holand.pdf.
Gans, D. and M. Jelacic. 2004. 'The Refugee Camp: Ecological Disaster of Today, Metropolis of Tomorrow', Architectural design 74(2): 82–86.
Golda-Pongratz, K. 2004. 'The Barriadas of Lima: Utopian City of Self-Organisation?', Architectural Design 74(4): 38-45.
Hill, J. 2003. *Actions of Architecture: Architects and Creative Users*. London: Routledge.
Holston, J. 1989. *The Modernist City: An Anthropological Critique of Brasilia*. Chicago: University of Chicago Press
Lefebvre, H. 1991. *The Production of Space*. Oxford: Blackwell.
Mumford, E. 2000. *The CIAM Discourse on Urbanism, 1928–1960*. Cambridge, MA: MIT Press.
Sert, J. 1942. *Can Our Cities Survive? An ABC of Urban Problems, Their Analysis, Their Solutions*. Cambridge, MA: Harvard University Press.
Trelcat, S. 2005. 'Brazil Builds, Le Retour', *L'Architecture d'Aujourd'hui* Brésil 359: 44.
Verde Zein, R. 2004. 'Architecture and Identity: Regional Study, Brazil', Berlin: Berlin University of Technology. Retrieved 5 September 2005 from http://www.architecture-identity.de.

Chapter 5

The Evolution of Informal Settlements in Chile: Improving Housing Conditions in Cities

Paola Jirón

Chile's marked demographic explosion, its accelerated urbanisation and the consequent concentration of its population in a few cities has generated significant housing needs, mostly manifest as housing shortages, overcrowding, sharing, land invasions and informal settlements. These settlements are scattered throughout the country's main cities as well as in small towns and rural areas, and are all understood as settlements lacking any of the three basic services: running water, electricity and sewage. Important efforts have been made over the years to improve the conditions of those living in such settlements, and Greene (2004) identifies five main stages: emergency eradication, new solutions, no state support, upgrading and upgrading with new solutions.

This chapter presents a brief history of informal settlements in Santiago de Chile. Beginning with the initial formation of *callampas* and organised land invasions, or *campamentos*, the chapter goes on to look at political motivations relating to housing involved in the relocation of hundreds of families during the dictatorship of Augusto Pinochet and the current democratic government's aim to eliminate poverty in Chile using housing as one of its main tools. This chapter also shows that the way the authorities have tried to correct, eliminate, control or promote informal settlements has varied over the years, from absolute control to complete support, and from total neglect to a more consensual way of approaching them.

Nonetheless, it appears that even the more democratic interventions have led to unsatisfactory ways of inhabiting the city, because top-down 'formalisations' of informal settlements erase the richness of everyday urban living. In other words, to approach improvements in quality of life merely as a formalisation of housing tenure, or housing structure, is equivalent to overlooking the complexity of poverty and the need for the creation of citizenship.

The Formation of *Callampas* and *Campamentos*

Since colonial times, living conditions in urban areas dedicated to lower income groups have been extremely precarious and highly segregated (de Ramón 1990; Sepúlveda 1998). Initially, the indigenous population was not allowed to site their dwellings within the city limits. This situation repeated itself later when lower income groups living in cities or those migrating from rural areas were forced to remain on the periphery. As de Ramón (1990) mentions, there are two main stages in housing occupation for lower-income groups. The first, from the 1830s until the 1940s, involved mostly legal forms of occupation which included rented land in the periphery or room rental in inner-city buildings, both with high levels of overcrowding and precarious living conditions. During this time illegal occupations were highly controlled and tolerated only on land with unclear ownership or on areas of public property such as outside city limits or on riverbanks. The second stage, from the 1950s to the 1970s, was marked by the illegal occupation of empty plots in different areas of the city (de Ramón 1990). These settlements presented a gradual yet continuous growth, with families or migrants arriving steadily until the plots were fully occupied. This settlement process soon began to be known as *callampas*, or mushroom settlements.[1] According to Sepúlveda (1998), *callampas* differ from illegal land invasions, or *tomas*, in that the first are not conceived as permanent solutions – the occupants remain there temporarily while waiting for a better housing solution – whereas the latter are planned occupations aiming for permanence and eventual upgrading. Both types were generally backed by political parties and usually presented some form of violent confrontation with the police.

Government policies varied throughout these years. In the 1950s, 'self-help' housing began to be used as a type of intervention that is still applied today. It encourages families to build their housing using their own labour with technical assistance provided by an external entity. Its origins are linked to an agreement between the governments of Chile and the U.S.A. (Hidalgo 1999; Haramoto et al. 1997; Greene 2004). In Santiago, this programme provided approximately 3,000 housing units, and it constituted a housing solution for families that lived in some of the most precarious settlements in the city (Hidalgo 1999). In the 1960s these programmes were included in the Eradication Programmes which involved moving urban dwellers either to finished units or, in the majority of cases, to urbanised plots where provisional housing was installed at the back of the plots for later self-building or formal construction by building companies (Hidalgo 1999; Greene 2004).

During the second half of the 1960s there was more influence from urban mobilisations. These were more than a political struggle to obtain land for housing, and became a type of social organisation that created social leaders and, later, became known as urban social movements. The Chilean experience during these struggles encouraged many authors to write about such movements, among them Manuel Castells (1983), who studied the impact of social movements in the development of contemporary cities.

Throughout this time, there was an increase in housing demand due to both the natural growth of the population and the rise of rural–urban migration. The state maintained its response from previous years, but the political context required faster solutions. One of these was Operación Sitio (Operation Site), focusing on self-built solutions. This programme was nick-named Operación Tiza (Operation Chalk), mocking the fact that, at the end, the plots were merely traced on the ground with chalk and the few initiated projects were very precarious. As a housing solution, Operación Sitio was similar to previous eradication and self-build programmes. Yet, these were considered to be new housing solutions and not provisional or emergency housing (Greene 2004). This alternative privileged access to land more than to finished housing units, whose construction would eventually be the beneficiary's responsibility. In Santiago, between 1964 and 1970, around 65,000 plots were provided through Operaciones Sitio (Hidalgo 1999) while over 110,000 were provided nationwide. This was fundamentally different to previous programmes: the quantitative leap represented the largest intervention ever carried out by the state up to that moment in Chilean history, and the start of progressive housing processes, in social as well as in physical terms, was then considered a real possibility (Greene 2004; Kusnetzoff 1987).

Social pressure continued and intensified at the beginning of the 1970s. At this point, Chilean cities evidenced almost three decades of illegal land occupations, and there was great dissatisfaction with the efforts made by the state in order to reduce the housing deficit. The housing deficit was growing steadily, reaching 156,205 housing units in 1952, 420,000 in 1960, and 592,324 units by 1970 (Hidalgo 1999; Kusnetzoff 1987). Homeless committees created by those encroaching on, sharing or living in illegal settlements started to put pressure on and negotiate with authorities and political parties. They soon became an organised, national dwellers movement, coordinated centrally, directed by proletarian parties and linked to the new revolutionary organisations which were emerging in the country at the time. The settlements originating from these movements were called *campamentos* (encampments), indicating their fragile and paramilitary character (Hidalgo 1999). According to Kusnetzoff, 'no less than 300,000 people came to live in the new encampments and entered with great dynamism into the political struggle within the city of Santiago' (Kusnetzoff 1987: 161). They came from *conventillos* (inner city tenements), *callampas* and *allegados* (sharers living in conditions of overcrowding).

State-sponsored self-building programmes were eliminated during President Allende's period (1970–73) because they were seen to affect workers' resting time, to increase unemployment and were technically inefficient and uneconomical (Hidalgo 1999). It was also argued that they were discriminatory against the poor (Greene 2004). Thus the government proposed an Emergency Plan to begin building finished housing units and proclaimed housing as a right for all citizens (Kusnetzoff 1987). However, during this time the peripheral growth in large cities of informal settlements or *campamentos* not only continued but greatly increased. In 1970, the *campamentos* in Santiago hosted around 60,000 people, but by 1973 around 800,000 families belonged or participated in this type of territorial and functional organisation (de Ramón 1990). These spontaneous land invasions did not comply with legal norms and administrative policies, ignored urban planning regulations and rendered master plans obsolete. Furthermore, most of these invasions were carried out in different parts of the city, not only on the periphery. By 1973, the periphery of the city of Santiago had been extended with spontaneous settlements to accommodate 17 per cent of the capital's population in approximately 10 per cent of the city's area (de Ramón 1990). Though they did not have legal or formal backing, these *campamentos* were considered the most important urban operation of the century and, although envisioned as provisional, they ended up being permanent (Greene 2004).

The Eradication of *Campamentos* to Make Land Available

The process of land invasion and *campamentos* was violently stopped by the military government of Augusto Pinochet in 1973. During seventeen years of dictatorship, the military government maintained strict control over land invasions and limited the informal growth of the periphery. However, self-building at the back of existing plots started to make up for the insufficient housing supply, increasing *allegamientos* (sharing) as a way to solve the housing problems for new families without access to formal housing. Thus the physical expression of the housing deficit changed shape in comparison to the old *callampas*. Sharing became the main problem, one that became progressively invisible since the increasing population was hosted within existing plots or dwellings, thereby significantly multiplying population densities.

By 1975 a new housing policy led by market forces was being defined (Gilbert 2003). The state supported the creation of an open housing market leaving the responsibility for construction in the hands of the private sector, thus eliminating the concept of housing as a right, and making it instead a good to be accessed via the market. By 1978, the quantitative housing deficit was somewhere close to one million housings units (Held 2000) and in 1979 a new urban policy was issued declaring land a non-scarce resource (MINVU 1979; Kusnetzoff 1987). Parallel to this, a new housing policy was created, providing the housing subsidy system that still operates today.

A further development was the eradication and relocation of peripheral-area dwellers to those older *campamentos* which still existed within cities. In 1979, there were 294 *campamentos* in Santiago housing 44,789 families (223,957 persons); and between 1979 and 1986 around 28,500 families were forcibly eradicated (Hidalgo 1999; de la Puente, Torres and Muñoz 1990; Fadda, Jirón and Allen 2000). These violent relocations freed up land that mostly lay in the richer areas of the city where land values were higher. These actions were a form of 'social cleansing' of such areas with the aim of removing obstacles to real-estate market development (Kusnetzoff 1987; Sabatini 2000).

There have been many studies describing the consequences of the 1980s eradications both on the housing market (Sabatini 2000; Kusnetzoff 1987) and on the affected population (Morales and Rojas 1986; de la Puente, Torres and Muñoz 1990). The studies agree that most of the destination areas provided inadequate infrastructure or facilities to welcome the incoming population due to their peripheral

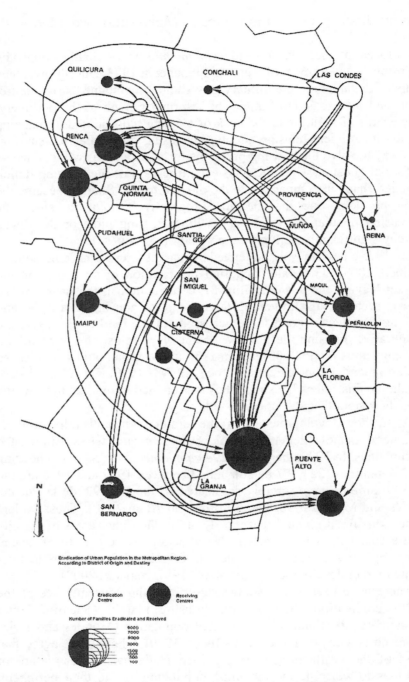

Figure 5.1 Eradication and Relocation Programmes in Santiago de Chile

location and a lack of investment. The housing provided included minimum plots and dwellers lived under conditions of 'dispersion, uprooting and isolation, which aggravated the social deficiency and lack of work for the majority of those displaced' (Kusnetzoff 1987: 169).

In some areas the official programmes of displacement and resettlement in the impoverished periphery were chaotic, as in the district of La Pintana in the south of Santiago, where during the brief relocation brief period of 1982–84 the population grew by 90 per cent to 148,000 (Kusnetzoff 1987). In 1984 there were only 'two doctor's surgeries in the area, a third of the population had no sewage service, half of the children had no primary schools, there were seven telephones for the whole community and unemployment was estimated at 60%' (Kusnetzoff 1987: 169). The relocation worsened the living conditions for most of those displaced. These housing programmes had an immense negative impact inside the city as well, as the new location of the eradicated settlements, due to the low cost of land, contributed to and accentuated the excessive growth of the city, not only generating increased segregation but also environmental problems (Hidalgo 1999; Kusnetzoff 1987; Sabatini 2000).

This housing policy continued to be applied, particularly through the Basic Housing Programme, until the end of the military period and throughout Chile's economic crisis. Although fewer houses were built than promised, and payment arrears increased from low- and middle-income groups, the policy remained in place, with increasing demands for more housing and an increased housing deficit due to the 1985 earthquake.

Counting the Poor: The Urge to Eliminate *Campamentos*

At the beginning of democratic period in 1990, the estimated housing deficit was around 900,000 units. One of the biggest fears of the incoming government was that massive land invasions would occur. This led to the implementation of new housing plans that could quickly respond to dwellers' demands and would avoid urban demonstrations. The overall policy remained the same, but the main innovation was the Progressive Housing Programme, oriented specifically to those sharing homes and the homeless. Through this programme, along with other interventions, the Ministry of Housing managed to provide a housing supply greater than the rate of formation of new households and largely contained new land invasions. During the next ten years there was a significant reduction in the housing deficit (MINVU 2004a/b), but this was primarily in quantitative terms because the quality of the housing provided, though an improvement on previous living conditions, generally proved unsatisfactory in terms of dwelling size, materials, interior distribution, location and scale of the housing estates.

The Ministry of Housing entrusted the University of Chile to carry out the first cadastre of precarious informal settlements in 1996. At that time there were 972 informal settlements with more than twenty households in the country, housing approximately 500,000 people (MINVU-INVI 1997). This initial survey served as the basis for the first housing programme that included a holistic view of poverty and demonstrated that through the provision of housing units only, the cycle of poverty would not be overcome but required additional dimensions including basic infrastructure, employment, training and community participation, amongst other things. This new programme, Chile Barrio, resembled the successful programme being applied in the favelas of Brazil, and included upgrading in cases where land was adequate and available, and relocation to other areas of the city when necessary. Though housing and infrastructure were two of the main aspects of the programme, it also involved community and social development, employment and aid (for small industry) and the strengthening of public programmes aimed at alleviating poverty.

The Chile Barrio programme generated high expectations, particularly due to its innovative design. However, soon after the programme became operational, various criticisms arose. There was consensus, confirmed by a national evaluation of the programme, that its aims and objectives were appropriate to tackle the problems of the low-income population living in informal settlements, particularly in terms of an integral understanding of the problem of marginality through a multi-sectoral approach. However, once in operation, the programme seemed less than ideal, particularly in terms of its social components, including community development and employment generation within the target groups. Furthermore, the institutional framework was incapable of dealing with the programme adequately, as timing and project execution was not efficient and, in terms of management and coordination with the different sectors, the multi-sectoral approach did not flow smoothly. Finally, the programme did not contemplate any follow-up, monitoring or evaluation system thus making it difficult to analyse its success (DIPRES 2002). The differentiated timing required for the housing and social objectives proved difficult in that the former involved a concrete result while the latter took more time to develop. In all, the programme ended up being yet another housing programme and not the integral proposal it had promised to be (SUR 2004). Though many of these criticisms were taken on board by the programme, it is uncertain whether they will be overcome as the formalisation of housing remains the most important product.

An additional issue arose after the original diagnosis. Because no monitoring or follow-up had been provided for, the diagnosis became static. A complementary cadastre was carried out in 2002, including micro settlements with less than twenty households, which accounted for a total of 1,282 *campamentos* nationwide (Ariztía and Tironi 2002). This meant that the dynamic and changing situation of informal settlements was not contemplated by Chile Barrio, nor was it meant to, because some government officials had expressed concern with including new settlements in the target population of the programme. They believed it would provide an incentive for the formation of more informal settlements seeking a fast route to solve their housing problem. However, in reality, some of the 'new' settlements had not been originally counted because they were smaller than twenty households and others, particularly those in rural areas, did not necessarily fall into the category of precarious settlements. Also, new informal settlements had been formed since 1997 by settlers trying to find ways of living in their district of origin through informal and formal means – that is, by land invasion as well as through formal application and negotiation with the Ministry of Housing.

The Chile Barrio programme ended in 2006 with the formalisation of the last settlements in the cadastre. However, although the housing target of the programme was reached, the other components, many of which take longer to implement and are harder to quantify, are yet to be attained. The programme offers many lessons and provides much room for improvement within itself and for other programmes following similar multi-disciplinary and multi-sectoral approaches to public policy. It has been suggested that the programme should evolve into one which will tackle the poverty and living conditions of the remaining precarious informal settlements, as well as inner-city vulnerable areas. It should also provide guidance to a new programme recently launched, Quiero mi Barrio ('I Love my Neighbourhood'),[2] aimed at improving the living conditions of those people living in housing estates built by the government over the past thirty years. However, the complexity of improving quality of life has to be learned prior to embarking on new or improved versions of the programme, particularly if it is to be emulated internationally as has been done with other Chilean housing programmes.

Improving Quality of Life? An Evaluation of a Resettlement Intervention

Various studies have analysed the impact of the Chile Barrio programme (CIS 2002; Contreras and Ugarte 2002; DIPRES 2002; FONDECYT 2000–2003; Saborido 2005; Siclari 2003). One of these studies, the 'Comparative Study of Quality of Life-Gender and Environment Triad' (FONDECYT 2000–2003),[3] included amongst its objectives that of assessing the quality of life of specific groups living in Santiago and, specifically, studied one of Chile Barrio's most notable interventions, the Oreste Plath Estate.[4]

The Oreste Plath Estate intervention aimed at formalising the housing, employment and community integration conditions of 326 families living in Parcela 30. This was an informal settlement where families had installed themselves, almost ten years prior to the intervention, next to a waste disposal site close to a riverbank. The houses were mainly of wood and light materials with only partial connection to water and sewage (44 per cent were without running water and almost 90 per cent without access to sewage), but all had illegal connections to the electricity supply (MINVU-INVI 1997). Furthermore, in terms of distance, the settlement had little access to health care, child care and educational services, and limited access to commerce, community and sporting centres. Moreover, its proximity to the waste site as well as its topographic conditions labelled it an area unsuitable for housing (MINVU-INVI 1997). The majority of the population was under twenty-four-years old with precarious employment and low education levels but they were highly organised with five housing committees. Most worked as independent rubbish collectors, recycling materials from the waste disposal site.

In 1998 the Parcela 30 settlement was eradicated and the residents transferred to the new housing complex of Oreste Plath close to the original settlement. The project was initially seen as a success and was even mentioned in the annual presidential speech of 1998 (Frei 1998). The overall project included 777 housing units distributed in three-storey building blocks ranging in size from 39 to 47 square metres. Within the project, 326 units belonged to the Chile Barrio programme and the other 451 households applied separately through the regular MINVU system (FONDECYT 2000–2003).

Due to the complex factors that determine quality of life (QoL), it is a difficult concept to apprehend, define and measure. The concept applied here does not limit itself to the 'private life level', but integrates

Figure 5.2 Oreste Plath: View of the Housing Blocks

all the elements, objective and subjective, of the conditions in which people live in an urban community, including their needs as well as their perceptions, expectations and levels of satisfaction (Jirón and Fadda 2003). This way of defining QoL is relevant when evaluating an intervention which attempts to provide an integral response to poverty. Housing is one of its components; since the housing process cannot be associated exclusively with the physical unit alone, it requires a vital analysis of the relation between the inhabitants and their habitat. This habitat includes the different scales at which people live (housing unit, surroundings, neighbourhood, city) and the various relations they form (family, neighbours, community, citizens). This makes the housing process more complex yet richer as it understands that improving housing conditions in material terms does not, automatically, imply an improvement of QoL, and, as will be seen, formalising informal settlements is a difficult goal to attain.

The following section presents the main highlights of an evaluation which started two years after the Parcela 30 settlement was relocated to the new formal housing complex in Oreste Plath. The evaluation consisted of analysing five major components of QoL, including human, socio-cultural, natural, physical and economic facts.

In physical terms, habitation of the new complex has led to the informal appropriation of common spaces, which is a widespread response in Chilean public housing interventions. Because the housing programme rarely responds effectively to the needs, household composition and everyday activities of families, it does not recognise the progressive dynamic of the housing process and the way urban dwellers appropriate space. Most ground floor apartments have been extended and there are appropriations and enclosures on the staircases which are used as bedrooms, kitchens, laundry rooms and drying areas,

Figure 5.3 Oreste Plath: Appropriation of Staircase Space

storage space or as gardens. These inevitable extensions, which were not contemplated in the original design, are constructed without technical advice and constitute a danger in terms of possible collapse, blockage of circulation routes and, due to the reduction of visibility, an identified security issue.

The estate was provided with a community hall, a childcare centre and municipal schools nearby. The complex lacks public sports facilities and, though green areas exist around the complex, their peripheral location discourages the community from using them on a regular basis. Moreover, a lack of communal and local services can be observed, including health (medical assistance or hospitals) and security. The spatial configuration of the complex does not make it easy to live there, as its morphology does not contribute to social interaction. The architectural typology does not have any formal relation with the site, and residual spaces with little illumination become unsafe, along with the empty areas which are not looked after by the residents.

Figure 5.4 Oreste Plath: Unused Green Areas

The poverty of the inhabitants can be seen as a major issue in this community which, although more stable, still remains vulnerable. About 65 per cent of the population is below the poverty line and there are high levels of unemployment. Credit capacity is low due to the informality of employment and, because most dwellers have outstanding debts due to the precariousness of their income, the possibility of saving is also minimal. Compared to how they lived before, in economic terms they feel worse off, particularly because of the increase in debt incurred by mortgages and basic services, which they did not have before. In terms of employment, their informal income from rubbish collection is no longer available, yet formal jobs have not been secured for the majority. Their economic situation requires many of them to seek help from the state, which promotes their dependency on welfare, with a high percentage receiving subsidies from the municipality in terms of food, water, electricity, healthcare and so on.

According to the residents, this vulnerability is complemented by the stigmatisation of the community due to crime, drug use, alcoholism and high rates of school dropout and teenage pregnancy in the neighbourhood. This situation affects citizen safety and raises concerns about the future of local children. The deteriorated environment strongly impacts on the perception of quality of life, even if people are not directly attacked (robbed, insulted or threatened). Women, for example, fear that their children will start taking drugs. Because of this, residents feel that they live in a 'dangerous neighbourhood'.[5] There is a sense of low social control of public spaces, all of which create opportunities for living in anonymity, gangs, fights, alcoholism, drug consumption and trafficking on the streets – a situation that was not found in the informal settlement where higher levels of solidarity and social cohesion existed.

The community also has had little involvement in any of the decision-making processes, from the original diagnosis prior to leaving the settlement through to the solutions provided. Hence, they feel low levels of empowerment and participation while, at the same time, they have high levels of expectation raised by the promise of future employment and educational training. Local inhabitants mention a negative change in the level of involvement as people are no longer committed to improving their habitat collectively as they did before. On the contrary, there seems to be an individualistic approach to community living, as if looking after each other were no longer necessary.

This situation generates speculation as to whether life in the previous settlement was better than in the current one. Most of those interviewed mentioned wanting to return to the informal settlement at Parcela 30. Although the assessment of housing satisfaction is, in most cases, positive, particularly in terms of ownership, it decreases as new issues arise over time: for example, people with whom they had no previous contact keep arriving from other settlements, an issue that generates tension and social dispersion. The inhabitants of Parcela 30 feel discriminated against by the non-Chile Barrio residents who have closed themselves off behind fences to avoid interaction with the new arrivals. Although the difficulties related to moving from an informal to a more formal settlement are recognised by the programme, its implementation was not made easier by the fact that the transition to Oreste Plath did not include any prior mediation or social discussion between the two groups moving in. Although it was ensured that those coming from the *campamento* would live in proximity to each other as a way of maintaining social ties, the division has also made the poor section of the estate highly segregated, stigmatised and rejected by the other group. Moreover, new expenses also arise and, with them, more debts. All this has a direct impact on the inhabitants' desire to leave the newly built complex, complemented by a poor image that makes them ashamed of living there.

The problems presented raise questions regarding how the Chilean housing process has failed to incorporate lessons learned from previous experiences or from international projects. It seems that there has been no change since Turner's writings on housing (Turner and Fichter 1972; Turner 1976), where local control in the housing process is seen as an essential condition for its success, which is measured in terms of residential satisfaction. This control does not necessarily mean self-building, but involvement in how and what processes take place with whom. From the start of this programme little consultation took place. Hence, it is not surprising that involvement or participation was also minimal and this, in turn, created little possibility for control in the decision-making process. The long-term results of this are evident in the absence of a sense of ownership and attachment to place as well as in the levels of overall dissatisfaction.

Moreover it is also surprising that, almost forty years since the debate started, the Chilean government has implemented exactly the opposite of what was being suggested at the time: large investment in housing as opposed to large investment in infrastructure and basic services. It is precisely in this respect that many of the flaws were found in the Chile Barrio programme: the removal of inadequate housing and the relocation to major housing complexes while neglecting the infrastructure and services originally lacking.

Understanding QoL in terms of its multiple dimensions helps us to understand the problems of the programme and provide recommendations for the future, not only for Chile Barrio but also for other programmes that are currently being implemented. This means that informal settlements cannot be formalised by cleaning or clearing away material poverty, particularly when the informal settlements carry with them poverty issues that are not easy to overcome, including social stigmatisation, limited opportunities for social mobility, weak social capital and intergenerational poverty. Furthermore, very seldom are the positive aspects of living in an informal settlement highlighted by formal housing interventions, including their previous strategies. Most traces of previous lives are erased, leaving the inhabitants without a history and the expectation that they will start their new lives from scratch. Achieving lasting change and real improvements in terms of quality of life involves time, and often time does not coincide with the framing of social policies. Lasting changes also require local control, and the way the Chilean system operates provides little room for this, from the administrative complexity down to a lack of trust in the ability of local residents to take control effectively.

Conclusion

The evolution of informal settlements in Chile is a complex issue that contains multiple dimensions. The country has striven to improve the living conditions of all its citizens, but the efforts that have been made do not respond adequately to the challenge (considering the degree of economic development of the country). Although interventions have lessened in terms of violent relocations, uprooting practices continue to create problems for informal settlements. Beneficiaries are often dissatisfied. Explaining that they feel like second-class citizens, many would like to return to where they used to live. It is understood that some of these original settlements cannot remain in their existing locations due to dangerous geographical conditions, but the relocation projects fail to recognise that the problem is not merely one of housing and that there are many positive aspects to the lives of dwellers in informal settlements.

The state response, though innovative and displaying an awareness of the complexity of poverty, does not translate adequately into practice. Chile Barrio did not offer an optimal solution since the programme's social components lagged behind due to implementation problems and institutional difficulties.

Despite the failures of the Chile Barrio programme, there have been some improvements in the way the state treats informal settlements and the poor. There have been a few land invasions over the past few years which, after careful negotiation with the authorities and the private sector, have resulted in participants securing the benefit of remaining close to sources of employment in areas where they have lived all their lives, as well as state support to stay. These cases have been few, very politicised and thoroughly documented.

There have also been evaluations and studies that suggest improvement in some areas, such as the promotion of participation (Siclari 2003), the reduction of the standardisation of solutions, and responses which act more on a case by case basis. Other advances include improvement in the social aspects of the programme which have proved to be the hardest to tackle and have largely remained unsolved; improved coordination among the different public institutions implementing social policies; the training of staff working in the programme, particularly in diagnosis, mediation and monitoring; enlargement of the scale of intervention from the neighbourhood to the city; and finally provision of an overall evaluation of the programme (Saborido 2005).

Chile Barrio's ideals of a territorialised, multi-sectoral, decentralised and participative approach seemed ideal for integral interventions aimed at improving urban quality of life; however, they clashed with the centralised and sectorial logic of Chilean public policy. This implies that in Chile the problem is far from resolved. Future trends are hard to anticipate, as the living conditions of those living informally, though precariously in physical terms, seem to provide higher levels of satisfaction than those whose living conditions have been formalised. There is a need to change the way housing is understood, moving from the attempt to formalise the informal in physical terms to the attempt to understand how people live on a daily basis and what improving the quality of life really means to inhabitants of informal settlements and urban dwellers in general. The social, cultural, environmental and legal aspects of daily living seem to be as important as the physical aspects. Therefore it is vital to increase our understanding of the everyday lives of urban dwellers.

Furthermore, if there is to be a shift away from paternalistic state interventions that have negative effects on the lives of informal dwellers, then there needs to be a shift in the way social policies are formulated, implemented, administered, monitored and evaluated, particularly if the aim is to improve dwellers' quality of life and not just their housing situation. Many blueprints regarding the aims and objectives of programmes and projects have little in common with their translation into practice. This seems to be a recurrent feature in Chilean housing programmes: the lessons from previous interventions do not seem to feed back into current projects. Although there are some major successes in the Chilean experience, more needs to be learned about how to give urban dwellers control over their housing.

Notes

1. In 1952 there were 75,000 people living in *callampas* (6.25 per cent) in Santiago; by 1966 there were 201,217 (8.05 per cent); in 1970 there were 346,380 (13.4 per cent); while by 1973, there were around 500,000 or 18 per cent of the city's population, living in this type of settlement (de Ramón 1990).
2. A national programme implemented by the Ministry of Housing to improve 200 neighbourhoods.
3. The 'Comparative Study of Quality of Life, Gender and Environment Triad' was a FONDECYT Research Project (No. 1000414). For further information, see: www.calidaddevida.uchile.cl
4. Named after a Chilean folklore researcher.
5. The estate is known as 'Choreste Plath', from the Chilean slang *choreado/a* which is commonly understood as 'angry' or 'enraged'. In that sense, *choreste* denotes the dangerous reputation of the area.

References

Ariztía, T. and M. Tironi. 2002. *Catastro Nacional de Campamentos 2002*. Santiago de Chile: Publicación Centro Investigación Social, Un Techo para Chile.

Castells, M. 1983. *The City and the Grassroots: A Cross-cultural Theory of Urban Social Movements*. Berkeley: University of California Press.

CIS. 2002. *Estudio Descriptivo de la Situación Post Erradicación de Campamentos en la Región Metropolitana Primer Semestre 2002*. Santiago de Chile: Centro de Investigación Social, Un Techo para Chile.

Contreras, D. and P. Ugarte. 2002. 'Para erradicar definitivamente los campamentos en Chile', *Revista de Economía y Administración* 143: 65.

de la Puente, P., E. Torres and P. Muñoz. 1990. 'Satisfacción residencial en soluciones habitacionales de radicación y erradicación para sectores pobres de Santiago', *Revista EURE* 16(49): 17–22.

de Ramón, A. 1990. 'La Población Informal. Poblamiento de la Periferia de Santiago de Chile. 1920–1970', *Revista EURE* 16(49): 5–16.

DIPRES. 2002. *Síntesis Ejecutiva N° 11, Programa Chile Barrio, Ministerio de Vivienda y Urbanismo*. Santiago: Ministerio de Hacienda, Dirección de Presupuesto, Programa de Evaluación de Programas Gubernamentales.

Espinoza, V. 1988. *Para una historia de los pobres de la ciudad*. Santiago de Chile: Ediciones Sur.

Fadda, G., P. Jirón and A. Allen. 2000. 'Views From the Urban Fringe: Habitat, Quality of Life and Gender in Santiago, Chile', in M. Jenks and R. Burgess (eds), *Compact Cities: Sustainable Urban Forms for Developing Countries*. London: Spon Press, 167–82.

FONDECYT. 2000–2003. 'Estudio Comparativo de la Triada "Calidad de Vida-Género-Medio Ambiente" en Tres Comunidades Urbanas del Gran Santiago'. Retrieved 20 January 2007 from: www.calidaddevida.uchile.cl

Frei, E. 1998. 'Mensaje Presidencial, Legislatura 338ª', Valparaíso: Sesión Ordinaria el Congreso Pleno, 21 May 1998.

Gilbert, A. 2003. 'Poder, ideología y el Consenso de Washington: desarrollo y expansión de la política chilena de vivienda', *INVI Boletín del Instituto de la Vivienda*, Universidad de Chile, 47: 133–56.

Greene, M. 2004. 'El programa de vivienda progresiva en Chile 1990–2002', Documento de Trabajo N° 78, Banco Interamericano de Desarrollo, Departamento de Desarrollo Sostenible en División de Programas Sociales, Estudio de buenas prácticas en vivienda económica. Retrieved 20 January 2006 from: http://www.iadb.org/sds/soc/publication_78_e.htm.

Haramoto, E., D. Jadue and R. Tapia. 1997. 'Programa de Viviendas Básicas en la Región Metropolitana', *Revista de Arquitectura*, Facultad de Arquitectura y Urbanismo, Universidad de Chile, 9: 32–37.

Held, G. 2000. 'Políticas de viviendas de interés social orientadas al mercado: experiencias recientes con subsidios a la demanda en Chile, Costa Rica y Colombia', *Serie Financiamiento del Desarrollo*, Santaiago de Chile: CEPAL/United Nations.

Hidalgo, R. 1999. 'La Vivienda Social en Chile: La Acción del Estado en un Siglo de Planes y Programas, Iberoamérica ante los Retos del Siglo XXI', *Scripta Nova* 3(45). Retrieved 20 January 2006 from http://www.ub.es/geocrit/sn-45-1.htm.

―――― 2002. 'Vivienda social y espacio urbano en Santiago de Chile: Una mirada retrospectiva a la acción del Estado en las primeras décadas del Siglo XX', *EURE* 28(83): 83–106.

Jirón, P. and G. Fadda. 2003. 'A Quality of Life Assessment to Improve Urban and Housing Policies in Chile', *World Bank Urban Research Symposium*, 15–17 December 2003. Washington, DC: World Bank.

Kusnetzoff, F. 1987. 'Urban and Housing Policies under Chile's Military Dictatorship: 1973–1985', *Latin American Perspectives* 14(2): 157–86.

MINVU. 1979. *Política Nacional de Desarrollo Urbano*. Santiago: Ministerio de la Vivienda y Urbanismo de Chile.

―――― 2004a. *Chile: Un siglo de políticas en vivienda y barrio*. Santiago de Chile: Ministerio de la Vivienda y Urbanismo de Chile.

―――― 2004b. *El Déficit Habitacional en Chile. Medición de los requerimientos de vivienda y su distribución especial*. Santiago de Chile: Ministerio de la Vivienda y Urbanism de Chile.

MINVU-INVI. 1997. *Catastro Nacional de Campamentos y Asentamientos Irregulares, Programa de Estudios Básicos*. Santiago: Ministerio de Vivienda y Urbanismo.

Morales E. and S. Rojas. 1986. 'Relocalización socio-espacial de la pobreza. Política estatal y presión popular, 1979–1985', *Documento de Trabajo No 280*, Santiago de Chile: FLACSO.

Sabatini, F. 2000. 'Reforma de los mercados de suelo en Santiago, Chile: efectos sobre los precios de la tierra y la segregación residencial' *Revista EURE* 26(77): 49–80.

Saborido, M. 2005. 'El Programa Chile Barrio: lecciones y desafíos para la superación de la pobreza y la precariedad habitacional', *Documentos de Proyectos, Naciones Unidas*. Santiago de Chile: CEPAL.

Sepúlveda, D. 1998. 'De tomas de terreno a campamentos: movimiento social y político de los pobladores sin casa, durante las décadas del 60 y 70, en la periferia urbana de Santiago de Chile', *Boletín del Instituto de la Vivienda*, Universidad de Chile, 35(13): 103–15.

Siclari, P. 2003. 'La participación en el Programa Chile Barrio: Evaluación en Curso y Propuestas de Mejoramiento', *Boletín del Instituto de la Vivienda*, Universidad de Chile, 18(46): 71–95.

SUR. 2004. 'Programa Chile Barrio 1998–2004. Lecciones y aprendizajes a partir del caso de Cerro Navia' *Seminario Internacional sobre Mejoramiento de Barrios*. Santiago de Chile: Corporacion de Estudios Sociales y Educacíon.

Turner, J.F.C. 1976. *Housing by People: Towards Autonomy in Building Environments*. London: Marion Boyars.

Turner, J.F.C. and R. Fichter. 1972. *Freedom to Build*. New York: Collier Macmillan.

Chapter 6

Housing for the Poor in the City Centre: A Review of the Chilean Experience and a Challenge for Incremental Design

Margarita Greene and Eduardo Rojas

Introduction

The present work focuses on issues of and solutions to the gentrification process that affects most urban rehabilitation programmes. These programmes, designed to tackle the obsolescence of city centres that affects most major Latin American cities, face a twofold challenge: on the one hand, the need to attract new investments to the area; and, on the other hand, the need to protect the low-income population living in the area and the heritage buildings that it may contain. These contradictory objectives are generally understood by the authorities that implement urban rehabilitation programmes, but in practice, in the majority of the cases, they focus in the physical aspects of the problem – the buildings – and overlook the social aspects involved. Since most rehabilitation programmes initially focus on the recovering of deteriorating heritage areas and buildings, they tend to give priority to direct and indirect investment in infrastructure, public spaces and buildings, as well as the protection of valuable yet endangered urban heritage buildings and areas. The poor population that uses these areas for lodging or for informal work tends to be overlooked; little attention is given to its displacement which in most cases is caused by the programmes created in order to rehabilitate the areas they currently occupy.

This chapter[1] argues that gentrification is a significant issue in contemporary public policy, not only because of its impact on social equality, but also because it undermines the social and political sustainability of rehabilitation efforts. The solution to the complex issues prompted by the deterioration of urban centres requires not only a careful treatment of the built form, but also, and centrally, a careful study of the impact that such a solution will have on the inhabitants of these areas.

The chapter is structured in five parts. The first two parts provide the basis for a better understanding of the socio-spatial processes that are occurring in Latin American city centres today. The first of these two parts describes the urbanisation process of Latin American cities, where the deterioration of the city centres is understood as the 'other side' of the urban sprawl, a by-product of the change from a traditional rural to a modern urban society. The second part presents some contradictory tendencies in the social process accompanying the rehabilitation of deteriorated urban areas, focusing specifically on the issues posed by gentrification and the plight of the urban poor.

The third and fourth parts of the chapter share some successful experiences of tackling the challenge of urban rehabilitation in Chile; that is, the provision of affordable housing solutions for the poor in dense urban centres. Thus, the third part describes the Chilean housing policy that provides the framework for the provision of such a type of housing, while the fourth part presents a sample of innovative designs that fit within that framework. The fifth and final part presents some concluding remarks and recommendations on protecting the poor residents of central areas from rehabilitation programmes. In brief, the experience seems to show that those rehabilitation programmes that include poor inhabitants require concerted local action within the framework of efficient housing and poverty reduction policies.

Urban Growth and Deterioration of Central Areas

Fuelled initially by rural migration and, lately, by the growth of an endogenous population, during the last century there was an increase in the number of urban conglomerates whose population exceeded 2,000,000 people. At the beginning of the last century, such conglomerates concentrated only 25 per cent of the population throughout Latin America, yet at the end of the century they housed nearly 75 per cent. Statistics show that at the beginning of the twentieth century, no Latin American city exceeded one million inhabitants while in the middle of the century there were seven; by the end of the century there were 49 cities which exceeded the one million mark. The structure of cities shows wide differences; on the one hand, there are huge urban conglomerates where 25 to 55 per cent of the national population lives – four of them rank among the ten biggest in the world (Mexico City and São Paulo with over 16.5 million, Buenos Aires with 11.6 million and Rio de Janeiro with 10.2 million inhabitants). On the other hand, there are many small municipalities that concentrate only a small proportion of the national population.

In general terms, urbanisation has been good for Latin America in economic terms. Greater concentration of the population in urban areas has been accompanied by the growth of per-capita income. In addition, the economies of more urbanised countries have grown faster than those of less urbanised nations (IDB 2004: 7–11). These outcomes result from the fact that the productivity of urban enterprises and labour is significantly higher than that of their rural counterparts. Urban areas offer better employment opportunities, higher incomes and better living conditions. In addition, the level of urbanisation has been recognised as an important factor in the reduction of poverty and improvement of social indicators because it is easier and cheaper to provide access to education, health and infrastructure services in urban areas than in rural ones. Spatial concentration makes the provision of basic services more efficient with the result that urban areas show a greater coverage of sanitation (drinking water, sewage systems, garbage collection and treatment) and access to health and education facilities than rural areas. Cities are Latin America's engines of economic growth and offer their populations the best opportunities for social and economic progress.

Notwithstanding the significant economic progress attained by Latin America in the last quarter of the twentieth century, poverty is still an issue. Moreover, in the future, poverty could be more dramatic for urban areas since recent estimates indicate that the number of urban poor is due to increase faster than those in rural areas. Today, urban poverty is a predominant social issue due to the fact that, fifty years ago, most cities were unable to integrate the massive influx of migrant populations into well-paid jobs and formal housing. This resulted in the emergence of vast settlements where the poor population lived with little or no access to urban facilities. Given that the percentage of the population living in poverty in rural areas has remained stable while the urban poor population has increased dramatically, this process has been described as the 'urbanisation of poverty'. According to World Bank (2000) data, 60 per cent of the total number of poor people in Latin America (113 million) and half of the extreme poor (46 million) live in urban areas, while approximately 20 to 25 per cent of the urban poor live in crowded slums.[2] However, at the moment, cities do offer a superior quality of life, along with greater opportunities for personal development. This is proven by the fact that the incidence of poverty among the urban population – affecting 28 per cent of the total – is half that of rural areas, and extreme poverty – affecting 12 per cent – is a third.

According to Ravaillon (2002), who bases his argument on cross-sectional data from thirty-nine countries and his work in India, there are identifiable conditions under which the poor urbanise faster than the non-poor, implying that the urban share of the poor is an increasing convex function of the urban share of the population. Latin America displays these conditions. By 2015 the rate of urbanisation is expected to increase further, with urban areas concentrating about 85 per cent of the population, up from 77 per cent in 2000. If poverty rates remain unchanged, by 2015 two thirds of the Latin American poor will be living in cities; that is, 22 million more people than in 2000, 9 million of which will be living in extreme poverty.

Urban Sprawl and the Abandonment of the City Centre

The environmental reach of Latin American cities is expanding rapidly. Cities keep growing on their peripheries and exercising mounting pressure on the environment by consuming large quantities of water and energy, land for urban usage and land, water and air to dump waste. Urban sprawl is fuelled by a complex set of factors. High- and middle-income households move to expansion areas on the periphery in search of bigger houses and to escape the congestion and pollution of the central areas. Commerce and services follow the richer groups, providing modern amenities and developing ad hoc services for the new urban culture (shopping malls, country clubs, gated communities). Expanding economic activities seek new developments on the periphery to establish new plants and office space, emptying the central areas which are then gradually occupied by lower-income families and by less dynamic activities, and eventually by depredatory activities, which in turn accelerate the abandonment of the area. The process is facilitated by a massive increase in car ownership and continual expansion of public transport networks, supported by the government along with the supply of public services, to reach the newly expanded areas on the outskirts.

Another factor is the lack of government action to control urban growth. In their analysis of recent transformations occurring in Santiago de Chile, which include the sub-urbanisation of the periphery, Greene and Soler (2004) link transformation not only to economic processes such as the impact of globalisation and the cultural changes it brings about, but also to what they call a 'non-transformation'. This term refers to the legal, normative and planning systems that have had practically no effect on the processes of transformation. They emphasise the importance of efficient urban planning, focused not on designing the desired future of urban space but on directing, orienting and giving shape to existing tendencies.

Urban development oriented towards the periphery can generate polycentric cities and bring some advantages: it is suggested that greater accessibility to urban services may reduce commuting distances and decrease congestion. However, it has a negative effect on traditional centres which, as explained above, are abandoned by members of the upper and middle classes who take with them the most dynamic economic activities and employment sources. This starts a process of urban deterioration that affects economic activities, inhabitants, buildings and monuments. In his description of this process, Bertaud (2002) points out that many cities, as they grow in size, depart from the original monocentric structure and move to a polycentric one. He observes that as a consequence of this process, the city centre loses its leading role to multiple clusters of activities spread over a vast territory which, in turn, requires people to travel longer distances.[3] Additionally, dominantly monocentric cities tend to have much higher densities close to the centre than cities that are polycentric. As can be observed in most Latin American cities, the decay of the city centre is further aggravated by the change from a monocentric to a polycentric urban structure.

The process of deterioration and the abandonment of city centres leaves large quantities of underutilised urban assets, including infrastructure, roads, public spaces, and public and private buildings. The underutilisation of city centre areas and the accompanying process of urban sprawl increase the cost of running cities, not only because of the additional expense of supplying outlying areas with sanitation and energy, but also because of the cost of transport, including both the construction of roads and the added cost paid by commuters.

It is important to understand these tendencies as two sides of the same process. In other words, peripheral growth and the development of multiple centres are the result of the abandonment and deterioration of original city centres (Rojas 2004: 2–10). Figure 6.1 illustrates the two population curves for Santiago de Chile. It is clear that while the city's population rose dramatically between the 1960s and 1990s, the population in city-centre areas shows a steady decline. The figure also shows the city's urban growth over the same years.

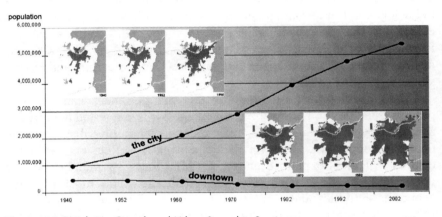

Figure 6.1 Population Growth and Urban Sprawl in Santiago

As the disadvantages of urban sprawl and city-centre abandonment became evident, governments initiated programmes to rehabilitate the central areas and attract a new population and urban activities. Initially the main concern was the loss of urban and historical heritage areas, yet most city-centre urban rehabilitation programmes to date are driven by concerns about the future of central areas and the impacts of their deterioration on the rest of the city. In most Latin American cities, there are city centre rehabilitation programmes currently in progress or under preparation.

The Urban Impact of City Centre Deterioration

Cities are composed of heterogeneous but interrelated neighbourhoods or districts. This implies that the problems of one area cannot be treated in isolation; the argument developed in the previous section offers an example of such interdependence. Poverty in the city centre involves multiple socio-cultural groups: poor people from the suburban slums who converge daily on the centre to carry out their activities, and poor people who live permanently in the city centre area either in formal or informal housing – in short, both residents and non-residents. These two groups differ for several reasons. Poor housing and insufficient access to services are not the same for non-residents and residents. The majority of non-residents are faced with severe difficulties in finding employment, have little access to public services and suffer from a lack of sanitation. In addition, non-residents suffer from tenure insecurity in relation to their property in the informal, peripheral settlements where they live. Residents, on the other hand, face severe overcrowding but have easy access to services and employment.

The dynamics of poverty are also different. While poor people in centres live under constant threat of being expelled as a consequence of urban renewal interventions, amongst other things, experience shows how poor people in the periphery always tend to progress, over time, towards more secure tenure and better services. The group of poor non-residents may also change in number and composition as the attractiveness of the centre changes, either creating new earning opportunities (pull factors) or inducing them to move to emerging sub-centres (push factors).

There is little data on the number of non-residents who depend on the city centre for their sustenance. Most of the existing information results from national censuses and refers primarily to residents. According to Wolff (2003), in Santiago de Chile, the ages of the population leaving from and arriving in the city centre are very different: the age of those leaving ranges between 0 and 44 while the age of those who arrive is generally over 65. Therefore, the central area is failing to maintain its younger resident population while attracting older, less dynamic groups.

It thus happens that the advantages obtained by the poor when they occupy the city centre on a massive scale are gained at the detriment of other users. In the city centre, the coexistence of poor – or low-income – people, with their informal economic activities, and the wealthier population which conforms to more formalised socio-economic structures, is difficult and problematic. In practice, such a situation has a different impact on the poor population according to their personal characteristics: age, gender, physical condition, race, culture, habits and household structure. These factors need to be taken into account when designing plans for the revitalisation of city centres.

Urban Rehabilitation in City Centre Areas

The revitalisation of urban centres is a complex endeavour requiring coordinated interventions in the economy, and the social and the physical structures of the area. This requires the joint action of several actors: the public sector, the community, consumers, investors and real estate developers. Furthermore, the rehabilitation process requires interventions in at least four areas of urban development: infrastructure; public services; quality of public spaces; and accessibility (Rojas 2004: 37, 38).

Launching a rehabilitation process requires not only strong public leadership and the drafting – and execution – of comprehensive plans which, in turn, require agreement between all stakeholders, but also heavy investment of public resources for prolonged periods of time. If the launch is successful, the area being rehabilitated becomes attractive to private investment as well as to new residents who would like to move in. However, it is only after a prolonged period of public investment that the rehabilitated area enters a sustainable stage when private investment begins to generate profits and public investment may be reduced (Rojas 1999: 29–34). The best signs of rehabilitation are the arrival of new economic activities and residents, and the corresponding rise of land prices.

The revitalisation strategies used at present vary from those that privilege physical dimensions to those that put the accent on social and economic variables. Nevertheless, none of these strategies will be sustainable if they do not attract inhabitants and economic activities to the rehabilitation area and, in so doing, generate a 'gentrification process'. The process is best described as an urban invasion by which the original population and economic activities are replaced by a new bourgeoisie and more productive activities. It has a dual connotation: on the one hand, it is a sign of the success of the rehabilitation process – the newcomers have greater purchasing power, can afford rehabilitated houses and support the expansion of commerce and services in the area, further fuelling the rehabilitation process; and on the other, it has a negative connotation as it expels low-income residents, particularly tenants who are excluded from the benefits of this revitalisation.

The gentrification process is pervasive in rehabilitation areas and raises a significant public policy issue as well as several practical issues. First and foremost, it creates an equality issue in as much as the displaced population ends up in worse conditions than they were before rehabilitation. They lose access not only to cheap and centrally located housing, but also access to a large pool of jobs, as well as to leisure and public spaces which are abundant in city centre areas. Most end up enlarging the ranks of the marginalised dwellers of informal settlements on the periphery of cities. Second, gentrification may endanger the long-term sustainability of rehabilitation processes, inasmuch as the affected population may stall, or diminish, the commitment of the public sector to invest and to support private projects in the area. A third ill effect of gentrification is the loss of social diversity in rehabilitated areas, a process which may, eventually, reduce the attractiveness of the area and create social tensions that may affect the process of rehabilitation.

Tackling Urban Poverty in City Centres

Policies and programmes devised to help the poor have evolved over time in tune with new ways of understanding poverty. Such new views are particularly significant to the field of urban studies. For a long time poverty was understood as the inability to obtain access to certain goods – the basic basket. Thus, it was directly associated with and estimated in terms of per-capita income. Then, fighting poverty consisted mainly of generating more income and relied heavily on economic policies. It became apparent, however, that some groups – precisely the informal groups – did not have access to some urban services that were considered essential to achieve a minimum standard of life. A set of 'basic needs' was defined and the 'unsatisfied basic needs' (UBN) indicator was developed; it considered five aspects of life: access to public services (electricity, drinking water and sanitation); rate of schooling (children of school age who attend school); dependency rate (number of non-working individuals per working person in the household); material quality of the house (walls, floor and roof); and overcrowding (number of inhabitants per room).

The UBN perspective had the advantage of bringing the built environment into the arena. When poverty was considered only from the income perspective, architects, urban planners and geographers had little, or no, contribution to make. With the development of the UBN, however, housing becomes defined as a basic need and is considered an important starting point in efforts to overcome poverty. In this way the UBN presented a new way of understanding poverty that allowed for a separation of needs and gave rise to alleviation programmes focused on these specific needs. An example of one of these need-specific programmes is the Neighbourhood Upgrading Programme (NUP), developed in many countries to improve the living conditions of the urban poor.

It is quite clear that by the end of the last century a new form of poverty, commonly referred to as urban poverty and mostly located in city centres, gained prominence. This category refers to groups of the population stigmatised by unemployment and economic inactivity. Such groups are dependant on institutional assistance – such as government benefits – and the young show high levels of school truancy. The new urban poor frequently suffer from the effects of drastic social segregation and, statistically, are prone to resort to forms of antisocial behaviour like delinquency and street violence. Tironi (2003) has referred to this idea as a 'ghettoisation' of urban poverty, characterised by spatial concentration, social homogeneity and a sense of segregation. Some of the main cities in Latin America show signs of this new urban poverty. Thus, if the UBN's position in relation to poverty brought the built environment into the social arena, this new manifestation of urban poverty becomes a challenge for all professionals involved in the production of the built environment who now need to find solutions requiring physical interventions in urban space.

Urban rehabilitation programmes aimed at central areas are usually motivated by concerns other than those of the poor, whose plight in the city centre is often little known, or is overshadowed by the huge social and urban problems presented by the informal settlements of the periphery. These interventions tend to be motivated by a desire to rehabilitate city centre areas rather then by social concerns for the urban poor. It is all the more important, therefore, that we recognise trends such as urban poverty and its ghettoisation and thus formulate successful interventions which might include the provision of affordable housing and the expansion and improvement of employment opportunities for the lower-income members of the population.

Inasmuch as affordable housing programmes involve a form of wealth transfer, they require financial resources in addition to those provided by local governments; usually they require transfers from higher tiers of government. Addressing repopulation issues in city centre areas thus depends intimately on the availability of efficient public housing polices. Similarly, the generation of new employment and the enhancement of existing employment opportunities available for low-income individuals in central areas require, in addition to a good business climate – which is mostly the result of sound macroeconomic policies – coherent labour training, technology transfer and micro-credit programmes.

Mitigating Gentrification

As stated above, gentrification has a dual connotation: positive, as a sign of the success of city-centre rehabilitation processes; and negative, as a burden imposed on the weakest members of society, the poor. Amongst the poor, however, the most affected are tenants that loose access to cheap and well-located housing.

While gentrification is an unavoidable effect of rehabilitation, programmes need to include measures to mitigate its most damaging consequences. Mitigation efforts are made simpler when rehabilitation programmes are the result of ample consultation between all stakeholders, and when they adopt an integrated approach to the problem. In other words, when rehabilitation programmes take into account not only issues affecting the physical fabric but also the social fabric of the area. Measures to mitigate gentrification may include pecuniary compensation for those who choose to leave the area. However, catering for tenants who choose to stay in the area requires more complex procedures. One option is to retain sufficient low-cost rental accommodation. This approach poses significant operational problems because private investors do not profit from investing in low-cost rental housing with high maintenance costs.

A second approach is to require developers to include in their projects a small proportion of affordable housing at prices below the standard market costs which is financed with profits obtained from other more profitable parts of the project, such as up-market housing units. This approach is feasible when the rehabilitation area fetches high prices on the market. Otherwise, requesting private developers to shoulder the cost of affordable housing may jeopardise the whole rehabilitation effort. The retention of the houses constructed in the below-market range is a problem because owners may sell their units to cash in on the price difference. In the United States, local authorities work through Community Land Trusts that retain ownership of the land or have the first option to purchase the houses that go on sale. Another option is to provide access to these houses as cooperatives, so that what the beneficiaries actually own are shares in the co-op which, in turn, regulates prices.

A third approach to retaining the poorer groups in the central areas is for the government to subsidise owner-occupied housing in the area for qualified low-income residents. This approach is currently practised in several countries and is the basis for the Chilean experience discussed in this work. As mentioned above, it relies on the availability of a well-functioning housing policy and on the availability of mortgage-based financing at reasonable cost.

Housing the Poor in Rehabilitation Areas: The Chilean Experience

As was the case in other Latin American countries during the twentieth century, the development of Chile was characterised by a demographic-territorial explosion, a rapid process of urbanisation and a significant concentration of the country's population in just a few cities. During these years the population grew from a little more than three million to more than fifteen million, while the concentration of the country's population in Santiago grew from 10 per cent in 1907 to 32 per cent at the end of the century. This led to significant housing problems, including a shortage in the provision of formal housing, overcrowding, household duplication – or *allegamiento*, the incorporation of other members, mostly married children, into the household due to a lack of alternative housing – land seizure and informal settlements.

Chile was one of the first countries to have governmental policies regarding housing issues. This concern was expressed in a legal framework for social housing that predates most other countries – the first national law on social housing dates from 1906 – and, since the middle of the twentieth century, the political and social importance given to the provision of dwellings available to all sectors of the population has prompted successive administrations to implement governmental programmes for low-income households. Until the early 1990s, and in spite of the government's efforts to provide finished houses or fully serviced plots, the growth of the population surpassed the annual provision of housing, a situation that became more acute with every passing year. In the 1990s, with the return of democratic government, and as a precaution against land seizures and the creation of informal settlements, a very aggressive social housing policy was implemented. It was aimed, mainly, at the production of more housing solutions using public resources while encouraging the involvement of the private sector in the construction and financing of houses. Nevertheless, while more housing units were produced than the average rate of population growth required, the quality of the housing built, as well as of neighbourhoods, deteriorated due to cost-cutting policies whose aim was to maximise the production of houses at fixed low budgets.

Public housing policies, which encourage low-cost houses to be built on the periphery of cities both in order to reduce the incidence of land cost and to respond to consumer preferences for suburban areas, have caused the sprawl of Chilean cities. As a compensatory measure, in the 1990s the central government added the rehabilitation of deteriorated central areas to its urban development objectives. Key amongst such objectives was the attempt to draw new residents to city centres which, for five decades, had systematically lost population. With this aim in mind, the central government set up a scheme whereby it financed a national programme to induce first-time buyers to purchase new or renovated houses in central areas. The government subsidised buyers with one-off upfront grants representing anything from 6 to 15 per cent of the dwelling's purchase price, depending on the total price. The so-called 'Urban Rehabilitation Subsidy' applies to houses in designated rehabilitation areas of deteriorated large city centres. This approach, however, caused the gentrification effect discussed above.

Thus, in 2002 the Chilean government produced the 'New Urban Policy' in order to address several aspects that had not been covered by the previous housing and urban development plans, most of which were strongly biased toward the quantitative side of the problem. The following section is a brief discussion of those Chilean housing policies and programmes which provide the background to analysis of the most recent proposals.

Chilean Housing Policy

In 1977 Chile introduced reforms to the housing sector that anticipated by almost a decade the fundamental policy shift that took place in housing agencies in other countries. In view of the fact that direct state provision never met the needs of the majority of the population, nor did it serve well the broader social and economic interest of the society, the government introduced public policy reforms and regulations enabling housing markets to work more effectively by transferring the bulk of the responsibility for the production and financing of housing projects to the private sector. These reforms were fundamentally consistent with the system known as the 'enabling approach' to housing policy (United Nations-Habitat 2005; World Bank 1993; IDB 1995). The reforms for the implementation of the enabling approach focus on three key areas: two on the demand side –the development of a mortgage-based housing financial system and the introduction of subsidies to low-income households so as to enable them to access private mortgages – and one on the supply side, the deregulation of land development in order to reduce costs.

Under this approach, historical difficulties which prevented the market from satisfying the needs of the low-income population were considered to reside in the insufficient purchasing power of these households. Therefore, the state adopted a subsidiary role to help households in need by supplementing their purchasing power with upfront subsidies in association with private banks which would provide complementary financing. Subsidies were financed through annual allocations given by the central government to the Ministry of Housing and Urban Development (MINVU). Middle- and upper-income households were expected to find financing in private banks mostly without government assistance.

Complementing the reforms, in 1978 the government introduced changes in the regulation of urban development that had the effect of liberating the urban land market. These reforms eliminated most land development restrictions arising from the strictly enforced urban-fringe and land-use regulations contained in municipal master plans, which had been implemented in the early 1930s. Rules for incorporating land into urban usage were simplified and the regulation of land usage made more flexible in order to allow urban growth to respond to market trends.

At the same time, the direct participation of the public sector in housing construction became practically non-existent. Its involvement was restricted to the provision of one-off direct subsidies to low-income households. The subsidy scheme was so effective that it was extended to other areas of urban development, notably to promote the rehabilitation of inner city areas by encouraging the construction of new housing in deteriorated areas of the city. Later, the scheme was also used to promote the rehabilitation of urban heritage areas.

However, reaching households in the first two quintiles of income distribution has proved to be difficult under this system. By focusing primarily on formal housing production, projects based on the enabling market approach do not attend to housing processes that provide shelter to a significant percentage of the population through both the informal acquisition of land and staged – and mostly self-financed – housing construction. However, this issue was addressed in the housing policy introduced by the MINVU in 2002, a policy which includes programmes that supply people with a core-housing unit at a reduced cost. In this programme, recipients are expected to expand their basic core unit into a full-sized house through self-construction or community help. Figure

6.2 summarises the financing scheme of the ten main social housing programmes implemented since 2002: five oriented to the low-income population, two to the low- and middle-income groups and three to the emerging middle-income groups.

Directed Towards	Programmes	House Value	Maximum Subsidy	Minumum Saving	Loan
Low-Income Population	Housing Solidarity Fund	10,326(*)	9,638 (+344*)	344	0
	Dynamic Social Housing without Debt	10,326 max	9,638	344	0
	Progressive Subsidy: First phase	4,819	3,442 to 4,543 5,163(***)	plot	0
	Progressive Subsidy: Second Phase	2,409 max	1,205-620	172	1,033 to 1,618
	Rural Subsidy	9,638 to 13,768	5,163 to 6,884	172 to 344	
Low- and Middle-Income	Special Housing	13,768 max	4,819	344 to 688	3,442 max
	Special Workers programme	12,047	3,088 to 5,163	1,377	
Emerging Middle-Income	Unified Subsidy	34,420	7,228 to 11,359 15,489	688	
	Urban Renewal Subsidy	34,420 to 68,840	6,884	1,442 – 6,884	
	Subsidy to Heritage Rehabilitation	41,304 to 68,840	8,605	1,442 – 6,884	

Notes: (*) This value can be increased with third party funds
(**) The additional US$344 corresponds to technical assistance
(***) The 5163 subsidy corresponds to beneficiaries who renounced to apply later for second phase subsidy

Figure 6.2 Current Housing Programmes (in US$)

It is important to note that among the programmes considered by the Chilean government, the one designed specifically to repopulate urban centres – the Urban Renewal Subsidy – is clearly not oriented to the urban poor but to households interested in buying new or rehabilitated houses in designated areas. On the other hand, all five programmes designed to help the population with the scarcest resources consider incremental subsidies, or building in stages.

The Housing Solidarity Fund is a flexible programme that provides the opportunity to address a wide range of housing needs, including minimum core units in the city centre. This programme, designed to provide housing solutions to families below the poverty line, is oriented towards organised groups, and finances the construction of one or more of the following housing solutions:

- A new dwelling consisting of a living and dining room, kitchen, bathroom and one bedroom
- Plot densification (construction of another dwelling on one plot)
- Dwelling construction on the same plot where families live
- Acquisition and improvement of existing dwellings
- Acquisition and rehabilitation of dwellings in *cités* (old inner-city minimum-standard dwellings)
- Acquisition, rehabilitation and subdivision of old buildings in order to convert them into dwellings

Chilean Housing Policy Applied to the City Centre

In order to promote the provision of affordable housing in city centre areas, some of which are under active rehabilitation, different local authorities and community organisations have taken advantage of the programmes advanced by the central government. A pioneering experience was the Santiago Development Corporation (CORDESAN). Faced with the abandonment of a critical portion of the central area of Santiago de Chile, CORDESAN carried out a comprehensive rehabilitation programme that included the removal of undesirable land uses from the area (a prison, various bus terminals and derelict vehicle depots), improvements to public spaces, rehabilitation of heritage buildings, construction of new facilities (a cultural centre at a heritage railway terminal) and the construction of new parks in the railway yard. In order to attract new residents to the area, CORDESAN undertook a pioneering housing project to benefit teachers in the municipal school system (a low-/middle-income group but with social prestige). With central government subsidies and bank loans, the beneficiaries acquired affordable houses built by private contractors. The project proved the feasibility of building new houses in the area at prices consistent with the purchasing power of potential beneficiaries (supported by government subsidies). This in turn attracted the attention of other potential buyers who approached the corporation in order to buy a house in the area. With a long list of potential buyers, CORDESAN then approached private developers to promote new investments. In the initial phases of the process, CORDESAN helped potential buyers to obtain central government subsides and certified the quality of the projects. Within a short time, the market for this type of housing gained buoyancy and as the income of potential buyers increased so the use of central government subsidies decreased (Rojas 2004: 163–78). As a result, a process of gentrification began within a few years as interest in new housing in the area moved from the initial low-/middle-income groups, to solid middle-income and, eventually, to upper middle-income groups. Supply followed demand and house-quality-motivated prices increased.

The strategies of CORDESAN have been successful in bringing new residents to a deteriorated portion of the centre of Santiago. However, it also underscores the difficulties in supplying houses affordable to people in the lower brackets of the income structure. The high cost of land in city centre areas and the cost of building a house are the major hurdles to be overcome. Of course, the high cost of land can be partially compensated for with high-density housing, and house designs that allow for construction in stages (by the owners themselves) can reduce the initial cost. However, these two solutions are somewhat contradictory. Incremental or phased house construction is easier to accomplish technically in one-storey houses on large plots, while high density calls for multiple-storey structures to reduce the cost incurred by land.

Incremental Design: Three Chilean Cases

Tackling these contradictory issues is the key feature of the most recent programmes to supply affordable housing in central urban areas of Chile. They rely on good design and, also, on the involvement of the community both in the design and execution of the project in order to achieve the goal. The following case studies illustrate three different situations found in central areas of Chilean cities, and offer interesting lessons for scaling-up programmes to mitigate gentrification in urban rehabilitation.

In the Comunidad Andalucía case, tenants of deteriorated houses in a central area of Santiago were to be evicted to allow for the urban renewal of the area. The promoters of the renewal project offered to subsidise houses on the city's periphery under the traditional housing programmes sponsored by MINVU. A small group of tenants accepted this solution while the rest fought to stay in the area given the proximity to their jobs and easy access to urban services. The project servicing this group aimed at producing houses whose cost complied with the parameters of affordability established by the MINVU, by using high density in order to maintain or limit the incidence of the cost of land.

The 'Proyecto Elemental' project developed a small in-fill site in the city centre of Iquique, a city in northern Chile. Families had begun to occupy the site illegally several years earlier and had proceeded to build precarious shelters without sanitation, which eventually became overcrowded. In addition to these poor living conditions, the settlement was affecting the development of the surrounding areas, mostly low middle-income neighbourhoods. The objective of the project was to allow all the families to remain on the site by providing housing solutions within the parameters of affordability set out by the MINVU.

The third case is somewhat different. It consists of a proposal to intensify the use of occupied residential plots in the first ring of growth surrounding Santiago's city centre. These areas, formerly on the city's periphery, became occupied by low-income people as part of government-sponsored housing programmes. As a result of urban growth, these areas are now relatively central and are highly valued as they have good urban facilities and easy access to jobs. Due to these areas' good location and relatively low density, new young families often choose to live with their parents rather than move to the new housing developments on the outskirts of the city. This proposal offers possibilities for the densification of plots by building extensions to existing houses or by building an additional house on the original plot. The three cases are also expressions of exceptionally good architectural design.

Case One: Low Height and High Density City Centre
The Comunidad Andalucía project commissioned architect Fernando Castillo Velasco, winner of the prestigious National Architecture Prize, to establish a model for the urban renovation of obsolete central areas without displacing low-income residents. The project brief specified providing affordable housing for 120 families who lived in old, deteriorated and overcrowded slums in Santiago's centre. Although the aim of the project was to fit within the budget offered by the

governmental funds, there was some flexibility due to a donation from the autonomous government of Andalucía, Spain, which was interested in promoting this type of good practice.

The approach adopted by the designer was to reduce the cost of the houses by providing a core unit to be completed by the beneficiaries. To achieve the high density required to meet the affordability targets, the houses were designed in two types: one in two storeys with access directly by outer stairs and the other in three levels with access from high-level open corridors. The ability to expand or complete the houses – what is called their incremental solution – was accomplished internally: the families would receive a cube – either two or three storeys high – with a central beam to receive the floor joists once the second or third storeys were built (see Figure 6.3). In this way the inhabitants received the full perimeter of the house but were left to finish their houses according to their needs and capacities (Eliash 1990). The design concept was developed in consultation with the beneficiaries, the importance of this communication perhaps being demonstrated by the fact that, on completion of the project, the houses have achieved a high level of consolidation with most second and third storeys finished. The final cost of the houses was above the government programme limits with the overruns covered by the grant from the government of Andalucía. Extra expenses stemmed primarily from additional structural costs needed to build five-storey houses to achieve the required density.

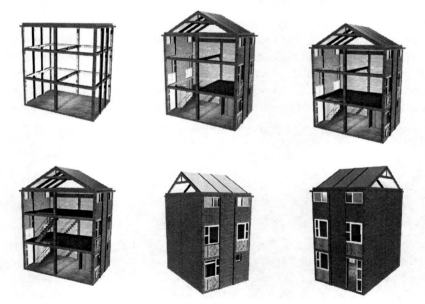

Figure 6.3 Low Height and High Density City Centre

Aside from the inventiveness of the design, which allows for a phased completion of the houses in a high-density situation, the project demonstrated the viability of building affordable housing for low-income households in central locations of the city, albeit at higher costs than in the periphery.

Case Two: Consolidation of an Informal Settlement in the City Centre
The architect Alejandro Aravena and a group of professionals from the Faculty of Architecture, Design and Urban Studies at the Pontificia Universidad Católica de Chile were asked by government authorities to assist in finding a solution to a complex problem posed by the need to settle one hundred families on a well located – and therefore expensive – half-hectare plot of land near the centre of Iquique, a medium-sized city in northern Chile. The inhabitants had occupied the land for at least thirty years, with no legal rights, no sanitation and in very precarious shelters.

The project was to fit within the budget provided by the Housing Solidarity Fund, one of MINVU's social housing programmes; therefore, the total cost per house, including the land, could not exceed US$10,300. At current building costs, this amount would allow, at most, the construction of structures with thirty square metres per dwelling, an area which is clearly insufficient to house a whole family. The designers chose, thus, to use the available resources to build the core of a house that could be expanded by their beneficiaries in the future. The initial unit would provide all the necessary components of the house: water, sewage and electric installations, and the kitchen, bathroom and stairs. The result was an ingenious 'parallel building' of houses built in twos, one over the other, allowing for horizontal growth at ground level for the ground floor houses and vertical growth for those above. The final houses, once enlarged by the inhabitants, would reach seventy-two square metres (see Figure 6.4).

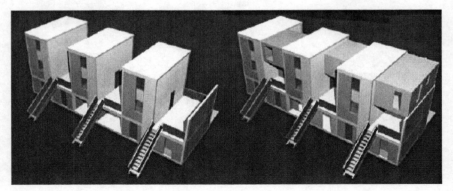

Figure 6.4 Development of an Informal Settlement in the City

The design process was carried out with community participation and several of the design options were adopted at the suggestion of the community. For instance, although the houses are built one over the other to achieve the required density, they do not have common spaces like doorways or stairs. This avoids the conflicts that plague apartment blocks.

The project demonstrated the viability of settling families in central locations within the limits of existing social housing programmes. The key element was the design of the houses that allowed the phased completion of the houses in a high-density situation. The project has been hailed as an example of good design and as a preview for an international competition to design the best housing solutions for centrally located sites in seven different cities around Chile. At the moment four of the projects have been built, while the other three are in different stages of design.

Case Three: Making Better Use of Residential Land: The Plot Densification Programme

The periphery of Santiago was built up to a great extent around what is known as '9 x 18 metre plot settlements', a phrase that refers to the dimensions of the plots produced by the public housing programmes of the 1950s, 1960s and 1970s. Some of these housing solutions initially offered only urbanisation – a plot with all the services attached to it, but no house – while others included two- or three-bedroom houses. With the rapid expansion of Santiago, these plots, which when built were located on the periphery, now form part of the consolidated city, and most inhabitants value their relatively good location highly.

At present, in addition to the house built by the original occupants, most of these plots have informal buildings at the rear of the plots where new families (often relatives of the original owners) with no access to formal housing live. These inhabitants share the sanitary facilities with the legal owners and generally live in precarious shelters. This situation often affects not only their own living conditions but also those of the original beneficiaries due to overcrowding. On the positive side, this spontaneous plot sharing has proved to be an efficient form of mutual help: aside from having a place to live, the younger families benefit from help with child care provided by the mostly elderly original beneficiaries, who also look after the property during working hours; in turn, the original occupants benefit from the rent paid by the new occupants, either in money or in kind (for instance by paying the bills).

Architect Francisco Vergara from the School of Architecture at the Catholic University of Chile conducted studio sessions with architectural students in order to design improvements to the housing conditions of these dwellers. The designs were further developed in the students' graduation projects and by the same (ex)students, now as young architects, in projects that continued to benefit from the support of the school's experienced lecturers. As with the other two projects discussed, the proposals had to fit within the parameters of the governmental social housing programmes. In this case, however, the quality of the solution benefitted from the fact that there were no land costs and an important part of the infrastructure was already built.

With variations to cater for local conditions, the solutions consisted mostly of a second house built at the rear or front of the plot (depending on the position of the original house) consisting of a first (twenty-nine square metres) and second storey (thirty-two square metres) without occupying the ground floor. This approach provides more privacy to both families and offers a new roofed area to the original house. The resources provided by the government allow for the construction of a finished house, given that there is no land cost and infrastructure costs are only for domiciliary connections. Approximately ten of these houses have already been built and they have had a great impact on the settlements both socially – by turning what was considered a survival strategy into a formal housing solution – and physically, as the three-storey constructions stand out visibly in the predominately one- or two-storey neighbourhood.

Final Remarks

The rehabilitation of deteriorated central areas is turning into a policy of choice for local governments in Latin America. Following good practices in the United States and Europe, and adapting them to local circumstances, many cities are succeeding in bringing new businesses and residents to their abandoned central areas. They are also encountering similar problems; in particular, the gentrification of the rehabilitated areas which expels lower-income households and informal businesses that previously benefitted from the low cost of living and the centrally located housing and workplace. The problem posed by gentrification in Latin America is as intractable as that faced by cities in the developed world. It cannot be avoided, only mitigated. Central to this effort is the capacity of the rehabilitation programmes to provide housing for the most vulnerable group: that of the tenants of low cost housing in areas around the city centre.

The presence of a good housing policy is a key factor in determining whether a mitigation programme can be implemented. As they involve wealth transfers to the beneficiaries – either to supply affordable rental housing or affordable housing in ownership – the programmes require grants to finance them. However, the availability of higher-tier financing on its own does not ensure success. The high costs of land purchase and house construction usually prevent the use of traditional social housing solutions in central areas. Phased housing construction, or so-called incremental housing, is one possible solution, although difficult to implement at the high level of density required to reduce the impact of land prices on the final cost. Successful implementation of this approach is heavily dependent on two other conditions: the active participation of beneficiary communities and good programme design and execution.

In all three of the cases discussed, the housing solutions were successful in large part due to the active participation of the communities involved. Not only did the recipients provide their opinions and input into the design process, but they themselves finished constructing the houses provided by the programme. Either through self-help or communal help, household members added floor space to the core units and improved or installed the finishings. This method relies heavily on the community's capacity to work together and support its members. It also puts a burden on rehabilitation programmes, which must provide technical support to the beneficiaries to ensure good-quality construction. The availability of micro credit for home expansion and improvements greatly facilitates the process.

The second condition, good design, is usually more difficult to achieve. The cases discussed are the result of somewhat exceptional circumstances: award-winning architects commissioned by the government, design work carried out to the standards of academic excellence, graduate students supervised over many years by leading teachers and practitioners in the field, winning entries in international design competitions. These conditions are hard to replicate. However, the three cases place a premium on social response and the dissemination of good practice and serve as both inspirations and benchmarks for 'real life' programmes that need to be implemented on tight budgets and work schedules.

Finally, in relation to the problem in hand – housing the poor in city centres – there are three important lessons to be extracted from the previous analysis. The first is the need to understand the role and timing of governmental action as enabling; that is, sharing responsibilities with the population and the private sector. This has to be understood not as government withdrawal but as taking responsibility for the dynamics of the process. For example, investors cannot individually halt the deterioration process of the city centres; they need well-timed actions that have to do with public space and public services. Second is the need to involve the community. The participation process should be seen as a reinforcement of social ties, not as a social cost or even as social investment but as pre-existing social capital that is an important resource to be recognised and harnessed. The inhabitants of the city centre most often correspond to a specific group – the urban poor – that needs to be attended to in differentiated ways that can be understood only through direct and close monitoring of the interventions. Finally, there is the need to consider incremental solutions – or buildings constructed in stages – oriented to the particular needs and specific attributes of the population and their social, economic and environmental circumstances, rather than solutions which deliver finished products for a faceless mass population. These incremental solutions can be understood, therefore, as forms of architectural design that develop, rather than seek to erase, informal building activities.

Notes

1. The authors are grateful to, and would like to acknowledge, FONDECYT for having financed this research through Project Number 1050928.
2. Slum incidence varies among countries and regions. Data from 2001 indicated that Central America showed the highest slum prevalence, at 42.4 per cent, while the Caribbean sub-region enjoyed a lower prevalence, with 21.4 per cent. At the time, South America, where urbanisation had reached a high and relatively stable level of about 80 per cent, had 35.5 per cent of its population living in slums (United Nations-Habitat 2005).
3. Bertaud (2002) outlines the circumstances that tend to accelerate the mutation toward polycentricity (a historical business centre with a low level of amenities, high private car ownership, cheap land, flat topography and grid street design) or tend to retard it (a historical centre with a high level of amenities, rail-based public transport, radial primary road network and difficult topography preventing communication between suburbs).

References

Bertaud, A. 2002. 'The Spatial Organization of Cities: Deliberate Outcome or Unforeseen Consequence?' *World Development Report Background Paper*. Wsahington, DC: World Bank.

Brakarz, J., M. Greene and E. Rojas. 2002. *Cities For All*. Washington DC: Inter-American Development Bank.

Eliash, H. 1990. *Fernando Castillo*: *De lo Moderno a lo Real*. Bogotá: Escala.

Greene, M. and F. Soler. 2004. 'Santiago: de un proceso acelerado de crecimiento a uno de transformaciones', in C. de Mattos, M.E. Ducci, A. Rodríguez and G. Yáñnez (eds), *Santiago en la Globalización*: *¿una nueva ciudad?*, Santiago de Chile: Ediciones SUR, EURE Libros.

IDB. 1995. 'Operational Guidelines for Housing', Publicaction SOC-111. Washington D.C.: Inter-American Development Bank.

——— 2004. *The Challenge of an Urban Continent*. Washington, DC: Inter-American Development Bank.

Ravallion, M. 2002. 'On the Urbanization of Poverty', *Journal of Development Economics* 68(2): 435–42.

Rojas, E. 1999. *Old Cities, New Assets*. Baltimore, MD: Johns Hopkins University Press.

——— 2004. *Volver al Centro. La recuperación de áreas urbanas centrales*. Washington, DC: Inter-American Development Bank.

Tironi, M. 2003. *Nueva Pobreza Urbana*: *Vivienda y capital social en Santiago de Chile 1985–2001*. Santiago de Chile: Ril Editores.

United Nations-Habitat. 2005. *State of the World's Cities 2004–2005*: *Globalization and Urban Culture*. New York: United Nations.

Wolff, P. 2003. 'Experiencias de Renovación Urbana: Acción de CORVi y CORMU en la Comuna de Santiago 1959–1973', Master's dissertation. Santiago de Chile: Instituto de Estudios Urbanos y Territoriales, Pontificia Universidad Católica de Chile.

World Bank. 1993. *Housing: Enabling Markets to Work, Housing Policy Paper*. Washington DC: World Bank.

——— 2000. *World Development Report*. Washington, DC: World Bank.

Part II:

Critical Practices

Chapter 7

Rules of Engagement: Caracas and the Informal City

Alfredo Brillembourg and Hubert Klumpner[1]

Introduction

In Caracas, a city ringed by verdant mountains and blessed with abundant rainfall, petrol is cheaper than drinking water. Caracas is flooded with oil money, but it has the largest, densest barrios relative to its size of any city of Latin America. Barrio, which literally means 'neighbourhood' in Spanish, is commonly used in Caracas to refer to the low-income urban settlements in which 55 per cent of the population lives on 33.5 per cent of the city's geographical footprint, in homes ranging from cardboard shacks to well-constructed, multi-storey buildings. The sites are often hazardous, and all have serious problems of access. Those homes built on the hillsides are highly vulnerable to mudslides. Those settlements encircling existing fixtures of city infrastructure – a water tank, market, sports venue, or industrial complex – are difficult to access and often have limited space for expansion which makes them extremely crowded. A third zone of housing runs along and just above the city's rivers and small creeks, which are prone to flooding, or follows the line of a highway, all of them hazards which must be negotiated by residents accessing their homes.

This is the informal city in Caracas. If one looks at it from a distance, one sees sprawling, rhizome-like shapes; one searches in vain for an ordering principle, a clear beginning and end, for ways to separate the whole into comprehensible elements. But close up, patterns begin to emerge and a certain logic – unlike that taught by conventional architecture or planning – can be discerned.

We do not believe 'informal' means 'lacking form'. It implies, for us, something that arises from within itself and its makers, whose form has not yet been recognised, but which is subject to rules and procedures potentially as specific and necessary as those that have governed official, formal city-making. Our work sets out to identify and describe that particular logic, to locate the order within the apparent disorder, so as to open up a productive dialogue about the relevance and the role of the informal city in the world.

In this chapter we wish to discuss Caracas and the informal city, and to position Caracas as an ideal laboratory for architecture and urbanism research in the 'global South'. We will describe the new urban context of informality in Latin America and the rest of the global South. We will describe informality's implications for urban theory, reimagining the barrio. We will talk about architectural practice in the informal city – what we call 'performative architecture' – using specific examples from our own architectural practice, Urban Think Tank. And we will conclude by presenting a rough agenda for architecture and design in the informal city, positioning architecture at the intersection of the economic, social, political and sustainable. Throughout we focus on the Caracas urban region because it is where we work and what we know, but we hope that our observations can be generalised to a certain extent to the rest of the global South, and specifically to Latin America. Moreover, we believe the lessons of the informal city extend to the developed world as well, where informality can also be observed.

Latin American Imaginaries

Is there any merit in generalising about Latin America from a single metropolis? In fact, almost all the big cities and many of the medium-sized cities of Latin America have two things in common. The first is an intense multiculturalism. Maybe this means the emblematic city of Latin America should be Miami, since this is the city in which all the countries of Latin America are represented. The multiculturalism to which we refer, however, is a three-way intersection of the indigenous population, and European and African migrations. In some countries there has been a large Asian migration as well.

These three cultural roots condition Latin America's contemporary development. They condition the way cities were founded and built, the way in which industry developed and the relationship between the city and the countryside. With regard to this relationship, the second characteristic that most big Latin American cities share is runaway growth since the Second World War. In colonial times, more than two thousand cities in the region were founded on the 'Laws of the Indies' of Philip II (Smith 2004: 39–53); but far more important for contemporary development is the urban explosion that has occurred in places like Mexico City, Rio de Janeiro, Lima or Caracas.

This explosion has no precedent in Europe or the United States. Caracas had approximately 500,000 inhabitants before the Second World War, but now has close to 6 million. This growth is particularly remarkable because it has generally not been accompanied by comparable industrialisation. Instead, it has produced a deficit in infrastructure, housing, education and all the needs of social reproduction. The result is that societies in the global South did not pass through an industrial age, but rather leapfrogged directly into the urban age, complete with vast and growing areas of poverty and exclusion. In Caracas, the two fastest-spreading housing types today are barrios and gated communities.

Caracas: Four Research Issues

When discussing the informal city in the global South, and specifically in Latin America, there are a range of urban locations suitable as test cases. But there are four factors that make Caracas a particularly good laboratory for architecture and urbanism research in the global South.

The first is that the city is profoundly modern, being almost entirely developed on the back of the oil boom that began in the 1950s. We could choose other cities if we wanted to emphasise other things, like Buenos Aires for its European-style architectural development or Rio de Janeiro for its picturesque setting and irresistible charm, but they are not as important in the contemporary development of urban Latin America. Caracas, in essence, is the idealisation of the postwar urban explosion. It is the ideal city to illustrate the challenges which not only most Latin Americans but most inhabitants of the global South have to face.

The second reason is that Caracas is a medium-sized metropolis in a mature state. With 6 million inhabitants, it is considerably smaller than the vast Latin American mega-cities like Mexico City or São Paulo. These cities are less relevant for our purposes, however, due to the fact that a majority of the world's urban population actually lives in medium-sized cities like Caracas, with between 500,000 and 6 million inhabitants, and this will be increasingly true in the future.

The third factor that makes Caracas vital for our purposes is that it has (relative to its size) the largest and densest informal urban settlements in Latin America, which are still growing and evolving. Currently, a little over one third of the city's geographical footprint contains 55 per cent of the population. Caracas is a model of accelerated growth, of the transformation of a magnificent valley complete with a tropical climate, abundant fresh water and fertile soil into a dramatic, over-extended, poorly-planned example of urbanisation. In this sense it is comparable to other Latin American cities, but it is probably the strongest expression of the friction – or even collision – between wealth and poverty. This has mostly to do with oil. The city's economic growth is tied not to an investment in diverse industries or commodities but to a single factor: petroleum rent. The result is a flourishing of services dependent on the government, at the expense of a diverse economy. This has created some advantages (liquidity) and some disadvantages (government monopolies).

Finally, there is the fact that Caracas is currently in political flux, and so it is ripe for the introduction of new ideas that will capture the imagination of politicians. The government of Hugo Chavez is attempting to reorganise Venezuela's role in the Latin American and international scene. The perpetual oil rent (2006 was another year of record-high prices), together with the government's desire for Caracas to become the centre of a new left-wing intelligentsia in Latin America, is driving the city to take a leading role in the Caribbean, as well as in the rest of Latin America. The implications for structural development are as yet unknown. Caracas today is the extreme representation of Latin America's utopian dream struggling to reinvent itself; the result is a period of uncertainty but also of great opportunity.

Informal City: The New Urban Context

We noted above that most medium and large-sized Latin American cities share an intense multiculturalism and a recent history of rapid physical and population growth. For the purposes of studying the informal city, growth is the most important factor. Runaway growth over the past half-century has changed the facts on the ground in modern Latin American metropolises, and it is absolutely fundamental that we – as architects, planners and urbanists – understand what has happened.

How, then, can we understand the informal city? Why is it that we know so little about these dense human agglomerations? Why do we treat these informal zones as blind spots in our cities? To answer these questions has become the mission of the Urban Think Tank over the last years. In addition, our book, *Informal City: Caracas Case* (Brillembourg, Fereiss and Klumpner 2005), presents new alternatives for understanding the processes involved in the formation and development of the 'unofficial' or excluded zones of Caracas (its barrios). For instance, it contradicts their standard characterisation as territories dominated by natural disasters, drug-related crime, illicit economies and impulsive squatter settlements.

In our view, two analytical concepts are particularly useful: regional urbanisation and informal globalisation. By regional urbanisation, we refer to the process by which cities not only expand rapidly, but develop into polycentric, networked urban regions. By informal globalisation, we mean the worldwide rise of the informal city. Its improvisation and flexibility make it a key aspect of, not an exception to, the globalised economy. We could in fact say we are witnessing the birth of twenty-first century urbanism.

These ideas are not meant to be concrete, crystallised designations. Like the image of the informal city itself, they are analytical guidelines, ways to capture the trends and coincidences we observe. They only have explanatory power to the extent that they are good descriptions of what is actually occurring in cities. But there are no easy explanations for informalism, and all we can offer are our own approximations.

Regional Urbanisation

Caracas right now is in the process of what we call regional urbanisation, something that has also occurred in Mexico City, São Paulo and Los Angeles. Regional urbanisation replaces old ideas of suburbanisation, of a core and a periphery. Cities are not simply growing outward from a centre; they are regionalising and developing into polycentric, networked urban regions: the geographer Edward Soja coined the term 'city region' to refer to this phenomenon. So we could say that metropolitan Caracas has six million inhabitants, while the Caracas 'city region' (which includes Los Valles del Tuy, Los Altos Mirandinos, Guatire, Guarenas and the Vargas coastal state) has twelve million and includes multiple orientations, multiple points of gravity. But it is important to remember that in addition to a regionalising process we are fundamentally talking about urbanisation. The majority of the world's population now lives in one of four hundred global city regions, each of which has a population of over a million people. Not only that, but it is estimated that all future world population growth will take place in urban regions. Venezuela is a perfect case study of this: a recent UN country report estimated that 87 per cent of the country's population lives in cities, with densities up to 678 persons per hectare, higher than Manhattan's 515 (United Nations 2001: 16).

In fact, when looking at regional urbanisation, it is also important to think about the way we measure and interpret densification. We focus on Soja's concept of 'city region' as the functional unit with which we need to be concerned because 'density' no longer appears to be a useful measuring tool. An example of this is the city region of Los Angeles, which has been growing very rapidly: there are now more than seventeen million people there and it is estimated that every hour twenty-three more people join them. At this point in time, what is typically considered the world's capital of low-density urban sprawl has actually surpassed the five boroughs of New York City as the densest urban area in the United States. Thus, if we use density as a measure of sprawl – or of sustainability, since we want compact cities – Los Angeles is the most compact, sustainable city in the United States, and Caracas the most sustainable in Latin America. This underscores the fact that density and sprawl are old concepts of the city and the metropolitan area.

The city region is an idea that is becoming more and more prominent. Economists and geographers agree that regional economies are the driving force in economic development. The environment and transportation need to be coordinated at this level as well. This is an urgent issue in Caracas right now, and in many other cities, and it highlights the importance of understanding urbanisation as *regional* urbanisation. As an indication of the prominence of the concept of city region, Urban Think Tank has been invited, on the basis of a methodology we presented to the Venezuelan Ministry of Transportation, to identify and study the country's fifty most strategically important cities, to develop their potential as network-nodes and to explore the possibilities of domestic and international connectivity.

Informal Globalisation

Our second analytical concept is informal globalisation. The informal city, long treated as an aberration or an exception to the standard of urbanism, is actually becoming the norm throughout the global South, and it does so as an integral part of the global economy.

Our research shows that in Caracas a growing majority of the city's inhabitants live in informal zones, and 80 per cent of new housing is self-built. The improvisation that characterises these zones resembles the 'plug-in, tune-up, clip-on' architecture of Yona Friedman (1999: 9–13). Unsurprisingly, this often collides with ordinances and laws, for example in Caracas where public spaces have been transformed into commercial strips and barrio houses project like rhizomes into the valleys. The informal city has generated its own modular design logic, and it needs to be better understood rather than ignored or treated like an aberration. This is a central tenet of our ongoing architectural practice and research.

Moreover, this informalisation needs to be seen as an aspect of globalisation. In contrast to traditional notions of urban informality as a consequence of scarcity, the informal city that has emerged across the global South coincides tactically with advanced capitalism. Its improvisation and flexibility make it a key aspect of, not an exception to, the globalised economy – equally in the barrios of Caracas and the shish-kebab stands of New York City.

It is important to recognise that when we talk about the informal city we are not simply talking about something criminal. By and large it is not illegal. It is simply extra-legal, outside the regulatory apparatus. It is also important to distinguish informal globalisation from the older idea of informalism as temporary, transitional, small-scale and concerned only with strategies for survival. The new informal concept is completely different, although it can sometimes look similar. It is permanent, established and large-scale. Sixty percent of the jobs in the global South are located here; they are products of informal globalisation.

You can also see this new informal economy in the industrialised world, in New York, London, Paris and Berlin. And the belief that in these cities an informal economy is a consequence of migration from the global South is an error. Immigrants do not have the power to implant these new economies; rather, they are responding to an effective demand for certain new ways to produce goods and services. Take Wall Street at lunchtime: a familiar image – the skyscrapers, the crowds, the odour of cooked meat on the street: street vendors selling shish kebab or Argentine *carne asada*. This is the encounter of the most advanced capitalism with the new informal economy, and it is why Hernando de Soto coined the phrase 'popular capitalism', given his admiration for invention in informal settlements (de Soto 2000: 86–92). The key is flexibility; the fact that it is cheaper is secondary. The deregulation of the economy has its output in this informal economy.

In Caracas, the barrios are also an exercise in sustainable development. Out of necessity, they produce less rubbish than other parts of the city. The few who collect this rubbish have formed a cooperative that sells recycled goods, and they are optimistic about the future of their enterprise, given the need for sustainability in cities. These are the new social-political actors that emerge on the critical economic terrain of new possibilities.

It is important that we do not look at informality as a sector existing apart from the 'legitimate' urban economy: it is superimposed, interlinked with the formal.

Demographic Transition

Regional urbanisation and informal globalisation: these are the two dynamics we believe are fundamental for understanding the new urban context of the informal city. But we also need to situate them in terms of the demographic transition: namely, urban and global populations are not going to continue to expand forever.

Historically speaking, we are in the midst of a short-lived explosion that peaked in the 1960s and is already beginning to trickle away. Two hundred years ago, population and economic growth rates skyrocketed and the transition to urbanity began, and within the next century, this process may well be complete as recent growth rates fall back towards zero (Kahn 1982: 30–32). The implication is not just that because Mexico City's population increased ten-fold in the last hundred years we should expect the same to happen again in the next hundred. Ours is the first generation to begin peeling away from the hyperbolic curve of growth. Consequently, our challenge is not to accommodate an ever-increasing population. Instead, our current challenge lies on issues regarding sustainability and redistribution. For this reason, the coming century will be crucial for creating a sustainable environment for human reproduction on this planet.

Reimagining the Barrio

The new urban context of the informal city raises implications for both theory and practice. In terms of the former, it requires a rethinking of the relationship between the barrio and the 'traditional' city.
•

The majority of citizens in metropolitan Caracas now live in the informal parts of the city, and the proportion continues to increase. This is a startling fact, and it suggests it is no longer possible to aspire to the concept of the nineteenth- or twentieth-century European city or to an urban beautification programme.

A new city is emerging for the majority of the world's population – one that undermines the dream of an ordered, planned and controlled environment based on the paradigms of traditional town planning. Even in cities like Paris, Berlin or New York, only a small percentage of the built surface corresponds to the ideals of an urban environment as imagined by the general public (just think of the Bronx, the poorest borough per capita in the United States). The regime of exclusion and the absence of beauty in the 'civilised' urban context raise a question: is it necessary to abandon the idea of the city as we know it completely before a new city can be realised?

For the great majority of the citizens of Caracas, this question has already been answered, yet the planning machinery in the city has failed to recognise the need for an updated understanding of the urban environment. Current initiatives – such as the CONAVI plan devised by the Venezuelan housing ministry – represent a rehashing of outdated housing concepts, smoothing the barrios into consolidated design districts and opening roads that bear no relationship to the inhabitants' concept of a village.[2] The failure to recognise the immediate problems facing the inhabitants of the informal zones of the city has led to a degradation of the environment, a compromise of infrastructure and increased violence and insecurity. The standard slum paradigm is clearly insufficient. We need to change the way we think of cities in the global South.

New Spatial Representations

To see the extent to which the current paradigm is insufficient, you only need to look at a standard map of Caracas and try to find the barrios. Despite being dense, even teeming with buildings and inhabitants, they are often represented simply as blank spaces. The implication is clear: informal zones and their inhabitants are not really part of the city, being considered temporary. But informal zones are not the exception – they are the rule. What does it mean to conceive of more than half the city as temporary or marginal?

Moreover, standard maps of Caracas show the city as a horizontal plane – completely flat. Yet the city is actually a staggering combination of mountains, hills and valleys. These topographical details tell a socio-economic story – patterns of wealth and poverty follow the curves of the hills – but flat maps are silent.

The problem is not just with conventional, static maps. To our knowledge, no architect has ever traced the changing geography caused by the development of low-income settlements on any city of the global South through the entire postwar period.

The Strength of Informal Settlements

We also need to reassess the informal city's institutions. We should not look at informalisation as social anarchy, or as the cast-offs of globalisation. The informal city has its own institutions, which have developed extra-legally to fill globalisation's gaps. The informal city has its own hierarchies and leaders, its own markets, its own economic order integrated into the world economy. Thanks to its sheer scale, the informal city is now finally emerging from the theoretical shadows. That is the case of Petare, in Caracas, which was considered the biggest barrio in the world. Yet, today, it is more accurate to describe it as the largest urbanised, self-built, suburban city. Not only does Petare offer housing and markets, but jobs and all forms of integrated public spaces.

When we think about informal settlements, there are certain conceptual dualities that are commonly deployed but are now out of date. 'Traditional' versus 'modern' is one of these: it is true that in the past informality was the traditional sector and formality was the modern, but today, when we find informal activities on the internet and at every level of the modern economy, this distinction is insufficient. The same is true for 'local' versus 'global'. Street vendors, for example, the epitome of the local, are now frequently supported by an entire complex supply chain that often stretches around the world. An informal supply chain might begin in Korean or Chinese production centres, then move to organising and distributing warehouses in abandoned historic city centres located in other countries and end with a person on the street selling pirated DVDs.

We should recognise the inherent strength of the informal city, which flows from its social adaptability. Self-organised informal urbanism organically addresses the shortcomings of modern urbanism; it fills the gaps.

The New Class

The final aspect to reimagining the barrio is updating our notions of its inhabitants. This is something that is particularly relevant in Caracas, given the political upheaval of the past few years, but it can be seen across Latin America. The barrio dwellers are a rising new class. They are dynamic, mobilised and increasingly powerful.

The rise of this new class is a consequence of the urban-growth dynamics mentioned earlier. The idea of popular capitalism as described by de Soto (2000) has brought about a true revolutionary change, but not one rooted in ideologies of the Left or Right. It is rooted in a socio-economic group that demands rights regardless of who is in power. The people of the new barrio class earn their living with their hands and build their own houses on the hills outside the regulatory system. They are routinely faced with urgent needs. They are likely to have an annual family income of between $1,000 and $10,000, to have never attended secondary school and university, and to have never held a formal job. They exert themselves on behalf of their own interests, but often see themselves as a progressive force. In fact, they embody Joseph Schumpeter's notion of creative destruction, of new growth sweeping away old institutions (Kahn 1982: 31). In contrast with the middle and upper classes, which have become increasingly economically conservative, the new barrio class is dynamic; through it, the new eats the old.

An essential aspect to the growing empowerment of the barrio dwellers is their increased political mobilisation. In combination with their large numbers, this means they are starting to fill a similar role as that of the middle class in North America and Europe as the electors of the government. The barrio has become politically vital in Venezuela and elsewhere throughout Latin America (it is the distorted equivalent of the 'moral majority' in the United States), but it remains to be seen whether the new class will benefit from its urban prominence.

Avoiding Catastrophe

What are the implications of informality for architects? What does the informal city mean for those who do their work in the global South, and what does it mean for those who see and hear about it from afar? Have architects become, or do they need to recast themselves as, agent provocateurs?

It is possible to differentiate between two types of planning. You can focus in your plans on what you hope to accomplish: best-case scenarios. Or you can focus in your plans on what you hope to avoid: worst-case scenarios. Successful architecture in the informal city follows the second model. Considering ideal conditions is a waste of time; the point is to avoid catastrophe.

Architecture in the informal city takes place in the context of urgency. This is obvious with the self-built houses that dominate the barrios. The 'ideal' house has a pretty, pitched roof. Roofs in the barrio are designed to allow for another house to be erected on top, usually by the future inhabitants. Four out of every five houses constructed right now in Caracas are self-built on appropriated land.

In the informal city, the architect has the potential to be an agent provocateur, to engage with what we want to call 'performative architecture'. Let us explain what we mean by this. A 'performative' is usually defined as a type of utterance that through its very enunciation accomplishes or generates a particular effect.

We believe architecture can be performative. That is, we see ourselves as agents or initiators of statements, either in built form or abstractly that can set in motion a series of social practices. This performative role of the architect can help delineate the contours of a community and in turn inject a certain collectivity into a community. In this role architecture also engages in a constant shaping and reshaping of the borders of the city by negotiating inclusions and legitimating exclusions.

Our Work

Urban Think Tank is our attempt to put these ideas into practice. After we left Columbia University in New York we were faced with the urban reality of Caracas. Through first-hand experience we discovered that not enough is being done to address the increasingly exacerbated urban condition. The city we experience has very little in common with the myth of the progressive modern Latin American city propagated by architects such as Carlos Raul Villanueva in Caracas and Oscar Niemeyer in Brazil. In the informal city we have the ability to challenge the materialistic treadmill of progress and object architecture and look for a practice of architecture based on other ideals – like real structural change for the global South.

We are immersed in what we call 'and/and' projects: the norm is adaptation to constantly changing conditions, building in a country under extreme economic and political circumstances. Uncertainty is the only constant in our daily routine as architects and, thus, we habitually begin many lines of work simultaneously – writing, mapping, researching, building and networking – that sustain one another, that interact synergistically and multiply. We are increasingly dissatisfied with an excess of computer-generated design and in our office we encourage first-hand, on-site experience. We find ourselves moving toward the pencil and the hammer, the physical three-dimensional model, the experiment combined with electronic tools.

Our practice is committed, first, to placing the social reality of a site at the forefront of political discussion. We are committed to building and sustaining dialogue between stakeholders and policy makers. Our non-profit research branch has developed into a school without the formalities of a school where interns from around the world mix with local community leaders in order to explore strategies for sustainable urban development in the global South. But our work does not merely contemplate the city. Rather, we initiate change in the city through direct intervention. The following are a few examples.

The Vertical Gym

Sports facilities stacked in the extremely dense environments of the informal settlements of Caracas offer the chance for integration and cooperation among the city's diverse communities. The Vertical Gym is dedicated to the belief that a physical structure can have a profound positive impact on social and physical interactions and a clear reduction in gang crime and health issues. It stands immediately outside the entrance to a barrio in Caracas's most affluent municipality and offers free services to all residents. It is a working alternative to the massive – and failed – social projects that sought to integrate citizens, but created just the opposite effect. Since the Vertical Gym's inception, crime has dropped sharply in the neighbourhood, exemplified by the astounding decrease in homicides from twenty-five each weekend to only five. The links between sports recreation and social well-being is so well established that it is mandatory by law in Venezuela that sports facilities be offered to neighbourhoods. But in great part due to urban space

Figure 7.1 Vertical Gym

limitations, these facilities have not been provided. The Vertical Gym manoeuvred around these obstacles and its positive effects are being thoroughly recognised.

House Core Unit

Caracas's informal city has spread through a region of dangerous, unstable and contaminated hills surrounding the main valley. Here one of the most pressing problems is the scarcity of water, and especially the lack of sewers and sewage treatment. A truly useful toilet in the barrio must meet certain requirements: it must be adaptable, functional despite resource deficiency, and built, altered and maintained self-sufficiently by the dwellers of the informal sector. Urban Think Tank's Core Unit is the culmination of each of these seemingly incongruous factors. With the incorporation of solar panels, a rain-catching roof and a storage tank, the design solution becomes a Core Unit from which the barrio house can grow. The toilet inside the unit is designed to separate off solid matter or sludge from the water, which, treated with chemicals, can be used as compost for growing medicinal herbs and vegetables on the roof of a single or communal home. Because of the lack of a proper collection system in the barrios and the fact that the sheer density of the urban landscape make even septic tanks impossible, the prototype is a solution that can feasibly be built and used by neighbourhood residents.

Prefab Modular Stairs

The issue of mobility within the barrios is both a cause for concern – in the case of lack of access – and a stimulus for community-building – in the case of the culture maintained within the boundaries of the informal city. Given the hilly geography of the barrios, stairs are central to this issue. But, overwhelmingly, the current stair systems within the barrios are old, worn and crumbling, where they still exist at all. Often there is no direct access between contiguous zones, and the lack of plumbing means that stairs often serve as drainage routes, to the detriment of the residents' health and safety. Urban Think Tank is implementing a prefabricated stair system to address these issues, in addition to issues such as cost, ease of construction, versatility and self-sustainability. The basis of the system is a familiar one in Venezuela: stilts, or *palafitos*. With the stairs raised off the ground the problem of rain and waste drainage is avoided, while the support tubing offers a way to run electrical wires and any other piping necessary. Barrio residents can install the stairs easily and cost-effectively as they are prefabricated and can be brought up the hills in pieces. Moreover, given the unstructured layout of the barrios, the versatility of the stairs allows them to be fitted to the neighbourhoods, not the other way around.

Conclusion: Transition to an Urban World

As we have shown in the projects described above, rather than producing a symbolic or autonomous architecture, our practice adopts concrete strategies that tend toward physical appropriation and production. It reflects our belief in politicising the urban sphere, and our interest in the performative elements of cultural-political practices. Moreover, we aim to reverse the top-down hierarchy of governance in the public sphere in favour of bottom-up, locally-driven action. Our clients are not corporations; they are cooperatives. This reversal sets up new paradigms for the dynamics of urban growth, the configuration of built form and social activities. Hence, we are not concerned with ideal situations because our work is about avoiding catastrophe.

We do not believe it possible to separate the concern for people from the concern for urbanism. The city's fate today is closely linked with virtually every aspect of human life. What is required is that people from a great many cities and a wide variety of disciplines consider evolutionary scenarios that lead from the present urban context of conflict and collision to a more just and sustainable future. We are not calling simply for open-ended or unfocused speculation; we live in an age of increasing specialisation, and for good reason. But the city is a complex system and specialisation must be supplemented by integration if we are going to adequately understand it. Architects, we think, are particularly well trained to integrate disciplines.

At Urban Think Tank we try to offer a platform for all disciplines to work. We meet to do research and to develop and build pilot projects aimed at making the city a better and more equitable place to live for all its citizens. In recent years we have invited people from a range of disciplines and from more than twenty countries to join us in taking a broad look at the whole as well as developing precise, acupuncture-like urban interventions.

We believe that in addition to the architectural and design dimensions, more and more we will need to consider environmental, economic and social questions as we intervene in the city.

Sustainable Development
Firstly, and most importantly, we need strategies for sustainable urban development. The example of Caracas illustrates how poverty colliding with development magnifies local geological and climatic hazards.

Particularly in urban areas, human activity has created a multiplicity of environmental problems, including climatic alterations, air pollution, diminishing fresh water, deforestation and soil erosion.

But solutions exist. Wealthy cities such as Caracas can reduce geological or meteorological risk through massive public works, for example by mitigating the risk of landslides with geo-textile nets and terracing over steep hillsides. In order to achieve sustainable urban development, we need:

- To understand and recognise the true scope, or footprint, of our urban areas
- To develop an approach to planning and architecture that acknowledges the centrality of resource management issues
- To protect our natural resources, which in Caracas are vast: the city has mountains, wetlands, a diverse ecology and more rainwater than it needs
- To redefine road and transportation infrastructure, *not* in order to reduce congestion, but to facilitate public transport, encourage air movement, create green ecological corridors and absorb carbon to produce clean air
- To redefine the uses and meaning of the city's parks: *not* just a space for public recreation, but also for water collection and storage, aquifers and ecology reserves
- To develop a new economic mechanism for reducing greenhouse gasses: we should pay the informal city to harvest carbon and give incentives for low carbon development

We believe our generation has the ability and the responsibility to address these sustainability issues. The question is whether metropolitan population growth in Latin America will level out as a result of foresight and progress toward more sustainable cities, or fluctuate as a result of those traditional scourges: war, conflict, famine and pestilence. If the curves of population and resource depletion do flatten out, will they do so at a level that will permit a reasonable quality of life, including a measure of freedom, and the persistence of a large amount of diversity? Or at a level that corresponds with a grey world of scarcity, pollution and regulation, with restrictions that make the coexistence of inhabitants and environment a mere question of survival?

Taking Informality Seriously
Architects, academics and politicians alike need to take informality seriously. We have entered an urban age where the city is the habitat for

the majority of the world's population and the informal city continues to grow. Yet, policymakers have reacted too slowly to this changed reality. The lack of attention to science and research in architecture and urbanism by policymakers who struggle to deal with the massive growth of cities remains astounding. For example, the situation in Caracas warrants the diversion of a greater portion of Venezuela's gross national product toward the city; however, paradoxically, the mayors and governors of Caracas have been spending progressively less on urgent urban issues. In sum, the distorted results of disparate and unrelated efforts have produced serious challenges in Caracas. Indeed, an undeniable crisis exists in the cities of Latin America. Thus there is a great need for understanding and integrating the various efforts at work in Latin American cities, and for bridging the disconnections between theory and practice, policymakers and stakeholders, North and South.

Now is a time of political change and upheaval in Venezuela and throughout the global South. Architectural and social structural change can occur in radical political cultures, as they did with the opening up of China, the fall of the Franco regime, the crumbling of the Iron Curtain.

As architects, we have to be aware of these possibilities, and we have to work to take advantage of them. Our work consists in proposing feasible design ideas to local stakeholders who have literally built their settlements with their own hands and whose voices go unheard in the corridors of power. We can do this by recognising their achievements and also by recognising the institutional shortcomings currently standing in their way. In short, we are talking about the politics of urban design and the design of urban politics.

Notes

1. With David Wachsmuth.
2. See the *Concurso de Ideas: Propuestas Urbanísticas de Habilitación Física para Zonas de Barrios Petare y La Vega (Caracas)* organised by the Consejo Nacional de la Vivienda (CONAVI) in 2000.

References

Brillembourg, A., K. Fereiss and H. Klumpner (eds). 2005. *Informal City: Caracas Case*. Munich: Prestel.

de Soto, H. 2000. *The Mystery of Capital*. New York: Basic Books.

Friedman, Y. 1999. *Structures Serving the Unpredictable*. Rotterdam: NAi Publishers.

Kahn, H. 1982. *The Coming Boom*. New York: Simon and Schuster.

Smith, J.S. 2004. 'The Plaza in Las Vegas, New Mexico' in D. Arreola (ed.) *Hispanic Spaces, Latino Places: Community and Cultural Diversity in Contemporary America*. Austin: University of Texas Press, 39–53.

United Nations. 2001. *The State of the World's Cities: 2001*. Nairobi: United Nations Centre for Human Settlements (Habitat).

Chapter 8

Integrated Informality in the Barrios of Havana

Ronaldo Ramírez

This chapter[1] examines informal activities carried out by individuals and communities living in the barrios[2] of Havana during part of the 'Special Period', the years of extreme scarcity experienced by the Cuban population in the 1990s. These activities, narrated mostly by their protagonists, form the basis of a research project carried out by an international team in Havana between 2002 and 2003. The chapter also explores conceptual understandings of urban informality and provides an overall view of this phenomenon in Havana. At the close, some tentative remarks are advanced on the significance that these informal activities have on the relationship between civil society[3] and the state in socialist systems.

Informality

The universe of informality in Latin American cities constitutes – since the acknowledgement of its existence in the early 1970s – a major chapter in the field of urban studies and policies.[4] While mainstream architects, planners and geographers had looked at the city in terms of space, forms and distances, the eruption of this vast, rich and heterogeneous universe pulled down the boundaries between these disciplines and other social sciences. It became possible to start filling in the blanks left by previously incomplete studies and to draw the contours of the real, underdeveloped, Latin American capitalist city.

The earliest studies of urban informality were descriptions of practices of poor households carried out outside existing regulatory frameworks (Lomnitz 1975; González 1990). While previous descriptions had qualified informal practices as abnormal or illegal, within the new critical framework they were defined as strategies socially necessary for the poor to survive, thus questioning the validity of regulatory frameworks. The recurrence of such informal practices in most underdeveloped cities led to a conceptualisation of the informal sector with clear borders, where the poor were the only actors of merit.

Awareness of both the importance and the complexity of the informal sector led to theoretical studies seeking to understand its real composition and dynamics. Out of these endeavours the informal sector has emerged as a complex system of social interactions. New concepts emphasise the flexibility of informality (Brillembourg, Feireiss and Klumpner 2005). These concepts acknowledge the presence of regulatory frameworks as the expressions of economic, social and political principles that organise different social models. They also identify patterns of regular practices that contradict some of those principles. For instance, some actions might be carried out by the poor to satisfy life's necessities but others may involve providing manufactured inputs to advanced industries (Sassen 2005). The actors in the informal sector tend to be multiple and they often move in and out through the rather porous borders of the sector. The state – or whatever institution that in a particular time has the recognised authority to impose the regulatory framework, to allow exceptions and to adapt it to changes – is another central actor. Understood in this way, informality plays an important role not only in exposing the miseries of a particular social model but also in provoking its change. For the same reasons, the existence of informality cannot be limited to the present, nor only to underdeveloped countries, for as Saskia Sassen writes, 'informality has long existed. Today, after a century of efforts by the regulatory state, we see an expanding informality in the global North that I characterise as a systemic feature of advanced capitalism, rather than an importation of the Third World' (Sassen 2005: 85).

Our effort to conceptualise urban informality has followed the same road. It has been strongly influenced by almost forty years of academic research and consultancy in poor informal urban settlements in Latin America, Asia and Africa. Along this road the informal sector moved from being a 'thing' into being a flexible process in which social actors confront each other according to an ever- changing set of rules. Theory told us about the existence of regulatory frameworks while practice showed how flexible and varied the applications of the framework could be. For these reasons, we verbalised the concept of urban informality as an 'arena of negotiations' that can be established for different purposes (Fiori and Ramírez 1992: 28). Some cases might have spatial implications; some might be related to cultural or other issues. We have been trying to define a system of social interactions in which combinations of actors, regulations and practices could be very varied but understandable throughout the world. We would also like to create a platform useful to study 'informality in the global North' (Sassen 2005: 85) as well as to examine informal initiatives in the barrios of Havana in the way we have been doing for the past twenty years.

Cuba and Social Equality

A discussion of urban informality in Cuba requires the identification of some of the attributes of its society and of recent historical events that have influenced such phenomenon. For more than forty years Cuba has been constructing a socialist society based upon the values of social equality. It chose from the beginning a radical path, breaking out of the dynamics of capitalism instead of trying to reform it. 'Three basic principles have guided Cuban government policies: universality, equitable access and government control' (Coyula and Hamberg 2005: 15). One of the most radical expressions of these principles has been to free the right to work and the value of labour from conditions determined by the market and by prestige. Every citizen has been able to find a working place and receive a low but similar salary with small variations.

At the same time these efforts have been undermined by a permanent scarcity of resources. According to some scholars, Cubans had become accustomed to a gradual increase in their general well-being before 1989 (Scarpaci, Segre and Coyula 2002). Incomes, although low, were supplemented by subsidised, rationed goods that seemed able to sustain the consumption of a family. Those conditions were possible only because of aid received from more developed socialist countries. The disintegration of the communist bloc at the end of the 1980s abruptly changed this situation. The Cuban government found itself without the resources to sustain the economy and to supply basic goods to the population. The country entered what Cubans call the 'Special Period' that lasted throughout the 1990s and to some extent continues today.

The government imposed strict measures of austerity and introduced some controversial market routines whose objectives were to stabilise the economy while preserving, as much as possible, socialist principles.

This chapter forms part of a larger examination of processes that might result from different forms of the relationship between civil society and the state. Particularly important are the possible influences of these relationships on the workings of an egalitarian society. For example, do policies guided by universalism, equity and state control lead to civil society practices resulting in a scarcity of resources? According to Coyula and Hamberg these principles 'have been responsible for most of the island's greatest achievements, but at the same time have produced some of its most thorny dilemmas and contradictions' (Coyula and Hamberg 2005: 23). To understand these contradictions it is necessary to carry out theoretical work beyond the limits of this chapter. However, the following analysis of a number of informal practices in the barrios of Havana should be understood as an attempt to contribute to that effort.

Havana's Informality

At the time of the socialist revolution of 1959, Havana was a city of 1,360,000 inhabitants, about 20 per cent of the total Cuban population. Housing was expensive and three quarters of Havana's families paid rent; evictions were frequent (Coyula and Hamberg 2005). 6 per cent of the city's population lived in shanty towns, while the majority of the poor lived in overcrowded *cuarterías* – endless subdivisions of dilapidated old mansions – and *ciudadelas* – purpose-built groups of small single-room units along a closed passage with shared services and kitchens (Scarpaci, Segre and Coyula 2002; Ortega 1996).

Among its first measures, the revolutionary government passed laws reducing the cost of rent by 50 per cent and forbidding evictions. During the first two years of socialist rule, Havana's largest shanty towns were demolished and their population relocated to newly-built large housing estates. During those two years state investment and improvements were spread throughout the country. After the second year, investment in the capital decreased considerably due to plans to reduce inequalities between rural and urban populations as well as to an anti-Havana sentiment which developed during the time of the revolution. The cycle of repairs, maintenance and replacement became progressively slower. Housing needs were not satisfied by the state and the quality of buildings in Havana deteriorated significantly. Although not as serious as in the capital, the situation was rather similar in the rest of the country. This was the context in which the population of Havana began to carry out informal interventions in order to improve their housing conditions. '[T]o the surprise of many, the Eleventh National Conference on Housing and Urbanism ... in 1984 revealed that the production of housing units by the population through self-help was practically double that of the state firms' (Scarpaci, Segre and Coyula 2002: 144).

The situation deteriorated even more during the Special Period. 50 per cent of housing units in Havana were classified as poor in 1996. There were sixty extremely poor barrios and more than 60,000 families lived in slums (Ortega 1996). By the mid 1990s, out of 4.6 million formally employed people in the country, hundreds of thousands were underemployed. In Havana nearly 60,000 were legally self-employed in 1994. An additional unknown number worked in the informal sector, performing both legal and illegal activities (Coyula and Hamberg 2005). According to Mario Coyula:

There always have been informal activities in Havana. While the state owns and controls nearly all aspects of the economy and most people work in state enterprises, there has been, since 1959, a fringe of *cuenta-propismo*,[5] people working privately to provide goods and services which were difficult to obtain through formal channels. These activities happened on a small scale and continued to take place despite being unacceptable before the 1990s. Yet, they grew considerably during the Special Period, particularly around activities promoted by the government as a means to create employment and support local consumption. International tourism and the legalisation of family remittances of dollars from the U.S.A. have produced and expanded the number of rooms for rent, street markets, small restaurants in private homes, planting and marketing of agricultural products, as well as other activities. Some of these activities are controlled and taxed by the government but many are not.

The field I am more familiar with is housing and planning in Havana. Informality has also been part of these activities. It takes place both in the peripheral municipalities and in the centre of the city. In the first we have illegal occupations of land, building and expanding shanty towns, [and the] enlarging of existing houses without permit or technical assistance. In Habana Vieja and in Centro Habana housing informality is very visible. More than half the population of Centro Habana live in *ciudadelas* and *cuarterías*. Many of them try to improve their residences. They create more space by building *barbacoas* and subdividing rooms.[6] They obtain more privacy by occupying public space adjacent to their rooms and building small toilets. When the families expand, some of these small invasions of public space are enlarged, becoming real nuisances to other residents, or small shacks appear on the roofs.

The role of the state in these processes has been contradictory. On one level the state considers informality as being close to illegality. There are clear regulations to order the demolition of any construction made without official authorisation, but the state shows considerable flexibility when it has to enforce the law. People are not trying to get rich but to solve real family problems. By and large, if the alterations are well done, if there are no physical dangers and the rights of the neighbours are not affected, the transgressor receives a fine but the work is allowed to stay. If the division of a house is also well done, there is again a fine and the new unit is incorporated into the housing stock of the city.

A similar approach has been followed with the shanty towns. No new big housing estates have been built in Havana since the first wave of development in the 1960's and 1970s, and it has not been possible to eradicate the residents of the remaining shanty towns. So the government started to upgrade their infrastructure and to provide building materials to the squatters to self-build their houses.[7]

A Change of Direction

A number of developments seem to have influenced Cuban urbanists, leading them to revise their approach to the social problems of Havana. One has been the growing realisation of the uselessness of building large housing estates to which populations in need of adequate housing are transferred. Another has been the lessons of the Special Period, which left a provider state with nothing to provide while people devised ways to satisfy their needs by themselves. Alongside this has been the realisation that for a long time the Cuban population has been able to build more housing units than the Cuban state. These, and other facts, have provoked a significant change of direction in some of the policies dealing with the social problems of Havana, requiring the participation of urban communities in the formulation and implementation of decentralised social policies that affect them.

The aspirations of Cuban urbanists to descentralise and promote popular participation, as well as recognition of the importance of the barrios, were reinforced by the creation of the Grupo para el Desarrollo Integral de la Capital (GDIC),[8] an initiative supported by the municipal government of Havana in 1987. The GDIC was established as an interdisciplinary agency, working with relative autonomy within the municipal structure. According to Gina Rey, its first director, 'the mission of GDIC was to define a strategic vision and a commitment to improve the urban living conditions of the population … its members clearly understood that this improvement had to be done with the participation of the people in the *barrios*, from the bottom-up' (Ramírez 2005: 150). Thus, one of its tasks has been to coordinate the participation of numerous groups in preparing the Strategic Plan of the city, the objectives of which are social and economic rather than physical. The GDIC also provided a major impulse to community participation with the creation and methodological guidance of the Talleres para la Transformación Integral de los Barrios (TTIB).[9]

The Cuban barrio is an urban area identifiable by its physical attributes and by its history and culture. It is not an administrative entity. There are poor and well-off barrios. The 1981 Census identified 380 barrios in Havana.[10] Their importance in the everyday life of the communities increased as a consequence of the Special Period when a severe disruption of urban transport reduced individual mobility and when the failure of state agencies to distribute goods stimulated the growth of local *cuenta-propismo*. All this led to the spontaneous reinforcement of informal networks in the barrios, networks which became very important in the life of local communities.

The *Talleres* began to appear in the barrios in 1988, as part of the movement to motivate new bottom-up social initiatives, and their crucial importance became more apparent with the social miseries beginning with the Special Period. According to Gina Rey:

> The *Talleres* were the fruit of a creative development in GDIC. After some discussions we knew that we had to put in place participative processes and that the starting point was the barrio … Our first idea was to move ourselves over to the barrios. But then it became obvious that there were conditions in the barrios to organise some form of locally based agency. We thought that it should be a very creative agency, not another bureaucratic entity. It needed to be seen as an open institution, collecting and processing the ideas of the community without imposing pre-conceived ideas of its own …

their working principles were to respect our 'integral vision' as a fundamental premise: that the work would be multidisciplinary, that the staff should preferably live in the barrio and be part of the community, that the *taller* should be in the barrio and have premises that will identify it as local, and that those premises should be centres of community activity, avoiding the image of a formal office with opening hours.[11]

There were at least twenty *Talleres* in Havana in 2002 and 2003, when our research took place. Each one had been installed after the request of barrio residents. They consisted of a small staff, frequently long-term residents in the barrio: one architect, one sociologist, a few social workers. Their tasks were initially carried out in improvised venues, but several *Talleres* were able to build adequate premises with rooms available for conferences, training programmes, meetings, celebrations and for the activities of local groups, such as the Círculos de Abuelos.[12] Their merits were recognised by most Havana institutions and by residents of the barrios.

The *Talleres* produce an annual 'Participative Diagnosis' detailing what their local communities consider urgent problems and the possible ways to solve them. This is followed by a 'Strategic Community Plan' where the problems are arranged according to their urgency and the realism of the proposed solutions. These documents are used to motivate and organise local initiatives, to lobby city and municipal authorities and to search for contributions from international aid agencies. The *Talleres* thus constitute loci where formal and informal community initiatives intersect with the state. They are agencies strategically located between the social base and the higher authorities. They are public institutions that frequently act as the advocates of civil society.

The Research Project

The primary data collected by the research project reconstructs the narratives of a number of community projects carried out in three barrios of Havana. These provide a valid foundation from which to explore examples of informal interactions between civil society and the state in a country like Cuba, with attributes different from the rest of the continent.

The first stages of the research showed that in those three barrios – El Canal, Pogolotti and Balcón Arimao-Novoa – the execution of Participative Diagnoses and a Strategic Community Plan had defined spaces ample enough for individuals, communities and organisations to propose, design and implement a variety of social projects. The information related to each project was provided by their authors, as well as by activists, beneficiaries and others, during private interviews and public discussions. This information was considered as valid by the research project once it had passed through three filters: first it was presented and discussed in a participative workshop attended by the whole staff of the local *Taller*, leaders of community projects, local activists, members of the Popular Councils and of mass organisations, municipal representatives, ordinary residents and the research group. Secondly, the main actors involved in each project were interviewed individually by the researchers and, thirdly, all was again discussed publicly in a second participative workshop.

Thirty community projects[13] in the three barrios were examined according to these conditions. Six of them are described in the following sections.

Barrio El Canal

El Canal, in Cerro municipality, is a poor barrio with badly maintained facilities and high population density. The *Taller* was inaugurated in 1996. Participative Diagnoses and a Strategic Community Plan resulted in twenty-seven community projects. Eleven of these satisfied the requisites of the research project and were analysed in the participative workshops. Eight of these projects had been initiated and carried out by individual or collective members of civil society and the other three by public institutions. Two of these projects are described below: the Ecological Community Garden/Agenda 21 and the Ecological Classroom. Both were initiated and implemented by individual members of the local community and were presented as a single project to the participative workshops by Justo, who also coordinated both.[14]

> The project started about 1998. A few friends and I were motivated by the idea of answering the needs of the Special Period, the scarcity of food, particularly vegetables and fruits, by making use of our own resources. We were inspired by the principles of Agenda 21. I was also familiar with the discipline of permaculture, that is cultivation without the expenditure of money, time or energy, using all spaces no matter how small because they are all useful for this kind of agriculture.
>
> We were too ambitious at the beginning. We wanted to change the cooking habits of Cubans, to move away from today's artificial food to natural ingredients, to convince everybody that it was

possible, that we had done it, that the resources were all around waiting to be used and that we were prepared to help. The Participatory Diagnoses carried out by the *Taller* had registered local concern with the environmental conditions in the barrio and we felt motivated to propose initiatives in this direction.

The idea of an Ecological Classroom arose as an instrument to implement our idea of helping ordinary people – like us – to obtain food using their resources. We prepared an educational project and planned to produce a regular bulletin. We thought that we would need to acquire a computer and printer, for which we would need money. Like most projects of this kind in Cuba, we were prepared to work as volunteers, receiving our salary from our regular employers. We submitted our project, with a request for six thousand dollars, to the National Environment Fund. And that was when the problems started.

It was a bureaucratic nightmare. The project was accepted but it was impossible to find a way to transfer the funds to us. First, the money could only be transferred to a bank account. But we were an informal community group unable to open such account. We negotiated with a Cuban NGO –which had an account – to present the project in their name. But there was a regulation, from the time when there were no NGOs in Cuba, that did not include such organisations among those authorised to receive government funds. After long negotiations the officials agreed to waive that obstacle. A new problem appeared: it was not possible to use money from the Ministry for the Environment to buy imported goods such as the computer. It was necessary to apply for a special license from the Ministry of External Commerce. So we decided not to buy the computer and instead to use the money to buy ordinary agricultural tools. But these tools could be purchased only from one authorised government agency that happened to be unable to sell to NGOs.

After several months of negotiations, we decided to abandon our association with the NGO and came back to the *Taller*. We reformulated the project from the beginning, now under the sponsorship of the *Taller*. Everything went well until we encountered the final obstacle. Ours was a community project based on a private plot and official regulations did not allow instruments and other goods purchased with government funds to be placed in a private location. At that point we gave up.

We came to the conclusion that the national institutional system was not designed to help community projects. Excessive centralisation, rigidity, the demands of the Special Period directing very scarce resources to the most urgent needs, all combined to leave no space for community projects to operate independently. We think that this situation is changing, but it is still a very slow change.

This experience influenced significantly our working style. We have redefined our strategy. Our project is recognised by all institutions. We had no problems working within the official framework, but we want to work within our municipality only. We see ourselves as a local Agenda 21. We do not have any dreams of national or international financing. We have even rejected the idea of seeking self-financing. For this we would have to enter into the world of *cuenta-propismo* that we hate.

We work mostly by example. What we do not do in our own garden we cannot ask other people to do. We want to show the people that all this can be done with the resources that are available to the community: the soil, the cans, the tyres that can be obtained from the refuse heaps, and the help, the exchange of products and the technical advice that can be obtained from friends. Today many people come from other barrios to see our project and [they] want to know about it.

Obviously we sometimes need tools, books, subscriptions or activities for which we need money. Up to now we have approached

Figure 8.1 Ecological Community Garden in Barrio El Canal. Agenda 21 Project

this through personal donations from friends and institutions. No bank accounts. No regulations. These are donations based on trust. Sometime during the project the idea of the Ecological Classroom was resurrected. The *Taller* has supported the project since its inception. We consider it the intermediary between us and government institutions. The contribution of the *Taller* may not be in the form of money but could be, for example, by opening the doors of municipal agencies to discuss the work of the project. It gives formal legitimacy to the project, it confirms that it is part of the community.

These two community projects were considered successful by the research project due to their continuity and their consistency with the original objectives. They expose the serious obstacles created by a rigid official administrative structure, but at the same time they show how, after exhausting negotiations, it was still possible to keep the projects alive with the support of the *Taller*.

Barrios Balcón-Arimao and Novoa

These two barrios, located in the western suburbs of Havana, have poorly maintained infrastructure and facilities. Most houses in Balcón-Arimao have two floors and brick walls. On the edge of the barrio there is a small shanty town. Houses in Novoa meanwhile are small prefabricated units. The *Taller* started to work in both barrios in 1998. The Participative Diagnoses identified fifteen community projects, some implemented before the *Taller* existed. Only nine of these, of which seven had been initiated or carried out by members of civil society, were examined in the participative workshops. Two projects are described below.[15]

Colouring My Barrio

This project consists of painting murals on the walls of the barrio. It started in 2000 and was initiated, promoted and directed by Jorge, a young local artist. It involves motivating other local painters to participate in voluntary work, to select walls and motifs, to obtain the necessary materials and do the actual painting. The project was explained to the participative workshops by Jorge:

This project was my personal initiative. I wanted to make a contribution to the barrio as an artist. My intention was to change the aesthetic of the barrio, where there was practically not a single work of art. I discussed it with the *Taller*, and they supported it. I then had several meetings with local artists and their reaction was enthusiastic.

Everybody wanted to participate. Very soon I had some fifty painters prepared to start working. Initially nobody was motivated by personal gain. If anything, there was a little bit of vanity.

We asked everybody for their views, consulted the opinions of the local community, the local institutions and the schools. Everybody wanted a mural. We started with two or three small murals. Now we have more than fifty. In the meantime we continue with our individual professional work. But at weekends we call the artists and we all go out to paint murals. No payment is involved.

Some experiences have been wonderful. In a school the murals were painted from drawings made by the children. They made many drawings and discussed them with us. We combined some of them to produce a final design which respected the children's ideas. Then, we invited the children themselves, their teachers, their parents and some neighbours, to do the actual painting. I engaged with the work only to complete some details. Then we wrote on the side of the mural the names of the children. It was a great experience of community participation. People have now developed a sense of ownership of the mural and respect and maintain it.

We do not impose our themes on the people. The subject matter of the murals is mostly related to national themes: flowers, butterflies, history and the flag. From the beginning, when we negotiated the authorisation to use public spaces, we made it clear that the imposition of subjects was not acceptable, and this has been observed.

We have also had some problems. Given the conditions of Cuba, it has been extremely difficult to obtain brushes, tools and the lack of paint nearly derailed the project. But most irritating has been the persistent negative attitude of the Municipal Culture Secretary. We needed their authorisation to paint on public walls. Their answers were always negative, petty obstacles, delays. There is this outside image, that in socialist countries artists are always being suffocated by the state. I think it is simpler. I think it is the reaction of functionaries, in any country, who resent a successful activity that they think should be under their control but is not. Ours is a spontaneous and unstructured project. We are not a registered 'association', nor do we wish to be. We are not registered formally or legally. We do not receive income, do not pay taxes. Therefore, to the Culture Secretary, we do not exist as a project.

When we started, some murals were defaced by local bully boys. Today that has changed. To paint in the streets is a festival

Figure 8.2 Colouring My Barrio Project in Barrio Balcon-Arimao

involving the community. There are cases of large murals on public walls which we expected would last no more than six months, and they are still impeccable after two years. The most important result of our work is that we are really changing the aesthetic image of the barrios and that the local people recognise this and like our work ... . They come and ask us to paint murals in their schools and in their streets. To me, personally, this is the most gratifying part of the work.

This community project was considered successful by the research project. It is an open-ended initiative which could continue as long as Jorge and his volunteers are prepared to maintain their contribution. It involves the participation of a larger community and the support of the *Taller* to overcome the bureaucratic obstacles posed by more formal local authorities.

Disco Cima 73

Zone 73 is a district in Novoa, a conflictive barrio with the highest record of delinquency in the municipality of La Lisa. The material and social conditions in the barrio were worsening rapidly by the end of the 1980s, at the beginning of the Special Period. In the absence of a *Taller*, four young men, some of them members of the local Comite de Defensa de la Revolución (CDR)[16] developed a number of activities to reduce the negative consequences of the crisis. They were José, Eusebio, Antonio and Rolando. Their leader was José, a charismatic local policeman with a master's degree in law. The project was described by Rolando:

> The conditions in the barrio were very bad. There was violence, especially amongst the young. We wanted to do something to improve all that and started collecting pieces of discarded, nearly rotten timber that were lying on the street and made a couple of small tables that we placed in front of the CDR house. Then we invited people to use them if they wanted to play chess or something. A friend gave us a radio and we added it to the tables. With that the place became a social meeting point, the only one in the barrio.
>
> We organised meetings and visited many houses to discuss things with the community. After a while we were able to make a list of problems. Some were beyond our capacity to intervene. But others, such as the frequent fights between groups of youngsters and the lack of places and activities for recreation, were problems we could do something about. We wanted to do it in such a way that it would change the attitudes of the people. We defined a set of principles: to listen to the people; to respect their interests and priorities; to trust their capacity to change themselves; to stimulate people by acknowledging their participation; to publicise each success so as to keep the community motivated. We also decided that all community projects should generate resources to be invested in benefits to the community.
>
> We organised a number of activities, one of which was the discotheque, Disco Cima 73, in the premises of the local agrarian market. The place worked as a market during the day and as an entertainment venue for the young on Friday, Saturday and Sunday evenings. It was a great success. The project was from the beginning conceived according to two simultaneous objectives: to satisfy cultural and social demands, and to produce an income. It was conceived as a work centre. It provided for the recreation of young people and produced financial resources that were invested in the barrio. It was possible to pay salaries in the discotheque for cleaning, security, acting as a disc-jockey, management and gardening. In the most stringent conditions of the Special Period about thirty local families were able to live from those salaries.

However, we had to close Disco Cima 73. At that time neither the government nor the CDR were in a position to understand or to authorise independent social activities that generated income through charging admission. The discotheque was sponsored by the CDR, an organisation which can provide services but cannot charge for them. This is done only by professional groups whose incomes are collected directly by state institutions, the same that paid their salaries and expenses. A few private initiatives were at that time authorised as *cuenta-propismo*, but they were strictly controlled. Once we received pressure from above, we decided to close the discotheque. It was a great disappointment for the young people in the barrio. As one of them said: 'it was as if a ton of ice had fallen on our heads. It was the only thing we had'.

This was one of the few community initiatives examined by the research project that failed. Notwithstanding the good intentions of the organisers, one of the quasi-commercial objectives of the project – admission charges to pay for salaries and services – collided head on with the prohibition on having a private income imposed by the Cuban state at that time. The involvement of the local CDR made negotiations difficult, a situation made worse by the non-existence of a *Taller*.

Barrio Pogolotti
At the advent of the revolution, Pogolotti was known as a violent barrio in a state of decay. This situation began to change in the 1960s when new buildings were started, houses were repaired and services improved. In 2002 the barrio had 10,000 inhabitants and included a small shanty town called Dust Island. Today, Pogolotti is considered a working-class barrio, with some serious social problems but not particularly violent. The *Taller* here was created in 1990. Participative Diagnoses and community planning exercises have been carried out annually since 1997. These have defined or identified forty-one community projects, ten of which were analysed in the participative workshops of the research project. Out of these ten projects, six had been started and carried out by community groups. The following sections describe two such projects.

Building Houses in Dust Island
The 1993 hurricane – known as the 'storm of the century' – devastated houses in Dust Island. In these circumstances the Martin Luther King Jr Memorial Centre[17] proposed to the *Taller* an emergency project to

Figure 8.3 Illegal Addition to a House in Barrio Pogolotti

finance and build twenty-five conventional houses in the shanty town. Central to the project was the participation of the local community both in the design and construction of the houses. Félix, a member of the Memorial Centre in charge of the project, explained how things went to the participative workshops:

This initiative was not designed with the logic of a conventional project. Four or five days after the storm we submitted the project: a couple of pages, a few sketches. No more than a week later, we received confirmation of financial support granted by an international aid agency. The idea was to identify a group of twenty-five damaged houses in Dust Island, to define the project with the assistance of their residents and to build the houses with their participation. But very soon the problems started. Some problems were institutional, some were structural and some were the consequence of our lack of experience and understanding of community participation.

Among the first problems we had was the fact that Dust Island was an illegal settlement. One thing is to help to improve informally a settlement like that, and another is to try to start a building operation that is supposed to be accepted formally and financed internationally. To obtain municipal permission was a difficult and slow process. Without this, it would have been impossible to receive the funds. Some of the structural constraints resulted from the contrast between the improvisations of participative actions and the over-regulation of most activities in Cuba. It wasn't a matter of going to the next corner shop to buy a missing tool. Particularly during the Special Period those shops did not exist and normally any purchase had to follow regular procedures.

The most important obstacle, however, was that in 1993 we – the Memorial Centre, the *Taller*, the local community and the country as a whole – did not have experience of community participation. Participation was spontaneous, emotional, disorganised, everybody wanted to do all things at the same time. We were not able to organise the participation of the involved community. There were problems each time we came together. Some resulted from the participants' lack of any knowledge of construction. Other problems resulted from personal interests such as 'let us build my house, or the house of my friend, first'. It was only after 1993 that the Memorial Centre started thinking about community participation and using these processes.

The participative project in Dust Island failed and was discontinued. Later the *Taller* and the Memorial Centre defined a new initiative to build sixty-three houses in Pogolotti under the management and execution of the Micro-Brigades, the building agency of the government, but the participatory concept of the initial project was lost. The new project built mostly conventional flats in buildings of two or three floors in Pogolotti and surrounding barrios. Twenty-five of them were assigned to Dust Island residents, but these never materialised. The Memorial Centre continued to be involved in community and participative projects in Pogolotti.

The Alafia Dance Group

The case of Alafia, one of Pogolotti's most important community projects, was presented to the participative workshops by Ramoncito, its director. He is a teacher and promoter of physical education and a local leader. He was born in Dust Island and lives in Pogolotti with his wife, Elda, who is a dance teacher. Both have been instrumental in the creation, development and success of the project. According to Ramoncito:

Alafia sprang from the realities of the barrio in 1991. When Elda and I went around the barrio about that time, we usually met groups of teenagers in the streets that did not know what to do with their time. The idea to work with them was born when we saw a group playing music with improvised instruments and dancing a conga.

We discussed several ideas with the *Taller* that was just starting to work. We first organised a youth club to which we invited all the kids that were interested. We had some brainstorming sessions to decide what to do. The majority wanted a group of music and dance. To start on this line we got the help of some professional musicians that live in the barrio and after a while we were able to work more or less regularly with a group of boys and girls. With them we made the first presentation [of the group] in Pogolotti during the barrio's anniversary. It was a total success. It was also a collective achievement because we had the help of the community: some gave us bedsheets to make the costumes and decorations, some had helped us with instruments and so on. Alafia was born that evening.

Nearly all the kids had serious social problems, so serious, indeed, that we nearly abandoned the project altogether at that point. Some boys had been in Re-education Centres, some were delinquents. We had a meeting in the *Taller* with the participation of the local Communist Party Secretary, the Reverend Raúl Suárez from the Martin Luther King Jr Memorial Centre, representatives of the Communist Youth, everybody. The decision was to go on, to help the kids with problems. We found practical ways to do so. In all this we had the contributions of the Memorial Centre, the *Taller* and the people of Pogolotti. From the beginning Alafia was a social project to rescue boys and girls in trouble.

The quality and prestige of Alafia are considerable. It has been the only amateur dance group in Havana of national and international recognised quality. It has performed in France, Denmark and Finland. It also has problems. The programmes are more sophisticated and require more expenses. The members of the group are older and need to earn an income but Alafia is officially an amateur group whose performances are not allowed to generate income for the group or for its members. With the help of some organisations we have been able to provide the members with opportunities to earn an income. Some have become bakers, others builders and teachers. Some have also moved out into the professional musical world. We maintain the original objectives. The group continues to accept kids with anti-social behaviour. Our objective is to reintegrate them into society as normal citizens. For this it is necessary that they see that new and attractive opportunities are accessible to them.

Alafia was one of the most successful and important community initiatives examined by the research project. It has created role models to move young people in Pogolotti and in other poor barrios out of anti-social activities. It stimulates a culture based upon music, dance and religions of Afro-Cuban origin that reach the very identity of people living in Havana's barrios. Its success has resulted to a large extent from the talent of the individual promoters of the project and the collaboration of the *Taller*, other local institutions and the mobilisation of the barrio residents. The future of Alafia will depend of the ability of the individuals and institutions involved in the project to overcome the problems created by its success.

Final Comments

As stated at the beginning, this chapter was motivated by an interest in exploring certain patterns in relationships between civil society and the state in socialist systems. The information obtained throughout the research project shows that in Cuba many initiatives by members of civil society were intended to benefit the community but opposed state policies, or were located on the margins of the state apparatus. Yet often such initiatives surmount the regulatory framework and are carried out successfully.

The research examined thirty projects in three barrios involving local communities. Twenty-one of them had been initiated and were implemented by individual or collective members of civil society, others took advantage of existing programmes or were initiated by the state. Fifteen of these projects were considered successful: either they have been completed and achieved their objectives, or they were on course to do so consistent with their objectives.[18] The six projects described in this essay – four of them successful and two which failed to achieve their goals fully – are considered representative examples of Cuban informality. They are initiatives by members of civil society to create conditions that may benefit the community. They take advantage of particular historical conditions. They are implemented, as explained above, following procedures opposed to or on the margins of the regulatory framework of Cuban society. In the six cases described the implementation involved negotiations of different degrees of intensity with institutions representing the state. The descriptions show some of the features of those negotiations: bureaucratic difficulties, apparently insurmountable obstacles, the bias and rigidities of functionaries, the exhaustion and exasperation of the promoters. But negotiations do not have prescribed results. The establishment of an arena of negotiations does not mean a form of warfare, of irreconcilable principles between the state and the communities. On the contrary, it is one of the forms of interaction between social institutions that keep a social system alive. However, as in other countries, not all negotiations are successful. Arenas of negotiation have limits, fundamental principles that neither the state nor the authors of the initiatives are prepared to negotiate. Beyond those limits there is no option but failure, illegality or rebellion.

Out of the six projects initiated by civil society that failed, there is one – Disco Cima 73, described above – that became unsustainable when its quasi-commercial objectives collided with laws concerning the earning of private income implemented by the Cuban state at that time. The other case of failure caused by similar circumstances was 'Pogolotti's Sacred Forest', not described in this essay, where the volunteers improving the physical conditions and the religious identity of a forest adjacent to Pogolotti abandoned the work when the state institution sponsoring the project changed its name and emphasis from religious to environmental issues. In only these two cases was the clash of principles between the state and particular civil groups responsible for the failure. The other four projects failed for a variety of reasons, such as absent leaders and lack of adequate finance, to mention a few.

Two still prevailing historical processes created conditions favourable to the emergence of the thirty community initiatives examined by the research project. One is the generalised movement of disciplines in the humanities and social sciences towards an urbanism defined at the community level as a multidimensional process that incorporates the participation of urban citizens and their integration in the city. The Cuban manifestation of this movement appeared as part of the drive of the urban and planning institutions in Havana towards decentralisation and popular participation and a recognition of the importance of the barrios, reinforced by the creation of the GDIC and the *Talleres*.

The other historical process might be defined as the need of the Cuban government and community to react against the negative impacts of the Special Period. The serious scarcity of goods and services forced communities to abandon a passive attitude of expecting the state to provide for their needs. People's reaction was to make their own initiatives using the new structures of participation mentioned above. The reactions of the state, although rather slow, have also been in the direction of change and flexibility. The result has been, as in the previous cases, the development of an environment that encourages informal civil society initiatives.

The six projects described in the essay show three characteristics that are also shared by the thirty projects included in the research project. The first is a good dose of realism. All of them are based upon the labour and contributions of their participants and of the communities they intend to benefit. Most of them avoid big expenses on materials, machinery, instruments or premises. When some of these expenses were unavoidable, the projects obtained the support of reliable institutions such as the Martin Luther King Jr Memorial Centre in Pogolotti, or devised strategies that allowed them to continue in case their source of funds failed, as was the case of the Ecological Community Gardens and Classroom in El Canal.

The sophistication of their components and the high professional quality involved in the design and implementation of the projects is another of their remarkable characteristics. In these very poor barrios in Havana live artists able to carry out projects such as Alafia or Colouring My Barrio and agricultural experts   able to organise the Ecological Gardens. High levels of education, artistic skills and organisational capacity are attributes shared by all the thirty projects. Similar levels of education and skills are also manifested by the staff of the *Talleres*. It is impossible to ignore the association between these conditions and the results – in quality and quantity – of the educational programmes of the Cuban government. As pastor Raúl Suárez, director of the Memorial Centre, said referring to Pogolotti, 'there are problems, but you also find that in the locally born population there are architects, artist, teachers, engineers and doctors' (Ramírez 2005: 157). Although this factor was not included in the research project, it is possible to argue that widespread high levels of education played an important role in motivating the residents in the barrios to put forward their ideas and strongly influenced the formulation and implementation of the thirty community projects.

The *Talleres* made, and continue to make, a significant contribution to the participation of the communities in the improvement of local living conditions in the poor barrios. Through community planning exercises they help these communities to identify their problems and to propose initiatives to resolve them. The staff of the *Talleres,* most of them local people, normally provide professional assistance to the residents in the design and implementation of projects. The *Talleres* played a significant supportive role in eleven of the twenty-one projects initiated by members of the local communities. This supportive role included bringing the projects to the attention of municipal and city authorities, seeking financial and other contributions from the state and from national and international NGOs and official institutions. The *Taller* for the Integral Transformation of the Barrios, the most unorthodox agency created by the Cuban government, is today a central actor in a process that simultaneously promotes and integrates informality in Cuban society. As Justo explained in one of the participative workshops: 'we consider the *Taller* as the intermediary between us and government institutions. It gives formal legitimacy to the project; it confirms that it is part of the community'.

This limited analysis may contribute to understanding the evolving relationships between civil society and the state in Cuba. There is a widespread conception that socialist societies are reducible to national institutions totally occupied or dominated by the state, a conception that denies any space or agency to civil society. However, the very brief and schematic description of Cuba's context presented earlier in the essay described developments that have taken place during the past eighteen years, characterised by a growing interlinking of state and civil society initiatives. This is consistent with the evidence shown in the cases described. The eruption of civil society initiatives in the barrios seems to challenge the image of inertia widely associated with 'socialism in power'. The content of these initiatives in Cuba is universally constructive and socially supportive. Governance is not remote, nor is it inhibited by the serious lack of resources or by dynamic local leaders and communities. All this may still be a very small part of a Cuban society undoubtedly under pressure from many forces. But it includes symptomatic, complex processes that raise questions not yet formulated that might contain the seeds for new forms of socialist organisation.

Notes

1. This chapter is based on a research project entitled 'Factors Affecting Success or Failure of Community Initiatives: Experiences from Havana, Cuba', which was carried out between 2002 and 2003 by Kosta Mathey, Reinhard Aehnelt, Octavio Tapia, Katja Buermann, Celeste Cuello, Daniel Fitzpatrick, Daphne Frank, Petra Luedike, Celeste Vargas and Ronaldo Ramírez. The research had the Cuban contribution of Rubén Bancrofft, Tania Gutiérrez and Gina Rey from the Instituto Superior Politécnico José Antonio Echeverría, and Rosa Oliveras from the Grupo para el Desarrollo Integral de la Capital (GDIC). The project was sponsored and co-financed by the Programme de Recherche Urbaine pour le Développement (PRUD) and the Fonds de Solidarité Prioritaire du Ministère des Affaires Étrangéres, France, and coordinated by the Groupement d'Intérêt Scientifique pour l'Etude de la Mondialisation et du Développement (GEMDEV) and the Centre de Documentation et d'Information Villes en Développement (ISTED), both of France. The Institutional partners were TRIALOG, the Technical University, Darmstadt in Germany, and the Instituto Superior Politécnico José Antonio Echeverría, in Havana.

   Neither the research project nor this chapter would have been possible without the collaboration of many people and institutions in Cuba and in the barrios of Havana. The author assumes responsibility for arguments and interpretations that might differ from the research project.
2. The term barrios ('neighbourhoods') is used throughout the text.
3. The term 'civil society' is a politically neutral sociological concept that designates individuals, groups, communities and institutions independently interacting with the state. Currently, the term has been corrupted in the political discourse of the U.S.A. by official institutions that ascribe political connotations to the concept of 'civil society' as a massive body of opposition both to the government and the social organisation of Cuba.
4. See, for example, Hart (1973), Bienefeld (1975), Lomnitz (1975), Turner (1976).
5. The term *cuenta-propismo* refers to small-scale private business.
6. *Barbacoa*: a makeshift mezzanine or loft-like structure that creates an extra floor.
7. Interview with Professor Mario Coyula, 2005. Professor Coyula is from the Instituto Superior Politécnico José Antonio Echeverría (ISPJAE), and has been s Director of Architecture in Havana and also Director of the Grupo para el Desarrollo Integral de la Capital (GDIC). He was interviewed for the research project. We are grateful for his contribution to this chapter.
8. Grupo para el Desarrollo Integral de la Capital, 'Group for the Integral Development of the Capital'. GDIC is used throughout the text.
9. Talleres para la Transformación Integral de los Barrios, 'Workshops for the Integral Transformation of the Barrios'. The term *Taller(es)* is used throughout the text to refer to these 'workshop(s)'.
10. More contemporary studies identify some 600 barrios.
11. Interview with Professor Gina Rey of the Instituto Superior Politécnico José Antonio Echeverria (ISPJAE), who was also Director of the Havana Provincial Planning Office and the first director of GDIC. She was interviewed for the research project, and we are grateful for her contribution.

12. *Círculo de Abuelos*, 'Grandparents Community Group'.
13. The thirty projects are: In barrio *El Canal*: 'Ecological Community Gardens', 'Agenda 21' and 'Ecological Classroom', both described in the text. The others are: 'Meeting with Hope' (activities with disabled children); 'Deserving of Love' (sexual education to adolescents); *'Alacrán* Troupe' (music and dance group); 'Key 40' (a women's programme); *'Cerro Union'* (a cultural project); 'Health and Healthy' (physical education); 'Migdalia's Party' (programme for third-age residents); 'Community House' (refurnishing of the *Taller*'s office for public use); and 'Tourist Itinerary' (physical improvement and security of the barrio).

    In barrios *Balcón-Arimao* and *Novoa*: 'Colouring My Barrio' and 'Disco Cima 73', are both described in the text. The other projects are: *'Haralaya'* (women's dance and cultural group); *'Fantasia'* (dance project for anti-social children); 'Health and Religion' (a research project); *'Tropicalle'* (programme for third-age residents); 'Cederista Family House' (a project to improve the social environment); 'Green Map' (environmental education for children); and 'Aids Prevention Centre'.

    In barrio *Pogolotti*: 'Building Twenty Five Houses in Dust-Island and Alafia', are both described in the text. Other projects include 'Food Conservation' (educational programme to conserve food by natural means); *'Mayanabo'* (children's dance group); 'Street-lighting' (an infrastructure project); *'Pogolotti*'s Sacred Forest' (environmental and religious project); *'Pogolotti*'s Forest' (environmental project); 'Building Sixty-Three Houses' (social housing programme); 'Recycling' (a domestic environmental project); and 'Community and Senior Citizen House' (building the local premises of the *Taller*).

    Seven additional cases, from the barrios *San Isidro* (located in Habana Vieja), *Cayo Hueso* and the Chinese Quarter (located in Centro Habana), and the small township of *Santa Fé*, were also examined by the research project as comparative references. Information concerning these cases did not pass through the same controls as the rest and, for this reason, they have not been included in this paper.
14. The local people who narrate the projects will be introduced only by their forename. Surnames are withdrawn as part of an agreement between them and the author of this essay.
15. The project Disco Cima 73 was carried out before the creation of a *Taller* in this barrio.
16. CDR is a socio-political organisation of the Cuban government, with cells in every urban block.
17. Martin Luther King Jr Memorial Centre is a Christian ecumenical association located in Pogolotti whose social work has been particularly important for the local community. Its role is similar to that of an NGO.
18. The other nine community projects initiated by government institutions, mainly by the *Talleres*, were all successful.

References

Bienefeld, M. 1975. 'The Informal Sector and Peripheral Capitalism: The Case of Tanzania', *Institute of Development Studies Bulletin* 6(3): 53–73.

Brillembourg, A., K. Feireiss, and H. Klumpner. 2005. 'Towards an Informal City', in A. Brillembourg, K. Feireiss, and H. Klumper (eds), *Informal City. Caracas Case*. Berlin: Prestel Verlag, 38–45.

Coyula, M. and J. Hamberg. 2005. 'The Case of Havana, Cuba', *Working Paper, David Rockefeller Centre for Latin American Studies*. Cambridge, MA: David Rockefeller Centre for Latin American Studies, Harvard University.

Fiori, J. and R. Ramírez. 1992. 'Notes on the Self-Help Housing Critique: Towards a Conceptual Framework for the Analysis of Self-Help Policies in Developing Countries', in K. Mathey (ed.) *Beyond Self-Help Housing*. Munich: Profil Verlag, 23–31.

González, A. 1990. 'Informal Sector and Survival Strategies: An Historical Approach', in S. Datta (ed.) *Third World Urbanization: Reappraisals and New Perspectives*. Stockholm: Swedish Council for Research in the Humanities and Social Sciences, 90–91.

Hart, K. 1973. 'Informal Income Opportunities and Urban Employment in Ghana', *Journal of Modern African Studies* 11(1): 61–89.

Lomnitz, L. 1975. *Como sobreviven los marginados*. Mexico: Siglo XXI.

Ortega, M.L. 1996. 'La Habana, Barrio de Atarés', in H. Harms, W. Ludeña and P. Pfeiffer (eds), *Vivir en el Centro: Vivienda e Inquilinato en los Barrios Céntricos de América Latina*. Harburg: Technische Universitat Hamburg-Harburg, 95–134.

Ramírez, R. 2005. 'State and Civil Society in the Barrios of Havana: The Case of Poligotti', *Environment and Urbanization* 17(1): 147–170.

Sassen, S. 2005. 'Fragmented Urban Topographies and Their Underlying Interconections', in A. Brillembourg, K. Feireiss and H. Klumpner (eds), *Informal City: Caracas Case*. Berlin: Prestel Verlag, 83–87.

Scarpaci, J.L., R. Segre and M. Coyula. 2002. *Havana: Two Faces of the Antillean Metropolis*. Chapel Hill: University of North Carolina Press.

Turner, J.F.C. 1976. *Housing by People: Towards Autonomy in Building Environments*. London: Marion Boyars.

Chapter 9

Formal–Informal Connections in the Favelas of Rio de Janeiro: The Favela-Bairro Programme

Roberto Segre

Latin America: Cities and Poverty

Historians and political experts have not yet agreed on the most outstanding characteristics of the last century. For some it was the shortest in history; for others it was the most intense because of the extent of its technical-scientific innovations and the fervour of the social revolutions that took place. Never before had revolutions occurred in such a brief period and over such an expansive area: Mexico, Russia, China, Cuba and other fleeting ones (Hobsbawm 1996). These revolutions represented the struggle of entire peoples against the widespread and increasing poverty of the world. They attempted to create just, balanced and optimistic societies that would eliminate the sharp contradictions inherent in industrial and financial capitalism. It is also valid to define it as the urban century: in the 1990s, for the first time in human history, the urban population surpassed that of rural areas. Marx and Engels's dream of doing away with the old antithesis between city and countryside has now become a reality, as Françoise Choay (1994) and Claude Lelong (1996) have argued. Today, as Paul Virilio (1997) has put it, it is possible to speak of the 'urban' and of 'urban archipelagos' where extreme polarities coexist in a territorial and ecological integration.

The last century can also be understood in terms of ambiguous antagonisms. Binary oppositions – such as dictatorship and democracy, reason and feeling, art and science, real and virtual, order and chaos, Left and Right, opulence and poverty – were diluted within imprecise limits, diffuse borders, intertwined processes, translucent and dialogic realities.[1] Equally, the formal city and informal city can no longer be separated by such sharp dividing lines. On the one hand the options are many and unexpected, as was shown by Deleuze and Guattari (1980) when defining the categories of fragment, labyrinth and rhizome; on the other, the speed of change in the world of today produces unexpected events: only Nostradamus could have predicted the collapse of the socialist system, the presidency of Nelson Mandela in South Africa, the attack on the Twin Towers in New York and the ascendancy in the world of Osama Bin Laden.

However, neither the vertiginous scientific advances nor the economic and cultural globalisation that have taken place since the second half of the last century have brought about significant improvements for the majority of the population. According to Sub Comandante Marcos (Marcos 1997: 5–7), of the 5 billion people who inhabit the Earth, only 500 million live adequately and almost a 1 billion live in slums (Davies 2004). Brazil, with a population of 170 million, of which 75 per cent are urbanised, has 90 million poor people, 62 per cent of the total, and 4,000 favelas scattered across the country (Taschner 2003). This undermines the image of the city as a place of formal and spatial coherence: the anonymous suburb predominates over symbolic centrality, the hegemony of extreme poverty invalidates the aesthetic designs and standards of the affluent society. In the metropolitan areas of Rio de Janeiro and São Paulo more than 6 million people live in precarious favelas or in overcrowded slums (Bonduki 1996).

Since the Second World War many attempts have been made to address the spontaneous habitat of the marginal migrants in Latin America. In the 1990s the Alliance for Progress emerged as an alternative to the Cuban model and backed the policy of the state as benefactor in the construction of gigantic housing districts – the Villas Kennedy and the apartment blocks on the periphery of Buenos Aires, Lima and Caracas – which aimed to replace the *villas miseria, callampas* or favelas (Eliash and San Martin 1996). The futility of this approach was demonstrated at the United Nations Habitat I conference in Vancouver (1976) when priority was given to the initiatives of community participation and self-built projects. This was the zenith of John Turner's thesis of self-help and mutual effort, which we unjustly criticised when defending the centralised planning system of Cuba (Segre 1975). In the 1980s, the so-called 'lost decade', negotiation and initiatives were paralysed due to the economic crisis generated by recession and the external debt of the majority of countries (Burgess et al. 1997). The advent of neoliberalism and globalisation led to new options in the 1990s. At the Habitat II conference, held in Istanbul in 1996, diverse policies were formulated based on popular economic management and the articulation between public structures and private initiatives from NGOs (Velázquez 1996; Bindé 2006). Improvements to the residential environment comprised not only housing but infrastructure and services to 'sew' together and integrate the formal city with informal settlements (Wainstein-Krasuk 1997). Such an outlook predominated in the actions driven by the municipal government of Rio de Janeiro during the twenty years.

Rio de Janeiro: From 'Solar' City to 'Dark' City

It would be difficult to disentangle whether the marginal settlements in Latin America appeared first in Havana or in Rio de Janeiro. Contemporaneously in 1897, two wars generated a defenceless and wretched population. In Cuba, the Spanish Governor General Valeriano Weyler i Nicolau, when faced with the advancing army of the liberators along the island, decided to expel the peasants from their lands and to concentrate them in the cities to remove logistical support to the Cuban combatants. Approximately 100,000 people arrived in Havana and settled on peripheral land in improvised huts of poles and palm leaves without water or latrines. According to the North American Consul, almost half of the residents died within a year because of typhus, smallpox, dysentery and cholera (Poumier 1975: 132; Moreno Fraginals 1996: 276).

In Brazil, soldiers of the Republican Army returned from the north-east to Rio de Janeiro after the massacre of peasants led by Antônio Conselheiro in the town of Canudos. Lacking accommodation in the city they settled in the hills (*morros*) near the centre, in the Morro de Santo Antonio as well as the Morro da Providência (Fessler Vaz and Berenstein Jacques 2003; Fessler Vaz 2002: 55). It was there that the term 'favela' was first used to refer to spontaneous settlements: it is derived from the name of a rough and wild leguminous plant commonly found in the *sertão* (semi-arid hinterland) as well as in the region of Rio. In 1904, this favela contained more than a thousand precarious dwellings (Zylberberg 1992; Zaluar and Altivo 1998).

By 2006, more than a century after that first favela developed in a city of almost half a million inhabitants, the population of the municipality had grown to 5.5 million (the metropolitan area has 11 million) and more than 600 favelas are scattered throughout its boundaries, in the *morros* next to the wealthy areas as well as in the poor settlements, whose constant growth has now reached 2 million (Arantes 1998: 8; Magalhães 2002). The 'broken' city is not segregated but constantly intermingles the opulent with the defenceless along the 'rio solar' of the south: the favelas of Vidigal next to the Sheraton Hotel; Rocinha at the entrance to the luxurious residences of San Conrado; Dona Marta in Botafogo; Pavao-Pavaozinho between Copacabana and Ipanema. These images represent the aesthetic and symbolic, natural and architectonic values which make Rio de Janeiro recognisable throughout the world (Ventura 1994).

From the administration of Francisco Pereira Passos (1902–1906) up to the military dictatorship (1964–1985), the government tried to eradicate the favelas, especially those situated in the centre and the south of the city, areas which were gradually taken over by the wealthy bourgeoisie of Rio de Janeiro. Pereira Passos wiped out the precarious settlements of the colonial city – *cortiços, estalagens, casas de cómodo, casebres* – and between the 1920s and 1950s the main central *morros* – *Castelo* and *Santo Antônio* – were eliminated, as well as some essential components of the urban historic memory of Rio: the first churches and convents of the colonial city were located in the Morro do Castelo (Abreu and Fessler Vaz 1991). Attempts at creating proletarian 'colonies' were not successful, from the Plan Agache to the government of Getúlio Vargas in the 1940s, to the laws forbidding the construction of new favelas or the extension of existing ones (1936). During the 1960s the governor of the Estado de Guanabara, Carlos Lacerda, and the military governments from 1964 onwards, applied the authoritarian-technocratic-rationalist pattern in their obsession to stamp out the favelas of the southern zone (Vainer and Smolka 1991). A total of 175,800 inhabitants from eighty settlements which were 'contaminating' the space of wealthy areas – Catacumba, Praia do Pinto, Macedo and Sobrinho, among the largest – were evicted between 1960 and 1975, without a doubt the largest urban 'cleansing' operation that has taken place in the country (Blank 1980; Queiroz Ribeiro 2003). This reversed the existing contradiction between the Cidade Maravilhosa of the rich which was expanding in the free spaces along the beaches, and the 'marvellous' views from the *morros* which were available only to the occupants of the *favelas* (Scholhammer and Hershmann 1997).

However, by not tackling the social and economic causes which generate poverty – the extreme poverty of the north-east of the country, persistent unemployment and the need for cheap manual labour by industry, construction and services – coercive actions were unable to stop the constant growth of the favelas, especially in the areas of expansion of the upper middle-class suburbs. This was the case of Miami Carioca in the Barra de Tijuca which generated spontaneous settlements in Jacarepaguá, such as the extension of the favela of Rio das Pedras. Between 1980 and 1991, while the urban population grew by 8 percent, that of the favelas increased by 35 per cent.

The Catholic Church played a fundamental role in 'humanising' the living conditions of the poorest population. In 1946 the Fundación León XIII supported the community action of residents ready to defend their original settlement, a decision which was ratified in 1979 by the Archdiocese of Rio de Janeiro in the Pastoral Letter on the favelas (Valladares 1983, 2006). Beginning in 1964, the authoritarian federal government insisted that low-cost house building plans must go through the Banco Nacional de Habitação (Duarte, Silva and Brasileiro 1996). Parallel to this, in 1968 the state of Rio de Janeiro created the Companhia de Desenvolvimento de Comunidades (CODESCO), which directed policies for improving and upgrading the precarious settlements. This was carried out with the support of the architect Carlos Nelson Ferreira dos Santos – one of the main champions of community participation – and other designers, who backed the population of the favela Brás de Pina in the struggle to prevent a planned eviction. 'Their success constituted the first experience of a community effort in which the inhabitants converted their cardboard and tin shacks into solid houses of brick and concrete' (Abreu 1997: 106). Once the dictatorship lost power in 1985, the city council and the state government backed participative planning and self-build initiatives (*mutirao*) in favelas and in peripheral marginal settlements.

Favela–Bairro: Reality and Hope for the New Millennium

In 1992 the UN Conference on Environment and development gave Rio a fleeting moment of splendour. During his term of office, the governor Lionel Brizola tried to improve the living standard of the poor population and commissioned Oscar Niemeyer to construct 350 schools for the education of the poor children of the state. However, the euphoria lasted only a short time. In August of that year President Collor was removed from office by a popular impeachment; in 1993 the slaughter of nine street children and twenty-one inhabitants of the favela Vigário Geral took place in front of the church of La Candelaria in the central historic district. To this was added the takeover and total control of the favelas by drug dealers and game operators (*el bicho*), which triggered 'Operación Rio' by the army in 1994, with the aim of controlling the expansion of street violence. The gradual deterioration of the urban environment, architecturally as well as socially, was demonstrated by the presence of 15,000 people sleeping in the streets, on pavements and under bridges and viaducts, and with 150,000 street sellers (*camelôs*) working daily throughout the city centre (Ventura 1994: 29–32).

When César Maia became mayor in 1993, a radical change took place in the urban strategy of the municipality. Under the leadership of Luiz Paulo Conde as Secretary for Planning, later elected mayor (1997–2000), and Sergio Magalhães, Housing Secretary during both periods, the city lived through a building fervour similar to the one that took place at the beginning of the century with Pereira Passos. It is unheard of in the history of the city for two renowned designers to take up important administrative posts (Guimaraens 1994). This does not mean that the previous mayors and governors did not promote essential public works but that they had limited environmental significance as their interventions were restricted to the beautification of the southern zone and to the development of infrastructural projects. Generic planning was now substituted by strategic and concrete projects (Portas 1996), defined by César Maia as 'urban acupuncture'. The interventions developed along two complementary axes: the Rio-Cidade Programme (Soter 1996) to reactivate the urban-architectural-aesthetic and functional identity of the public spaces of seventeen barrios, and the Favela-Bairro Programme (Soter and Laranjeira 1999) aimed at the transformation of precarious and marginal settlements to turn them into an integral part of the 'formal' city, provided with essential basic services (Zein 1996).

The originality of both initiatives stems from the importance given to the aesthetic attributes of urban design. To regenerate the everyday beauty of the living spaces of the sections of society most in need constitutes a basic objective, as contrasted with the limitless suburban extension of the 'grey' or 'shapeless' city and with the bureaucratic, technocratic and functionalist actions of state and municipal organisations. In view of the impossibility of addressing the actual housing itself, which in the majority of cases the users manage to build for themselves, the aim was to radically improve the collective environment of public space which is so often abandoned and deteriorates in great housing projects: that emaciated no-man's-land of streets, squares and parks. It was thought that the anonymous character of vacant urban sites, lacking in character and function, should be able to contain essential community buildings, and with quality design it should be possible to break definitively with the image of the architecture of poverty and thus rescue the inherent socio-cultural values of the community.

The favelas are creative places: the inhabitants have generated theatre groups such as the internationally renowned Vidigal; the famous dance schools in Maré; the well-known songs and baroque images of the carnival Escolas do Samba – the Império Serrano in the *morro* of Madureira and those of Mangueira and San Carlos – and it is no coincidence that Michael Jackson and Spike Lee made a video clip in Doña Marta in 1996. Such creativity and inventiveness also appear in the urban dimension, in the articulation between professional culture and popular knowledge, between public power and participative democracy.[2] The knowledge produced in the favelas finds itself integrated in a global system made possible by the development of computer technologies, a system which does not have economic or social barriers. It could be said that it is a sign of the inventiveness of the favelas' inhabitants that the 'Rio businessman Rodrigo Biaggio created an NGO – Committee for the Democratisation of Informatics – which trained more than 600,000 people in the *favelas*' (Cerqueira 2005: 32). As the late Betinho, a sociologist who fought tirelessly for the cause of the defenceless, declared, 'the way to democracy in Rio goes through *Favela-Bairro*. For the first time intelligence has gone hand in hand with dignity to transform the city' (Conde 1998: 8).

To achieve this objective – the multiplication of the intelligentsia in urban space – the municipal government *(Prefeitura)* called a public competition for each of the projects, which mobilised the majority of professional firms in the city. The innovative character of the proposal filled the president of the Inter-American Development Bank, Enrique Iglesias, with enthusiasm. The bank offered to contribute more than $500 million to finance the works as they considered it paradigmatic for the whole of Latin America, both for the quality of design and for the articulation achieved between public power and private initiative.[3] It was exciting to witness the enthusiastic response not only of young professionals but also of older prestigious architects – including the brothers Roberto, Acácio Gil Borsoi and Paulo Casé, among others (Casé 1996) – who were usually dedicated to the design of hotels, offices or high-cost residential buildings, but who understood the importance of this project to the city. The first fourteen communities of the first phase were followed by another seventy-three, benefiting a population of more than 200,000 inhabitants. 'At the end of the year 2000 the interventions had reached 150 communities, which benefited almost half a million people' (Conde and Magalhães 2004: 56). Whilst at the beginning only medium-sized favelas (2,000 to 4,000 inhabitants) were included, in 2006 the municipal government, under the leadership of César Maia, planned to undertake the restructuring of some of the largest, Jacarezinho and Rio das Pedras, which house up to 50,000 people. Moreover, Luiz Paulo Conde, the vice-governor (2004–2008) of the State of Rio de Janeiro, called for a public competition for the development of ideas for urban interventions in the favela of Rocinha where over 50,000 people live.

The originality of the Favela-Bairro Programme lay in the conceptual and methodological work that preceded the project. The competition did not require rigid design criteria but a general approach to the problem. Considerable flexibility was generated by the range of dissimilar situations in the settlements: ecological, topographical, infrastructural, social, cultural and industrial (Duarte, Silva and Brasileiro 1996).[4] The participants adopted the shared parameters of the selected example and defined their plan of action. Once accepted, the essential research for the urban and architectural proposal got started, the realisation of which depended on the participation and approval of members of the community. Thus the project was not the result of an a priori approach but was a response to specific conditions. This resulted in a range of solutions with different degrees of emphasis, from ones that gave prominence to social structures to those where form and space design were the priority (Ventura 1997; Ribeiro 1996). In this sense, the essential points of the programme, defined by Jorge Jáuregui, are illustrative:

a) To democratise the enjoyment of the city by making it accessible to all citizens

b) To favour the connectivity of the urban structure as a whole, addressing the divided city, that is to say, the deficit of city, especially but not only in areas of poverty

c) To guarantee accessibility to all places in the city and to increase connection and integration with the environment

d) To avoid removing anyone from their place in order to avoid severing existing social linkages (except in areas of high risk or where it was necessary to create open spaces to allow conviviality)

e) To respect the history of each area and the investments made by each inhabitant through their own efforts

f) To open up places in the existing urban fabric by introducing spaces and buildings as urbanistic-environmental re-articulators and *re-qualifiers*

g) To encourage community participation through 'listening' to the inhabitants' requirements, establishing differences between stated and latent demands

h) To create new *centralities* and empower the existing ones as well as increasing the connectivity between them

i) To produce a drastic change in the image of the area, making it possible to change the inhabitants' own perception of it, thus enunciating a thoughtful position with regard to their own environment.

j) To produce cohesion by articulating heterogeneous logics, unifying the city without homogenising it, looking for the coexistence of the city of flows with the city of places (Jáuregui 2003: 8–9).

Amongst the many diverse favela projects which were completed in the first phase in 1997, we will analyse two in more detail. The work in the favela of Fernao Cardim was carried out by Jorge Jáuregui and Hamilton Casé Planejamento Arquitetonico e Ambiental.[5] The favela has a population of three thousand inhabitants and is located in Méier, an industrial area in the north of the city, in the district of Engenho de Dentro. It sprang up in the 1950s when dwellers set up their improvised dwellings on both banks of the contaminated Faría Timbó River, which periodically flooded the muddy land of the settlement. With its persistent deterioration, lack of basic services and urban chaos, it approaches the image of hell on earth.

The designers adopted connection with the formal city – via a main axis of vehicular circulation in front of the favela – and river management as the primary elements of the project. Once canalised, planted with trees and furnished with street furniture, the river ceased to be a feared threat to the dwellers and instead became the main space for social interaction. The irregular side streets were surfaced, a range of small squares created in open areas for children and old people and public space was brightened up with the aesthetic attributes of the designed environment. The change that took place in the quality of life of the population was impressive and it was noticeable how each dwelling owner along the riverbank started to make changes to the front of their homes to go with the improvement of the main axis of the favela. The architectural climax was achieved in the access square, with a succession of new 'pieces' introduced by the designers. Counterpoised by a banal MacDonald advert, the square – framed by craftmen's workshops, a sports field, crèche and block of flats built for those who had to be rehoused to make way for the new public spaces – is the abstract symbol of the project's existence. The architectural language of these interventions was based on the existing typology of bricks and tiles, recovering the articulations and transparencies implicit in the constraint-free composition of the dwellers' buildings.[6]

Work in the favela of Parque Royal was carried out by Archi 5 Arquitetos Associados. Parque Royal has a population of almost 4,000 inhabitants and lies in the district of La Portuguesa in the Isla del Gobernador, on the bank of the Bay of Guanabara and in the vicinity of Galeao International Airport. While in Fernao Cardim the structure of the favela had been organised around the axis which penetrates its interior, here the young designers of Archi 5 opted for clearly defining the edges of the settlement. Apart from the irregularity of the layout, one of the main problems of spontaneous popular housing is the lack of defined limits and its continuous cell-like growth. The expansion of Parque Royal with fragile wooden dwellings on stilts was endangering the mangrove swamps of the Bay of Guanabara. Therefore, it was decided to establish two curvilinear axis-limits: the first along a fast traffic route which connected it with the formal city; the second aimed to recover the quality of the environment and the landscape of the bay's coastline. Eliminating the precarious dwellings, rehousing the inhabitants and designing a promenade and a cycle way transformed the most deteriorated spaces of the favela to create a convivial environment, which in the future will compete with the promenades along the beaches of the southern zone. Faced with the impossibility of penetrating the existing densely interwoven fabric, the social functions were linked together along the axis defined by the rapid traffic route, with partial penetration achieved through the main square and the community centre. The new axis established by the stadium, primary school, crèche, the new housing block and the centre for job retraining, form a series of architectural links which integrate with the complementary environmental inventions. Apart from the 'rossiana' style of the housing block, the design adopts a contextual language with generous open spaces for social activities.

Poverty, Society, Urbanism and Architecture

The impulse achieved through the Favela-Bairro programme was halted at the beginning of the twenty-first century when César Maia returned to the municipal government. Ironically it was during his term of office in 1993 when Luiz Paolo Conde and Sergio Magalhaes began the ambitious project. In Brazil there is continuous conflict between the political parties which alternate in power at the different levels – federal, state and municipal – of government. In the case of Rio de Janeiro, Maia did not wish to continue the initiatives of Conde and the antagonisms continued between the state and the municipality because Conde was secretary of the environment and urban development at the time (2003 –2006). This effectively meant that investment in the programme stopped and support for solutions to the social and community problems of the favelas was withdrawn.

In recent years much has been written about the successes and failures of this experience. Both local and international researchers have criticised the policy of 'city marketing' carried out by municipalities following European models, such as Barcelona. 'These are based on cosmetic actions and the presence of international "superstar" architects to attract foreign investment and international tourism' (Sanchez 2003: 27). In the case of Rio de Janeiro this dynamic was linked to the Panamerican Games in 2007, which required that urban violence be controlled. In this context the Canadian academic, Anne-Marie Broudehoux, has described the Favela-Bairro programme as a showcase for political propaganda rather than an effective intervention that managed to reduce injustice and social conflicts. She has asserted – wrongly – that the aesthetic attributes of the architecture took precedence over the economic, social and cultural concerns of the inhabitants in the settlements (Broudehoux 2001).

We are confronted here with an unjust 'sociological' vision reminiscent of the extreme ideological posturing of the old communist Left. The interventions in the urban spaces of the favelas were ambitious, not just aesthetic. They aimed to break the traditional separation between the formal and informal city and to establish principles of permeability between spaces which have been historically segregated; to improve the environmental conditions of the community; to revalue public space; and to provide precarious settlements with essential infrastructure and social services. In other words, the Favela-Bairro projects aimed at eliminating the ghetto image which, since the beginning of the twentieth century, has been the dominant way of understanding and viewing favelas. In the original plan, once the initial works were completed, the role of the municipality would be to support the residents in improving their own houses, to participate in the maintenance of buildings and urban infrastructure as well as to promote the participation and education of citizens in the care of the social life of the community, all initiatives which have still not been implemented at the necessary level. Undoubtedly the broader problem of the favelas has social and economic dimensions which are beyond the reach of urban design and architectural interventions.

Even though the Favela-Bairro programme was halted, it was assumed by many that the living conditions of the poorest in the population would improve with the election of the popular government of Ignacio Lula da Silva in 2002, which led to the creation of a Ministry for Cities and, in 2004, the new Statute for Cities which favoured the distribution of land and property titles to the inhabitants of favelas and peripheral settlements. However, in his speech to the United Nations, the Minister for Cities, Olivio Dutra, stated that the population of the favelas in Brazil had increased by 150 per cent between 1999 and 2001, mostly in the large metropolitan areas (Celestino 2004). This was for a number of reasons: continuing migration to the cities of the rural population from the north-east, the absence of low-cost housing projects, and the high unemployment rate. Almost 3 million people were without work in the six largest metropolitan regions, reaching 9.6 per cent of the population of Rio de Janeiro and 14.1 per cent of Sao Paulo. It has become clear that despite the efforts of the government to tackle the deep-rooted poverty of the majority of the population – with measures such as increasing the minimum wage and the creation of the *bolsa familia*[7] – Brazil continues to lead the world as the country with the largest difference between the income of the rich minority and the poor majority.

In conclusion, the Favela-Bairro programme aimed to restore the urban qualities of the poorest settlements in both the central and peripheral areas, and to integrate them into the multifaceted complexity of the metropolitan context. However, the economic and social reality of the country, the acute contradictions between different social groups and the progressive segregation and separation of residential areas make the coexistence and connection between the rich and poor hard to achieve. The violence generated by desperate poverty and the vicious control of drug traffickers over the favelas – which has increased in the early years of the twenty-first century – inhibit the impact and future prospects for architectural and urban design interventions. However, undeniable and tangible improvements have already been achieved: many thousands now enjoy improved living conditions and the inhabitants of the upgraded favelas are more aware of the cultural and aesthetic values of their new social environment which offers them a real sense of identity and humanity. These are the objectives for which we, as Latin American architects, struggle, with the aim of reversing the centuries of exploitation and injustice which are dominant in our hemisphere. However, to achieve these goals requires substantial transformations in social and economic structures across the region. Such transformations may already be taking place in some countries. It seems as if the leftist governments of Lula in Brazil, Evo Morales in Bolivia, Hugo Chávez in Venezuela, Daniel Ortega in Nicaragua and Rafael Correa in Ecuador have identified many of the needs of poor people in their countries, although too little has been done so far. If politicians do not respond to the claims of the community, the possibilities for architectural transformation will remain slim.

Today the dialogue between elite culture and popular traditions is consciously deepening. It is no coincidence that the topic of Third World housing and its problems is present in debates, exhibitions and projects taking place in the First World, for example in the work of Rem Koolhaas (Koolhaas et al. 2001) and in the dominant themes of the 2002 Venice Biennial.[8] The historic divergences have been converted into urgent convergences. Architecture is returning to its ancestral social meaning of expressing the everyday needs of pleasure and beauty through the vital rescuing of lost human dignity. From the suffering humanity of Latin America we find fragmentary hopes for the twenty-first century.

Notes

Translated from the original Spanish by Angela Uribe de Kellett.

1. See 'El torbellino y el holograma', interview with Edgar Morin, Buenos Aires: Centro de estudios latinoamericanos, April 1993, 12.
2. In the last few years there has been a growing interest in the forms of cultural expression that emerge out of the favelas, as well as in the development of the creative abilities of its inhabitants. On this topic, see Altivo (2001) and Berenstein Jacques (2001). Additional material can be found in Varella et al. (2002).
3. See Magalhães (1997).
4. Duarte, Silva and Brasileiro (1996) contains the methodological proposals of the first stage of the Favela-Bairro programme.
5. They were also in charge of the historic favela of Vidigal. To see the main completed projects of the Favela-Bairro programme, see Revista (1997).
6. Apart from this project, Jorge Jáuregui was involved in many others. Those in Vidigal, Rio das Pedras, Morro dos Macacos, Fubá-Campino and Salgueiro are among the most outstanding. All his work has a strong theoretical and philosophical base which makes it stand out amongst the best works of the past twenty years. This earned him the sixth Verónica Rudge Green Prize in Urban Design, awarded by the Harvard Graduate School, in 2003 (Machado 2003).
7. The *bolsa familia* is the government's flagship poverty reduction programme, and is aimed mainly at poor families in the north-east. It is an income transfer scheme which gives poor people a monthly cash allowance, provided that they meet certain criteria. It represents an important incentive for parents to invest in their children's education and health and provides financial incentives to keep their children in school.
8. At the 8th Biennial of Architecture in Venice in 2002, Brazil presented the favelas as the central theme of its exhibition, curated by Elisabete and Gloria Bayeux. See França and Bayeux (2002); see also Fiori (2001).

References

Abreu, M. 1997. *Evolução urbana do Rio de Janeiro*. Rio de Janeiro: IPLANRIO.

Abreu, M. and L. Fessler Vaz. 1991. 'Sobre os origens da favela. Novas e velhas legitimidades na reestructuração do território', *Anais do IV Encontro Nacional da ANPUR* (Salvador, Universidade Federal da Bahia) 481–92.

Altivo, M. 2001. *As cores de Acari. Uma Favela Carioca*. Rio de Janeiro: Fundação Getulio Vargas.

Arantes, G. 1998. 'Rolo Compressor', *Jornal do Brasil* (Rio de Janeiro) 18 March.

Berenstein Jacques, P. 2001. *Estética da ginga. Arquitetura das favelas através da obra de Hélio Oiticica*. Rio de Janeiro: Editora Casa da Palavra, Rioarte.

Bindé, J. 1996. 'Sommet de la ville: les leçons d'Istambul', *Futuribles* 211: 77–95.

Blank, G. 1980. 'Bras de Pina. Experiência de Urbanização de Favela', in L. do Prado Valladares (ed.) *Habitação em Questão*. Rio de Janeiro: Zahar, 93–124.

Bonduki, N. 1996. 'Habitação, mutirão: a experiência da administração Luiza Erundina em São Paulo', in N. Bonduki (ed.) *Habitat. As práticas bem-sucedidas em habitação, meio ambiente e gestão urbana nas cidades brasileiras*, São Paulo: Studio Nobel, 180–94.

Broudehoux, A. 2001. 'Image Making, City Marketing and the Aesthetization of Social Inequality in Rio de Janeiro', in N. AlSayyad (ed.) *Consuming Tradition, Manufacturing Heritage: Global Norms and Urban Forms in the Age of Tourism*. London: Routledge, 273–297.

Burgess, R., et al. 1997. 'Contemporary Spatial Strategies and Urban Policies in Developing Countries: A Critical Review', in R. Burgess, M. Carmona and T. Kolstee (eds), *The Challenge of Sustainable Cities: Neoliberalism and Urban Strategies in Developing Countries*. London: Zed Books, 111–24.

Casé, P. 1996. *Favela. Uma exegese a partir de Mangueira*. Rio de Janeiro: Relume Dumará.

Celestino, H. 2004. 'Favelização e impotência', *O Globo*, 1 May, 3.

Cerqueira, S. 2005. 'O sonho de Bggio', *Veja Rio*, 7 December, 32.

Choay, F. 1994. 'Le règne de l'urbain et la mort de la ville', in J. Dethier and A. Guiheux (eds), *La ville. Art et architecture en Europe, 1870–1993*. Paris: Éditions du Centre Georges Pompidou, 26–35.

Conde, L.P. 1998. 'Ciudadanía e democracia', *Jornal do Brasil*, 7 April, 8–9.

Conde, L.P. and S. Magalhães. 2004. *Favela-Bairro: uma outra história da cidade do Rio de Janeiro*. Rio de Janeiro: Vivercidades.

Davies, M. 2004. 'Planet of Slums', *New Left Review* 26: 5–34.

Deleuze, G. and F. Guattari. 1980. *Mille Plateaux. Capitalisme et Schizophrénie*, Paris: Minuit.

Duarte, C., O. Silva and O. Brasileiro. 1996. *Favela, um bairro. Propostas Metodológicas para Intervenção Públicas em Favelas do Rio de Janeiro*. São Paulo: Grupo Habitat, UFRJ, ProEditores.

Eliash, H. and E. San Martín. 1996. 'L'abitazione sociale e la costruzione della periferia urbana in America Latina', in R. Gutiérrez (ed.) *Architettura e Società. L'America Latina nel XX Sécolo. Dizionario Enciclopedico*, Milan: Jaca Book, 53–63.

Fessler Vaz, L. 2002. *Modernidade e moradia: Habitação coletiva no Rio de Janeiro*. Rio de Janeiro: 7 Letras.

Fessler Vaz, L. and P. Berenstein Jacques. 2003. 'Pequeña historia de las *favelas* de Río de Janeiro', *Ciudad y Territorio. Estudios Territoriales* 35(136/137): 259–72.

Fiori, J. (ed.) 2001. *Transforming Cities: Design in the Favelas of Rio de Janeiro*. London: Architectural Association.

França, E. and G. Bayeux. 2002. *Brasil: Favelas Upgrading*. São Paulo: Pavilhão Brasileiro, Fundação Bienal de São Paulo.

Guimaraens, C. 1994. *Luiz Paulo Conde: Un arquitecto carioca*. Bogotá: Escala, Universidad de Los Andes.

Hobsbawn, E. 1996. *Era dos extremos. O breve século XX. 1914–1991*. São Paulo: Companhia Das Letras.

Jáuregui, J. 2003. *Estratégias de Articulación Urbana. Proyecto y Gestión de Asentamientos Periféricos em América Latina. Um Enfoque Transdisciplinario*.

Buenos Aires: Secretaria de Investigaciones en Ciencia y Técnica, Facultad de Arquitectura, Diseño y Urbanismo, Universidad de Buenos Aires.

Koolhaas, R., et al. 2001. *Mutations*. New York: Actar.

Lelong, C. 1996. 'Una nueva forma urbana: el archipiélago', *Ciudad y Territorio. Estudios Territoriales* 28(110): 824–25.

Machado, R. (ed.). 2003. *The Favela-Bairro Project. Jorge Mario Jáuregui Architects*. Cambridge, MA: Harvard University Graduate School of Design.

Magalhães, S. 1997. 'Entrevista a Sérgio Magalhães, Secretário Municipal de Habitação do Rio de Janeiro', *Arquitetura IABRJ* 79: 6–9.

——— 2002. *Sobre a Cidade. Habitação e Democracia no Rio de Janeiro*. São Paulo: ProEditores.

Marcos, Sub Comandante. 1997. 'Porque combatimos', *Cuaderno Mais!* October.

Moreno Fraginals, M. 1996. *Cuba/España, España/Cuba. Historia común*. Barcelona: Grijalbo Mondadori.

Portas, N. 1996. 'Urbanismo e sociedade: construindo o futuro', in D. Pinheiro Machado and E. Mendes de Vasconcellos (eds), *Cidade e Imaginação*. Rio de Janeiro: PROURB, FAU, URFJ, 30–39.

Poumier, M. 1975. *Apuntes sobre la vida cotidiana en Cuba en 1898*. Havana: Editorial de Ciencias Sociales.

Queiroz Riberio, L. 2003. 'Segregación, desigualdad y vivienda: la metrópolis de Río de Janeiro em los años 80 y 90', *CyTET, Ciudad y Territorio. Estudios Territoriales* 35(136/137): 295–314.

Revista. 1997. *Revista Favela-Bairro*, 3rd edn. Rio de Janeiro: Prefeitura da Cidade do Rio de Janeiro, IPLANRIO.

Ribeiro, M. 1996. 'Favela Bairro inaugura nova era', *Jornal do Brasil*, 5 September.

Sánchez, F. 2003. *A reinvenção das cidades para um mercado mundial*. Chapecó: Editora Universitária Argos.

Scholhammer, K.E. and M. Herschmann. 1997. 'As cidades visiveis do Rio', *Lugar Comun. Estudios de mídia, cultura e democracia* 1:11–19.

Segre, R. 1975. 'Práctica social y práctica arquitectónica en los barrios de América Latina', in R. Segre (ed.) *Las estructuras ambientales de América Latina*. Ciudad de México: Siglo XXI Editores, 227–76.

——— 2002. 'América Latina. Urbanidad del siglo XXI. Suburbios, periferias, franjas y archipiélagos', in *Iberoamérica Arquitectura 02. III Bienal Iberoamericana de Arquitectura*. Seville: Tanais Ediciones, 36–43.

Soter, A. (ed.) 1996. *Rio Cidade. O urbanismo de volta as ruas*. Rio de Janeiro: Prefeitura da Cidade do Rio de Janeiro, Mauad.

Soter A. and A. Laranjeira (eds). 1999. *Cidade Inteira. A Política Habitacional da Cidade do Rio de Janeiro*. Rio de Janeiro: Secretaria Municipal de Habitação, Prefeitura da Cidade do Rio de Janeiro.

Taschner, S.P. 2003. 'O Brasil e as suas favelas', in P. Abramo (ed.) *A cidade da informalidade. O desafio das cidades latino-americanas*. Rio de Janeiro: Sette Letras, 13–42.

Vainer, C. and M. Smolka. 1991. 'Em tempos de liberalismo: tendências e desafios do planejamento urbano no Brasil', in R. Piquet and A.C. Torres (eds), *Brasil.*

Descamihos da Modernização. Térritorio da Desigualdade. Rio de Janeiro: Zahar, 19–32.

Valladares, L. (ed.) 1983. *Repensando a Habitação no Brasil* . Rio de Janeiro: Zahar.

――― 2006. *A invenção da Favela.* Rio de Janeiro: Fundação Getúlio Vargas.

Varella, D., et al. 2002. *Maré. Vida na Favela.* Rio de Janeiro: Casa da Palavra.

Velásquez, I. 1996. 'Repensar lo Urbano. Hábitat II: la cumbre de las ciudades en Estambul', *Arquitectura Viva* 49: 96.

Ventura, Z. 1994. *Cidade Partida.* São Paulo: Companhia das Letras.

――― 1997. 'A boa nova que vem lá de Serrinha', *Jornal do Brasil*, 8 March.

Virilio, P. 1997. 'A catástrofe urbana', *Caderno Mais!*, 28 September, 5–4.

Wainstein-Krasuk, O. (ed.) 1997. *Hábitat y Vivienda: el gran desafío.* Buenos Aires: Secretaría de Investigaciones en Ciencia y Técnica, Facultad de Arquitectura, Diseño y Urbanismo, Universidad de Buenos Aires.

Zaluar, A. and M. Altivo. 1998. *Um século de Favela.* Rio de Janeiro: Fundação Getulio Vargas.

Zein, R.V. 1996. 'De volta à cidade maravilhosa: a renovação do Rio de Janeiro busca superar a degradação urbana'. Projeto Design, São Paulo, SP, n. 201, 42–55.

Zylberberg, S. 1992. *Morro da Providência. Memorias da 'Favela'.* Rio de Janeiro: Prefeitura da Cidade do Rio de Janeiro.

Chapter 10

Spatial Strategies and Urban Social Policy: Urbanism and Poverty Reduction in the Favelas of Rio de Janeiro

Jorge Fiori and Zeca Brandão

Since 1994, the municipal government of Rio de Janeiro has been implementing a slum upgrading programme called Favela-Bairro, a name which signifies the transition from slum to neighbourhood. The programme gained international recognition as one of the most advanced of its kind in the developing world. Indeed, it became paradigmatic of a new generation of slum-upgrading and urban-development programmes (Fiori, Riley and Ramírez 2000). Not only did it aim to achieve a very large-scale intervention but it proposed a multi-sectoral and integrated approach which introduced a series of new ideas vis-à-vis previous generations of slum-upgrading policies and programmes, both in Rio and other cities in Brazil and abroad. Not least among these ideas was the renewed emphasis on spatial strategies and design as playing a very important role in addressing issues of social and spatial segregation in the city. This chapter focuses specifically on this subject, for it is our contention that the Favela-Bairro programme helped to bring back the role of urbanism – as a spatial discipline and practice – to the forefront of the pursuit of improving urban social policies. In its varied and rich search for spatial tools of analysis and intervention, the

Favela-Bairro programme also seems to have contributed to the development of an appropriate urbanism which addresses the particular conditions of irregularity and informality in the city.

For many decades now slums and squatter settlements have become a central feature of cities across the world, especially in the developing world. Overwhelming evidence indicates that the numbers of people living in urban slums have increased continuously almost everywhere – both in absolute as well as relative terms – particularly under the impact of structural adjustment programmes and neoliberal globalisation policies. 'In 2001, 924 million people, or 31.6% of the world's urban population, lived in slums. The majority of them were in developing regions, accounting for 43% of the urban population, in contrast to 6% in more developed regions' (UN-Habitat 2003: xxv). It is projected that the number of slum dwellers will increase in the next twenty-five years to around 2 billion if no appropriate action is taken (UN-Habitat 2003, 2004; Garau et al. 2005).

In view of the strong connection between slums and circumstances of extreme poverty these statistics are, indeed, frightening. But it is even more worrying if one considers that programmes and policies which claim to address the social and physical problems of slums have been around for decades as well! So, why have different approaches and recipes to scale-up to the social and spatial dimensions of the problem failed so consistently? What has gone so badly wrong in this history of failures, from the early policies of slum eradication, state mass housing and the blind belief in the powers of urban planning; through the experimentation with affordable, unsubsidised, replicable, site-and-services and upgrading projects of the 1970s which took place in the context of the crisis of modernisation and the questioning of modernist traditions in planning, urbanism and architecture; to more recently the neoliberal ambitions of scaling-up by means of market liberalisation, deregulation and institutional reforms which were supposed, eventually, to let their benefits filter down to the poorest members of society? While the answer to the latter question still defines an area of considerable controversy, there is convergence around the general idea that scaling-up involves and requires a more complex multi-dimensional and integrated approach than those used in the above-mentioned strategies.

We have argued in previous publications that a new generation of slum-upgrading and urban-development policies started to emerge in the mid 1990s, and the Favela-Bairro project belongs to it. This new generation of policies aimed at connecting a variety of components that are not new in themselves (Fiori 2001; Fiori, Riley and Ramírez 2001,

2004). What could be considered new are the way these components are combined and the search for synergies across a variety of social, political, institutional and spatial processes, all of which are interconnected and operating at different scales simultaneously. Scaling-up, in our view, is a function of the way in which those processes interact. However, instead of giving an almost exclusive priority to the social and political processes – as in most of the relevant literature – we argue that consideration of the spatial processes, and the formulation of strategies to deal with them, are an essential part of any integrated approach to scaling-up in poverty reduction initiatives. Scaling-up to the level of social needs in urban areas in general, and in relation to slums and squatter settlements in particular, is inexorably about reaching the dimension of the city itself through the articulation of its multiple scales. This requires engagement with urbanism and appropriate spatial design strategies, perhaps the most absent and least spoken of component of the many attempts, over almost forty years, to develop a comprehensive and coherent approach to scaling-up in slum upgrading and urban poverty reduction.

The Place of Urbanism: Abandoned or Misconceived?

We argue that there has been a growing 'despatialisation' of slum-upgrading strategies over the years. Yet, this is the result of past policies that were profoundly marked by a spatially deterministic approach. Throughout the world, the heroic days of slum eradication, mass housing and modernist urban planning were characterised by a strong belief in the power of architecture and urbanism to promote development and to shape social relations. Almost invariably, the critique of such attitudes was equally spatially deterministic, as it turned design into one of the main scapegoats for the failures of the period. Justified criticisms increasingly gave way to a powerful anti-design discourse – often defensively adopted by architects and urbanists themselves – with the result that, slowly but surely, the baby was thrown out with the bath water.

The emergence of informal urbanisation as an object of analysis and as a field of action coincided with the appearance of the dominant critiques of modernism in the 1960s and early 1970s. From the works of John Turner, Charles Abrams or William Manguin, to the spatial analyses of Habraken or Christopher Alexander and the studies of the different members of Team X, there was an enthralment with the spontaneous, the organic, the self-organising as another way of doing or, as it has been called, the order behind the apparent disorder so inimical to the modernist logic (Castillo 2001). Beyond acknowledging the absence of architects and designers within spontaneous settlements and cities, there was in fact an increasing valorisation of that absence. The bottom-up, self-produced logic of these 'unplanned', 'undesigned' and unregulated spaces was seen as creating more appropriate responses to the objective and subjective conditions of their users.

The critique of particular spatial and design practices and their inability to deal with the real city opened the way to a growing dismissal of design itself. At the same time, an increasing emphasis on the local and contextual – in opposition to the artificial ambitions of modernist planning which dealt with the city as a whole through a homogenising approach – led, in our view, to a growing loss of the city scale and, ultimately, of the city itself. It is here that we can locate the beginnings of what we have called the 'despatialisation' of the debate and the strategies to deal with the urban slums and squatter settlements of the developing world. This became particularly apparent in the emergent discourse of 'urban development planning' which focused on the cities of the developing world, and whose emphasis shifted entirely towards the social and political processes of the city (Safier 1983; Sprenger 2006).

This discourse converged fully with the emergence of one of the most influential concepts in the analysis of postwar developing countries and cities, that of the informal sector. This concept addressed both institutional and socio-economic aspects of the processes of the production of goods, provision of services and formation of settlements which happened outside existing regulatory frameworks and which diverged from the dominant forms of capitalist production, even if subordinated to them. Although different theoretical and ideological perspectives varied in their interpretations of the informal and in their understanding of the relationship between the formal and the informal, they all shared – in drastic contrast with the dominant views of the past – the sense that the informal represented a universe of resourcefulness and inventiveness which required support and enhancement rather than eradication. The means to achieve this, however, has remained, until today, one of the main areas of dispute and debate in the field of development policies, not least because in so many parts of the developing world, the informal has become the 'dominant' way of producing and delivering goods and services and constructing cities. The question arises as to how to deal with the informal and, more particularly, with an urban informality that has become constitutive of the urban condition itself.

The radical change in the understanding of informal settlements led, at the end of the 1960s, to a new set of policies in the form of sites-and-services and slum-upgrading programmes and projects. They combined the discourse about the merits of self-organised and self-produced settlements with the search for minimising costs through extreme reduction of quality standards, something which was then rationalised under the concept of 'progressive development' – that is, housing and settlements which were under permanent and continuous processes of transformation (Turner 1972). A decade of those policies and programmes produced results which have been the object of extensive analysis. There is agreement, however, that on the whole they have never risen to the scale of the challenge and have only resulted in isolated and fragmented interventions.

The reasons for such a failure were multiple and it is beyond the scope of this chapter to expand on them. It is important to note, though, the total lack of an urban and spatial perspective on those experiences. Generally, upgrading projects followed a very 'introverted' logic, concerned mainly with the provision of very basic sanitation and infrastructure, essentially making them works of urban engineering. There was little attention to the creation or enhancement of internal spatial qualities through design and, particularly relevant to our discussion, almost no consideration about questions of connectivity of settlements with their immediate surrounding as well as with the city as a whole. Even in the context of greatly ambitious upgrading programmes – such as the Kampung Improvement Programmes in Jakarta and Surabaya that have been underway since the late 1970s (Silas 1984) – scaling-up was seen mainly as a function of the numerical multiplication of projects without much attention to the quality of their spatial connection with the overall city and no particular interpretation of how the informal and the formal logics of city-making meet.

In many respects, this was a very 'schizophrenic' period. The new set of policies, informed by new understandings of informal processes in the city and a critique of modernist planning, still aimed at 'formalising' the informal city in line with the principles and rules of the modernist tradition. New approaches often coexisted with the old planning departments going about in their old ways but stopping short of eradication in the hope that, sooner or later, the logic of the formal city would somehow prevail through the slow-motion upgrading of the informal one. Their practice, however, was much less ambitious and much more incoherent than even that. More often than not, upgrading projects were implemented in a piecemeal manner, with their 'back' turned on the city, reinforcing a logic of isolation if not 'ghettoisation', totally disconnected from any plan or overall city strategy. In fact, in many cities – including Rio de Janeiro – those projects were being implemented at the very same time that all city maps and plans ignored the existence of favelas.

It would be wrong and unfair to blame the failures of those experiences on the defendants of an organic, self-produced logic of spatial organisation. More out of expediency than principle, their discourse was appropriated – or misappropriated – by governments and international agencies attempting to reduce costs and often neutralise social pressures. The fact is, however, that no critique of the failures of upgrading policies and programmes of the 1970s to scale-up to the breadth and depth of social need ever raised the spatial dimension as an important part of the equation. Neither have they tried to articulate a different understanding of the role of urbanism and spatial strategies in it.

While slum-upgrading programmes and projects continued through the 1980s and early 1990s, they did so in an even more isolated and fragmented manner. The main thrust of housing and urban development policies in those years – strongly influenced by the hegemonic neoliberal policies and structural adjustment programmes of the time – moved away from upgrading projects and from carrying out physical interventions in order to focus on the redesign and reform of institutions. In terms of urban planning, there was a growing fascination with the emergent discourse of 'strategic planning' which, superseding physical master planning, aimed at setting up institutional structures for the formulation of strategic visions of competitive cities in a 'globalised' market. Although strategic planning would then revalue architecture and design as central tools in the creation of the infrastructures of competition and in city marketing, none of this was directed to the question of how to address the informal and irregular city. Furthermore, that revalorisation never regained a proper sense of city scale due to the recurrent inability of strategic planning to address the multiple and contradictory logics inherent in the development of the contemporary city.

By the early 1990s, the worsening conditions of poverty and social exclusion in most of the developing world which resulted from the implementation of neoliberal policies was increasingly acknowledged. Ideals of the minimum state and of market liberalisation as an instrument of universalisation and accessibility to social goods came under strong criticism, even by some of the institutions that helped to shape and propagate those ideas (World Bank 1997, 2000). Questions of poverty and social policy – with a particular focus on the urban context – came firmly back into discussion. The agendas for urban development in the 1990s started to articulate different understandings of the relation between economic growth, state reform, poverty reduction and sustainability (World Bank 1991). By no means did this become an arena of consensus but certainly there was a reinvigorated debate which returned to issues abandoned during the years of unrestrained neoliberalism.

New conceptualisations of poverty emerged, emphasising the multiple and heterogeneous nature of poverty and the need for much more integrated and multi-sectoral approaches to it (Moser 1995). The debate about informality gained new impetus, with analyses of its multiple articulations with poverty and social exclusion and the wide spectrum of conditions it now encompasses in the context of policies of deregulation, minimisation of the state and the new circumstances created by so-called globalisation (Gerxhani 2004). It is in this context that once again housing – in its multi-dimensionality and its long-established links with health, personal safety, income generation, productivity, educational achievement and so on – returned as a key policy area in poverty reduction. Housing policy in developing countries in the 1990s, however, continued to be almost entirely associated with slum upgrading, slums being one of the most visible expressions of poverty in general and of shortages in urban facilities and housing in particular.

A central feature of housing and slum-upgrading policies of the 1990s especially relevant to this paper was the re-emphasis on the project level. These projects, however, have taken a very different form from those of the 1970s, reflecting a new ambition for multi-sectoriality and scale and a different understanding of the relationship between the project level and its multiple scales of interaction, both spatially and politically. It is in this context and embodying many of these aspirations that the Favela-Bairro programme emerged in 1994.

The evolution of ideas and practices associated with what we have referred to as an emergent new generation of slum-upgrading policies in the 1990s has produced a gradual resurgence of the discussion about the role of architecture and urbanism. This appears, on the one hand, in the work of international agencies and policy-orientated institutions and, on the other, in the analyses of many academics and practitioners revisiting the subject of informal urbanisation.

The UN-Habitat report on 'The Challenge of Slums' (2003), for instance, dedicated a whole session to the spatial dimensions of slums while the Task Force of the UN Millennium Project on Improving the Lives of Slum Dwellers (Garau et al. 2005) made explicit allusion to the contribution of the design disciplines. In fact, some of its members went on to organise a Global Studio – which met in Istanbul in June 2005 and in Vancouver in June 2006 – with a view to elaborate further on this question. While these developments were extremely interesting, they have tended to fall short of elaborating on possible tools of spatial analysis and interventions, as well as on the question of how the spatial 'meets' the social. In many ways, these attempts to reintroduce design into the debates about slum upgrading and poverty reduction strategies – especially in the case of people and agencies involved in policy formulation – have tended to reiterate the old arguments about the need for social and political engagement by design professionals, while acknowledging the greater complexity of their involvement in an intricate web of disciplines, sectoral policies and institutional arrangements.

However, several new studies published almost at the same time attempted to advance the understanding of informal urbanisation as well as explore its implications for planning and urbanism (among others, Berenstein Jacques 2001a, 2002; Brillembourg, Feireiss and Klumpner 2005; Castillo 2001; Roy 2005). While sharing many of the views of the early writers on the self-generated informal city and its merits, they moved the debate forward in one significant manner: rather than seeing the informal as a sector, or as segments of cities, they regarded it as constitutive of the urban condition itself. Urban informality is inexorably interwoven with the city as a whole – at all scales and levels – and has to be seen as another way of being in the city and constructing it. The above-mentioned authors – emblematic of the main positions in the debate on the subject – share the view that informal urbanisation is in direct opposition to dominant practices of urban planning. However, the implications of their analyses, for planning in general and urbanism in particular, are considerably different.

In her inspiring writings, Ananya Roy, for instance, calls for a new epistemology of planning, conversant with the informal 'generalised mode of metropolitan urbanisation' (Roy 2005: 147). In order to understand informality not as the object of state regulation but as produced by the state itself, she then invokes the concept of 'state of exception' developed by Giorgio Agamben (1998) which suggests ways of using exception strategically. Roy, nevertheless, dismisses urban upgrading as part of the ideology of space:

> In such policy approaches, what is redeveloped is space, the built environment and physical amenities rather than people's capacities or livelihoods.... such an emphasis on the physical environment is an 'aestheticisation of poverty', one that equates upgrading with

aesthetic upgrading rather than the upgrading of livelihoods, wages, political capacities. It is an expression of ... the search for rational order in aesthetic terms, the belief that an efficient city is one that looks regimented and orderly in a geometrical sense. (Roy 2005: 150)

It would appear that, at this point, we are back into spatial determinism in reverse. Conflating any spatial strategy or any type of upgrading with rationalist regimented geometries misses entirely the opportunity and need for a serious rethinking of the meaning and tools of 'another' urbanism. Opposing spatial strategies to social and political objectives and dismissing them as an 'aestheticisation of poverty' fails completely to acknowledge the need for a multidisciplinary approach to urban poverty reduction which includes the spatial and to engage with necessary discussions about the relationship between socio-political and spatial processes.

From a different angle, Paola Berenstein Jacques (2001a, 2001b, 2002), in her fascinating analysis of the aesthetics of favelas, reflects on the different temporalities of city-making and argues that informal urbanisation is not, nor can be, planned. It is in fact inimical to the very concept of planning. The informal city is characterised by a never-ending process of self-production and self-construction which conflicts with the logic of plan and project – among other things, because these are always guided by the need for an 'end'. The inside-out logic of spaces in continuous movement – from the scale of the shelter, through the neighbourhood, to the city and the territory – will invariably produce different spaces to those of the planned city. The informal city, as a space in movement, with its own culture and identity – where the movement of space dictated by the needs of the actors defines the space itself – will negotiate its own way through the rest of the city. It does not need control or 'integration'. It might need micro interventions that follow the natural and spontaneous flow of informal urbanisation without ever trying to fix or preserve that which, by definition, always moves. Compelling as her analysis is, it begs the question of how the conflict and negotiation of different logics of city-making happens and whether this sort of 'urban acupuncture' is sufficient to address the spaces and politics of the encounter and the intermixing of those different logics.

José Castillo's (2001) views are not dissimilar to those of Roy and Berenstein Jacques regarding the nature and scale of the self-producing logic of informal urbanisation and the inability of dominant planning practices to deal with it. However, more in line with Roy's arguments, Castillo does not see the informal as unplanned but, rather, as a minimum and unorthodox way of planning where decision making and transformation go hand in hand. In his view, informal urbanisation provides more complex ways of dealing with time, urban hierarchies and the symbiosis between space and users. These should inspire architects and urbanists to rethink the relationships between programme and form (Castillo 2001). He calls for an end to the obsession with control and for architects and urbanists to embrace the real, everyday generic city which is looking more and more like the informal city – in his view, the ultimate indication of the legitimacy of the informal urbanisation. He coins the term 'urbanisms of the informal', for the plural not only 'embraces the complex and heterogeneous forms and procedures that represent these urban phenomena but also engages them both as practice (as in urban planning and design) and as a body of knowledge, a new episteme' (Castillo 2001: 110). Unlike Roy, however, Castillo clearly does not deny the need for urbanism and design but, similar to the work of Brillembourg, Feireiss and Klumpner (2005), he calls for a different way of conceiving and practising it. There is not much elaboration, however, on the nature of the specific tools of spatial design and urbanism which, informed by urbanisms of the informal, can contribute to the creation of cities of greater integrity, inclusion and diversity.

In our view, far from the aims of 'integration' and regimented homogenisation, the challenge for urbanism as a spatial practice is how to address the encounter and coexistence of different and often contradictory logics of city-making while contributing to a process of redistribution of power, resources and means of access to the benefits of city life. Urbanism is about applying appropriate tools and instruments of design which can enhance connectivity across diverse urban conditions while contributing to redesigning urban institutions and regulations so that they can take such diversity into account. In this sense, each intervention in the city is also, by definition, about transforming the nature of the city itself, rather than just requalifying a part of it.

Only too often planners and urbanists have been busy addressing 'pieces' of the city as if they were disconnected from the city as a whole and its multiple scales. More worryingly, they have attempted in vain to 'fit' those pieces into a set of rules which lost their legitimacy long ago. In the best cases, as often with squatter settlements, these pieces are dealt with as 'zones of exception', which is not quite the same as redesigning the rules themselves. This tradition of planning and misguided urbanism is one that only replicates a logic of disembeddedness and fragmentation.

Indeed, when the UN predicts that there will be nearly 2 billion urban slum dwellers in the next twenty-five years, it is not only because of the lack of policies and programmes to deal with them, it is also, and very substantially, because of the policies themselves. Misconceived approaches and practices keep multiplying the problems they aim to resolve while, at the same time, becoming more irrelevant to the scale and complexity of social needs. Nothing illustrates better this contradiction than the lack of proportion between the projected needs and the puzzling 'ambitions' of the goals of the UN-Habitat and the Millennium of reaching, through the implementation of their policy proposals, 100 million slum dwellers by 2020 (Satterthwaite 2004).

In many ways, it would not be an exaggeration to say that dominant planning practices have continuously reproduced and reinforced the creation of ghettos, enclaves and enclosures in the city – be it those of the poor or those of the upper classes. We believe that this is, at least in part, a reflection of the above-mentioned loss of scale and 'despatialisation' of urban planning and strategies in general, and in their approach to the informal city in particular. Developing or requalifying any area or site in a city involves the search for internal synergies and virtuous relations both within the area itself as well as in its relation with the surrounding context. It requires engagement with the different scales of the city. Indeed, the former is not possible without the latter. There is a need to move away from 'introverted' and disconnected interventions into a much more 'extroverted' approach to the urban project. This is even more relevant in areas of poverty and informality and it is as much about social, political and institutional processes as it is about spatial ones. This requires appropriate tools of design, beyond master planning and land-use exercises. We argue that only in this way can a true urbanism emerge, one which fulfils its social and political role.

The paralysing fears of many progressive planners that, by opening up informal settlements to the dynamics of the city and its markets through increased connectivity, they will facilitate gentrification, are entirely contradictory with their ambitions of making those areas a part of the city and its institutions. Experience shows that introverted 'acupunctures' and minimalist interventions have not contributed to substantial social improvements and changes in informal settlements or to the necessary transformations of urban institutions and regulatory frameworks. Indeed, this so-called – and often misnamed – 'gentrification' has often been the result of isolated interventions and upgrading rather that the result of a comprehensive and systematic attempt to link individual projects to a multi-scale approach which would contribute to the requalification of the city as a whole. That is, re-qualification that reflects respect for the different conditions, logics and cultures of city-making without fear of connecting those conditions both spatially and socially, thereby contributing to the creation of inclusive institutionalities.

Such ambitions cannot be the result of good design practices alone. These practices are inexorably and complexly interwoven with the social and political processes of the city. No institutional reform, for instance, is going to come about without social organisation and political mobilisation. This is not an argument either for a mechanistic interpretation of the relation of spatial and socio-political processes or for a revival of old spatial determinisms. In many ways, it could be said that the spatial and the social constitute quite autonomous spheres which concern and condition one another. Good design and urbanism can help create platforms for other social and political developments in the city. It will not, however, automatically create inclusive and just cities. But neither will just cities come about without appropriate spatial and design strategies.

Favela-Bairro in the Context of Housing Policy in Rio de Janeiro

The favelas of Rio de Janeiro have long been recognised as one of the most visible manifestations of poverty in the city and as a symbol of the inequalities that exist between rich and poor. While the favelas of Rio de Janeiro may not uniformly house the poorest of the city's poor, their residents suffer from sub-standard services and infrastructure, ill-health, low levels of educational attainment, social stigmatisation, violence, insecurity of employment, and low and unstable incomes (Fiori, Riley and Ramírez 2001). During the 1980s, the percentage of people living below the poverty line in Rio increased from 27.2 per cent to 32.5 per cent and Rio became the city with the highest number of absolute poor people in Brazil. Throughout the decade, the population living in favelas grew by 50.7 per cent (Lago 1992) and, in addition, there was a marked increase in violence within and around Rio's favelas associated with the illegal trafficking of drugs and the violent and repressive style of the police.

Favela-Bairro is a large-scale comprehensive upgrading programme for medium-size squatter settlements in the city of Rio de Janeiro. It has the financial backing of the Inter-American Development Bank and was launched in 1994 by the Housing Department of the municipal government of Rio de Janeiro. In 1994 there were around 660 favelas in the municipality of Rio de Janeiro, housing over one million people. The programme aimed to upgrade all Rio's favelas of between 500 and 2,500 households by 2004. Medium-sized favelas make up nearly one-third of all favelas in Rio, but house around 60 per cent of the favela population of the city. In 2006 the programme had already reached 556 thousand people in 143 settlements (Prefeitura do Rio de Janeiro 2003a), although many of the projects were still unfinished. In addition to Favela-Bairro, Rio's Housing Department operates other upgrading programmes for both large and small favelas. Of the many programmes covered by the city's housing policy during the last decade, Favela-Bairro is undoubtedly the one with most resources, the largest scale and the one that has achieved the highest political profile. In fact, it is the largest squatter-settlement upgrading programme implemented in Latin America to date, a programme which continues to attract international recognition due to its ambitiousness and comprehensiveness.

The first stage of the Favela-Bairro project consisted of a competition for ideas which provided the basis for the methods that were applied. The competition took place in March 1994 and was organised by the Institute of Brazilian Architects in conjunction with the municipal Planning Institute (IPLANRIO) and the Municipal Housing Department (SMH). Of the thirty-two multidisciplinary architect-led teams that entered the competition, sixteen were selected to design projects for favelas that were chosen on the basis of criteria developed by the SMH.

From a multi-sectoral perspective, Favela-Bairro aimed to go beyond sanitation and basic infrastructure and address a variety of social needs through the improvement and construction of facilities and spaces internal to the settlements, as well as through enhancing the connectivity of the favelas with the city fabric and its institutions. The Favela-Bairro project can be described as a programme of physical and social transformation encompassing: the installation and upgrading of basic infrastructure such as water, sewage and drainage systems; the upgrading of public and domestic lighting networks; the opening and paving of roads and walkways connected to the urban systems of circulation and transport; the elimination of housing in areas of geological instability or natural risk; the construction of new housing for essential resettlement; the setting up of rubbish collection systems; the commencement of land tenure regularisation processes; the opening of new public squares and spaces to promote social interaction within and across settlements; the construction and reformation of buildings and their use through the implementation of social projects such as nursery schools and community centres, and income generation and training projects; the construction and operation of new sports and leisure facilities; the construction of commercial facilities and kiosks; the construction and operation of social and urban advice centres; and, finally, reforestation projects (Fiori, Riley and Ramírez 2000).

Favela-Bairro does not meet the housing needs of individual residents but instead addresses the collective needs of the favela as a whole. Thus, upgrading projects for each favela build upon – and respect – the existing layout of houses, roads and walkways, leaving them unaltered so that they form the basic structure of the upgraded settlement. It is, therefore, through the construction and upgrading of collective space and infrastructure, as well as through the implementation of social projects, that the programme seeks to generate profound changes in the communities, establishing transformations in the quality of life and the environment, whose results will be felt in the entire city (SMH 1995a).

As with the initial sixteen projects, each new upgrading project has been designed and formulated by a team of architects and social scientists, with the construction work undertaken by private firms and utility service providers. All this is done through competitions open to public tender. The implementation of the social projects requires the involvement of various departments within the municipal government, as well as non-governmental organisations. At the same time, local residents participate in processes of consultation and project approval, while helping to disseminate information and to carry out maintenance activities. Through the involvement of a wide range of private architectural offices and multidisciplinary teams, and by instigating regular discussions of new ideas, the municipality intended to renew the housing approaches of its own technical personnel.[1]

Design Strategy and Tools of Spatial Intervention Used in the Favela-Bairro Programme

We believe that the Favela-Bairro programme is part of a new generation of urban social policies which revalorise spatial strategies and design as intrinsic components of a multi-sectoral and integrated approach to slum upgrading and poverty reduction. Rather than presenting here an analysis of the relationship between spatial, social and political-institutional processes in Favela-Bairro's approach and experience, or an evaluation of the socio-spatial impact of the programme, we want to highlight briefly its general spatial design strategy and some of the tools of intervention employed.

In our view, the central concept underpinning the Favela-Bairro's design strategy is that the urbanisation and requalification of each favela depends on its increased connection with the different scales of the city. This reflects itself in a two-way process of 'opening up' the city to the residents of the favelas by making certain urban facilities accessible to all residents at different scales – from the favela itself to the infrastructure, services and labour markets of the entire city – while increasingly opening up the favelas – with their economic resources, local culture and locational advantages – to the city. The latter is often referred to as the creation of 'urban cells' in favelas; that is, a set of services and facilities within a favela for the use of people from outside. Additionally, Favela-Bairro has aimed to develop its design strategy through a difficult and delicate balance between preservation and renewal, integration and respect for diversity.

While this general approach has provided a framework for all the design professionals working on Favela-Bairro projects, each practice applies its own spatial strategies and design tools. Three of these design tools will be described below as a means to illustrate the general approach. They are: the improvement of accessibility and mobility to and inside the settlements; the creation and enhancement of public spaces; and the introduction of 'city images' into the favelas.

Upgrading Accessibility and Mobility

Most favelas contain significant diversity in the forms of occupancy and their constructive urban patterns. Even in the old, consolidated communities, there are areas of relatively recent and still disorderly occupation. While the great majority of dwellings in these consolidated areas are located along roads and better-defined pedestrian streets, in more recently developed areas houses are precariously built along narrow and sometimes dead-end footpaths. The lack of connection between areas within the same settlement – due to poor circulation systems for both cars and pedestrians – results in deficient internal social integration.

The situation is even worse in the favelas settled on steep hillsides. These have precarious circulation systems formed mostly by narrow footpaths which occasionally represent 90 per cent of the circulation network, a situation that makes walking up and down the hills very hard for the dwellers who live at the top. In some cases, there is only one vehicular access route for the entire settlement.

Consequently, the programme considers it crucial to improve the condition of vehicular and pedestrian circulation inside the favelas. Upgrading the circulation system as a whole is essential not only to facilitate the movement of residents inside the settlements, but also to allow access to the services provided by ambulances, fire engines, refuse collection, police cars, as well as for the distribution of gas and electricity. The improvement of vehicular access and circulation has also facilitated the delivery of supplies to small commercial areas located inside most settlements.

Stairways, ramps and funiculars were constructed in the settlements located on the hillsides, aiming to join their different levels together. In order to facilitate pedestrian flow and internal social integration in these steep areas, some architects proposed a series of interconnected 'meeting platforms' which, while being dedicated mainly to leisure activities, contained kiosks, telephone booths, mailboxes, garages and refuse collection points. These meeting places are connected by roads which also channel the pedestrian flow, offering better conditions for circulation. The network of plateaus – which are never more than twenty metres apart – and roads implies that all the residents of a favela have equal access to nearby facilities. The plateau system formed by the meeting platforms was proposed for several settlements.

Figure 10.1 Different Types of Vertical Circulation: Ramp

Figure 10.2 Different Types of Vertical Circulation: Stairway

Figure 10.3 Different Types of Vertical Circulation: Funicular

In order to prevent favelas remaining like ghettos, physically disconnected from the rest of the city, architects have tried to link them with the rest of the urban network. To this end, main roads have been extended into the favelas and public transport has been provided along those new roads.

These urban corridors also function as places of integration, connecting favelas with adjacent neighbourhoods. In most projects, architects have located a series of urban facilities – such as community centres, nursery schools, public squares, commercial kiosks and sport facilities – along these roads. In this way, a kind of linear centrality has been created by the principal urban-architectonic events proposed for the area. In some cases, a single major road leading through the settlement from one side to the other, can act as a connecting 'boulevard' along which all the favela's activities are distributed.

Another design strategy used by many architects was the creation of a ring road surrounding the settlements that would allow easier access to all its parts and that could eventually transform the internal streets into access roads to other areas. In order to give more functional consistency to those ring roads, public services and collective activities were located along them. Therefore, ring roads helped to improve access to the favelas, but also played the role of connecting most of their public inner spaces.

Creation and Enhancement of Public Spaces

One of the main priorities of the Favela-Bairro project has been the creation and improvement of public spaces. Public spaces such as squares, streets, sports grounds and the like have been introduced in order to encourage social integration among the residents. Public spaces also introduce a range of urban values into slums, values which reinforce their link with the city and the population of Rio de Janeiro.

In previous publications we have reviewed proposals by different architects for squares with different characteristics and typologies (Brandão 2004). Some of these squares were located at the fringe of squatter settlements and were intended to bring together local residents and people from outside. Other squares were located inside the favelas themselves and designed to be predominantly used by their own dwellers. While the former kind of squares strengthens integration with the city, the latter reinforces the internal cohesion of the community.

The squares located on the fringes of settlements were usually conceived to play two important roles. Firstly, they would play a symbolic role as landmarks highlighting main access routes to specific communities. These consisted of public spaces designed to a high specification, which often created visual connections across different neighbourhoods. Secondly, they would function as primary public spaces to encourage social integration with adjacent neighbourhoods.

Although the Favela-Bairro project's main emphasis is to provide

Figure 10.4 A Typical 'Entrance Square' with a Row of Commercial Kiosks and a Landmark

Figure 10.5 Public Spaces Boosting the Self-esteem of Community Members

Figure 10.6 An Avenue along the Canal is Proposed as a Structural Axis to Connect All Local Interventions

basic infrastructure to people in the favelas, its contributors remain aware of the symbolic value of public spaces and their part in consolidating the self-esteem of their residents. It is understood that if the residents have a positive image of the public spaces they use daily, a sense of pride would arise which is crucial for the community to develop. Moreover, by improving the quality of existing public spaces or creating new ones, the programme assumes that systematic improvements will follow throughout the favela. In this context, the improvement of public spaces plays a relevant role not only in promoting social integration and boosting the dwellers' self-esteem but also keeping the upgrading process alive.

Introducing 'City Images' While Preserving Local Character

Another guiding principle of the Favela-Bairro programme was the acknowledgement of diversity among squatter settlements. The programme recognised that the favelas of Rio de Janeiro were spatially and culturally different despite having similar problems. Therefore, individual projects should reinforce the cultural identities and spatial features of each area. Architectural proposals needed to be compatible with the particular character of each settlement.

In order to design a project for these areas, architects and urbanists had to be able to identify what each favela offered to its resident community. Only then was it possible to suggest changes for improving the physical conditions while preserving their identities. In other words, the greatest design challenge for all the design teams involved in the programme was to transform squatter settlements into neighbourhoods without destroying their individual character.

However, another requirement set by the programme, which should be seen as a guiding principle, made the design process more intricate: the municipality also wanted the architects to insert urban elements from the 'formal' city into the informal settlements. The aim was to break up the symbolic barriers between the slums and their surrounding neighbourhoods by introducing urban images into the settlements that would be understood as 'city images' by both residents and outsiders. In other words, architects should conceive urban interventions of high visibility and legibility that would be capable of transforming the environmental perception of those sites into integral parts of the city. These punctual interventions would work as bridges linking the squatter settlements to surrounding areas, while also preserving the character of the site. To achieve such a well-balanced design was undoubtedly a difficult equation.

The visual integration of the settlements into the 'formal' city has been one of the most contentious issues generated by the Favela-Bairro projects. For some critics (Berenstein Jacques 2000; Andrade 2000; Montefusco 2002) this is an attempt to transform squatter settlements into formal districts in an authoritarian manner, by architects imposing their views. Critics doubt that there is a need for visual integration and suggest that such an approach has imposed an aesthetic which will eventually homogenise the urban fabric of the city. According to them, this kind of physical intervention has usually weakened rather than strengthened the identities of slums.

However, most architects responsible for the Favela-Bairro project support the idea of introducing 'urban symbols' into the squatter settlements.[2] They claim that projects must both supply the infrastructure of provision and connectivity to the favelas as well as create urban images which increase the perception of these settlements as parts of the city. They believe that to transform the favelas into established neighbourhoods of the city is also a matter of perception, which requires the production of a mix of urban forms and images which contribute to the blurring of the borders between the 'formal' and 'informal' city and the articulation of the different logics of city-making. Although it is the infrastructure that gives the favelas the condition of being neighbourhoods, it is the urban images and forms that mean they are perceived as integral parts of the city. According to these architects, it is important for the success of the programme that the local residents and the population as a whole start to see the favelas as neighbourhoods, as this enhances the self-esteem of the former and the level of acceptance of the latter.

While the general argument about the introduction of new 'city images' seems relevant, the interpretation and implementation of this has changed considerably in the work of different architectural offices and from project to project. Similarly, although all projects clearly adopted a contextual attitude during the design process, the interpretation of which physical and cultural aspects should be preserved varied considerably. The balance between preservation and change, and between local identity and integration, is a delicate and complex matter. It is beyond the scope of this chapter to assess the impact of these interventions within the Favela-Bairro project. However, it is undoubtedly the case that the collective search for such a balance has produced remarkable results, substantially different from what had been achieved by previous generations of slum-upgrading programmes.

All the design tools highlighted here operate at different scales and aim at creating greater social and spatial connectivity between the favelas and the city. Undoubtedly, the most important common feature of the design approach in the majority of the Favela-Bairro's projects has been the linking of the infrastructures of access and circulation with the articulation of different types of public spaces and the provision of services to and from the favelas. While the undisputed priority of any slum-upgrading programme with ambitions of scaling-up to the level of social needs should be to open up the city and its institutions to all the residents of favelas, perhaps the greatest test of the strategy advanced by the Favela-Bairro programme lies in the attempt to open up the favelas to the city.

Final Considerations

The Favela-Bairro programme itself was the result of a process of scaling-up from isolated pilot projects to a policy level, which formulated for the first time the understanding that reaching the scale of social needs in the favelas required reaching the scale of the city. Scaling-up in this sense became by definition a complex mix of social, political, institutional and spatial processes. Favela-Bairro acknowledged the need for a spatial strategy that could articulate individual favela projects to a strategic vision for the city and valued the role of architecture and urbanism in the implementation of an urban social policy. Good design of buildings, infrastructures and public spaces was seen as necessary not only to improve conditions and enhance certain processes within a favela but also to ensure the connection and interaction of the favelas with the fabric of the city and its institutions. Indeed, this was seen as a necessary if not sufficient condition for true scaling-up in poverty alleviation.

However, while the official claims about the results and achievements of the programme thus far are, as indicated above, impressive enough, it is difficult to confirm the fulfilment of the strategic aims of Favela-Bairro. In areas where the programme was implemented there has been improvement in physical conditions and the enhancement of connectivity, a noticeable increase in the value of land and property with little displacement and expulsion of people, and a high level of approval by the residents. Yet, even if the number of people reached by the programme is significant, the number of beneficiaries of the social initiatives (education, health and income generation) is still limited. The indirect impact in terms of economic opportunities, employment and social conditions – a central part of *Favela-Bairro's* social-spatial strategy – is uncertain and has not yet been properly assessed. Such an assessment would require different and much more complex methodologies of evaluation than the ones which have been used so far.

After six years of considerable development (1994 to 2000), the programme slowed down significantly in the last few years. Increased violence associated with the presence of drug trafficking in the favelas has generated a different climate and this has substantially affected the implementation of the programme, although it still continues. More importantly, changes in the city's political administration and discontinuities in terms of important institutional modifications introduced in the 1990s, together with low levels of user participation, have undoubtedly undermined the impact of the programme and its sustainability. We have argued in the past that the institutional transformations and the social mobilization, as well as the participation which underpin these transformations, provide the basis – and conditions of sustainability – for the development of such a socio-spatial strategy and the synergies it requires in order to operate (Fiori, Riley and Ramírez 2004).

Adriana Laranjeira (2006), who worked within Favela-Bairro for many years, suggests that, despite the very innovative nature of the programme and its strategic ambitions, it did not play the structuring role expected and necessary in order to generate a different way of thinking and producing the city. In her view, the undeniable improvements found in specific projects are not reflected in an equally perceptible and consistent change throughout the city as a whole.

In a way this is reminiscent of past times. Some critics of the Favela-Bairro programme point their finger at the importance given to spatial and design matters. It would appear, though, that the shortcomings are much more of a political nature and rather than dismissing such a valuable experience, the limitations of Favela-Bairro might help us reflect on the huge complexities, contradictions and time scale of the articulation of political, social and spatial processes. Furthermore, it seems difficult to dissociate some of the indisputable social achievements of the programme from its rethinking of the role of spatial strategies and urbanism in slum upgrading and poverty alleviation. It is our contention, thus, that the guiding concepts behind the Favela-Bairro programme, those which made it one of the most important experiences of slum upgrading and poverty alleviation in the developing world, remain extremely relevant today.

Notes

1. Source: interview conducted in 2002 with S. Magalhães, head of Rio de Janeiro's Municipal Housing Department (1993–2000).
2. This point is derived from interviews conducted in 2002 with a number of those involved in Favela-Bairro projects: D. Anastassakis (Invento Espaços Anastassakis &

Associados Ltda, Rio de Janeiro); P. Benetti (Fábrica Arquitetura Ltda, Rio de Janeiro); P. Case (Paulo Casé e Luis Acioli Arquitetos Associados Ltda, Rio de Janeiro); J. Jáuregui (Planejamento Arquitetônico e Ambiental Ltda, Rio de Janeiro); and P. Moreira (Archi 5 Arquitetos Associados Ltda, Rio de Janeiro).

References

Agamben, G. 1998. *Homo Sacer: Sovereign Power and Bare Life*. Stanford, CA: Stanford University Press.

Andrade, S. 2000.*Três Momentos Cariocas de Atuação em Projetos para Favelas: Pedregulho e Catacumbas, Brás de Pina e Favela-Bairro*. Master's dissertation. Rio de Janeiro: Universidade Federal do Rio de Janeiro.

Berenstein Jacques, P. 2000. 'As Favelas do Rio: Um Caso Limite'. Unpublished paper. Rio de Janeiro: Universidade Federal do Rio de Janeiro Faculdade de Arquitetura e Urbanism / PROURB (Programa de Pós-Graduação em Urbanism).

————— 2001a. 'The Aesthetics of the Favela: the Case of an Extreme', in J. Fiori and H. Hinsley (eds), *Transforming Cities: Design in the Favelas of Rio de Janeiro*. London: AA Publications, 28–31.

————— 2001b. *Estética da Ginga*. Rio de Janeiro: Casa da Palavra.

————— 2002. 'Cartografias da Maré', in D. Varella, I. Bertazzo and P. Berenstein Jacques (eds), *Maré: Vida na Favela*. Rio de Janeiro: Casa da Palavra, 13–65.

Brandão, J. 2004. *The Role of Urban Design in Strategic Planning: The Case of Rio de Janeiro*. Ph.D. dissertation. London: Architectural Association School.

Brillembourg, A., K. Feireiss and H. Klumpner. 2005. *Informal City: Caracas Case*. Munich: Prestel.

Castillo, J. 2001. 'Urbanisms of the Informal: Transformations in the Urban Fringe of México City', *Praxis* 1: 102–11.

Fiori, J. 2001. 'Why Favela-Bairro?', in J. Fiori and H. Hinsley (eds), *Transforming Cities: Design in the Favelas of Rio de Janeiro*. London: AA Publications, 8–12.

Fiori, J., E. Riley and R. Ramírez. 2000. *Urban Poverty Alleviation through Environmental Upgrading in Rio de Janeiro: Favela Bairro*. London: Development Planning Unit, Univerity College London.

————— 2001. 'Physical Upgrading and Social Integration in Rio de Janeiro: The Case of Favela-Bairro', *DISP* 147: 48–60.

————— 2004. 'Melhoria Física e Integração Social no Rio de Janeiro', in E. Fernandes and M. Valença (eds), *Brasil Urbano*, Rio de Janeiro: Mauad.

Garau, P. et al. 2005. *A Home in the City*. London: Earthscan.

Gerxhani, K. 2004. 'The Informal Sector in the Developed and Less Developed Countries: A Literature Review', *Public Choice* 120(3/4): 167–300.

Larangeira, A. 2006. 'La gestión de la informalidad en Rio de Janeiro y Brasil. La frágil sintonía entre los avances del marco regulatorio y la concreción de cambios consistentes en la realidad urbana', *Cuaderno Urbano* 5: 187–214.

Lago, L.C. 1992. 'Política urbana e a questão habitacional: novas tendências face à crise econômica brasileira', *Cadernos Instituto de Pesquisa e Planejamento Urbano e Regional/Universidade Federal do Rio de Janeiro*, 6(1): 41–7.

Montefusco, A. 2002. *Os Olhares da Favela.* Master's dissertation. Rio de Janeiro: Universidade Federal do Rio de Janeiro.

Moser, C. 1995. 'Urban Social Policy and Poverty Reduction', *Environment and Urbanization*, 7(1): 145–58

Prefeitura do Rio de Janeiro. 2003a. *Favela Bairro: Monitoramento e Avaliação.*

———— Prefeitura do Rio de Janeiro. 2003b. *From Removal to the Urban Cell; the Urban-Social Development of Rio de Janeiro Slums.*

Roy, A. 2004. 'Transnational Trespassings: The Geopolitics of Urban Informality', in A. Roy and N. AlSayyad (eds), *Urban Informality: Transnational Perspectives from the Middle East, South Asia and Latin America.* Lanham, MD: Lexington Books, 289–317.

———— 2005. 'Urban Informality: Toward an Epistemology of Planning', *Journal of the American Planning Association* 71(2): 147–58.

Safier, M. 1983. 'The Passage to Positive Planning', *Habitat* 7(5/6): 105–16.

Satterthwaite, D. 2004. *The Millennium Development Goals and Local Processes: Hitting the Target or Missing the Point?* London: International Institute for Environment and Development.

Silas, J. 1984. 'The Kampung Improvement Programme of Indonesia: Comparative Case Study of Jakarta and Surabaya', in G.K. Payne (ed.) *Low-Income Housing in the Developing World.* Chichester: Wiley, 69–87.

SMH. 1995a. *Programa Favela Bairro. Especificação para Elaboração de Projetos.* Rio de Janeiro: Secretaria Municipal de Habitacião.

———— 1995b. *Política Habitacional da Cidade do Rio de Janeiro.* Rio de Janeiro: Secretaria Municipal de Habitacião.

Sprenger, S. 2006. *Space Matters.* MSc dissertation. London: Development Planning Unit/University College London.

Turner, J. 1972. 'Housing as a Verb', in J. Turner and R. Fichter (eds), *Freedom to Build.* London: Macmillan, 148–75.

UN-Habitat. 2003. *The Challenge of Slums.* London: Earthscan.

———— 2004. *The State of the World's Cities.* London: Earthscan.

World Bank. 1991. *Urban Policy and Economic Development: An Agenda for the 1990s.* Washington, DC: World Bank.

———— 1997. *The State in a Changing World.* Washington DC: World Bank.

———— 2000. *World Development Report 2000/2001: Attacking Poverty.* Washington DC: World Bank.

Chapter 11

Urban and Social Articulation: Megacities, Exclusion and Urbanity

Jorge Mario Jáuregui

Figure 11.1 Aerial View of Rocinha

In Latin America, as elsewhere in the world, the last thirty years have revealed a new phenomenon provoked by a process that has two main components: on the one hand, the confluence of an increasing interconnection of and dependence on the movements of capital (financial globalisation), and on the other, the substitution of technologies originating in the transition from the mechanical to the electronic age, affecting administration and management as well as production processes. This phenomenon – which has been described in various ways, but is mainly known as postmodernisation and/or globalisation – has had numerous urban consequences. It contributes to a geographic dispersion of economic activities, caused by the systemic interconnection of economic activities, and to the renovation and expansion of central urban functions. But it also intensifies the social exclusion of large sectors of the population, resulting in marginalisation, violence and the destruction of congenial living conditions. This is clearly manifested in the production of the 'broken city', in the tension between the so-called 'formal' urbanisation and 'informal' areas of uncontrolled sprawl.

The structure of such informal areas in the 'broken city' – with its conflict-ridden but interconnected formal and informal elements – can be seen as an urban expression of a global pattern. The process of increasing integration at a global level is characterised by the formation of a worldwide network of interconnected megacities, which form a new topography throughout the world. Yet, it also creates new conditions of centrality. This is true both at the 'macro' (global and continental) as well as the 'micro' level (the inner core of each urban structure). On these two levels, the formation of new geographies of centrality can be perceived as a metropolitan network of urban nodes, on the one hand, and as a rhizomatic city pattern, on the other. By rhizomatic pattern, we refer to a type of structure that denies a synthetic relation between its elements; a structure that refuses a hierarchical order and possesses a patchwork quality, a radical heterogeneity.

Paradoxical Processes and Urban Intelligence

The paradox currently evident in the urban field is that while telecommunications maximise the potential of geographic dispersion, the process of economic globalisation imposes a logic that requires the consolidation of strategic places with large concentrations of infrastructure, labour, services and buildings. In addition to these new centralities, the combination of new organisational capacities and technologies, as well as the growth of new economic sectors in Latin America, generates an enormous increase in marginality. The variety of processes related to the reterritorialisation of people and economic and cultural practices has its urban expression in the growth of the informal sector of the economy – that is, the occupation of sidewalks, public squares and residual spaces by illegal vendors and miscellaneous artisans in both the planned and unplanned areas of the city. Thus in the increasingly interdependent economy which is extremely 'sensitive' to turbulences, the 'local' turns international by adopting guidelines of behaviour and consumption originating from very distant realities; and the 'global' becomes 'local' by showing anomalous 'insertions' in the midst of the emergent urban network.

In terms of the kind of interventions made in larger Latin American cities, this interpenetration of the so-called 'local' and 'global' creates a demand for a concept of urban intervention capable of simultaneously articulating a range of scales. These scales include physical aspects (urban, infrastructural and environmental heritage), social issues (cultural, economic and existential), ecological challenges (natural and psychological environments), as well as those related to the safety of all citizens. In the current condition of simultaneous global interconnection, uncontrolled urbanisation and social exclusion, urban and social articulations cannot resign themselves to searching for guidelines, speculating on potential orders and schemes or imagining abstract forms of interpretation. The contemporary city is a process whose order and complexity are always in mutation and, thus, it demands new conceptual and instrumental devices in order to operate effectively.

Strategic urban articulation must be included in the development of urbanity for all. It must address, and battle against, the exclusion of the underprivileged majority in order to improve the quality of life of the entire population and the urban structure as a whole. This approach brings to the forefront the central question of the connectivity between the so-called 'formal' and 'informal' components of the city. In many of the largest Latin American cities the percentage of the informal city is greater than the formal city. This is the case of Caracas, where the informal sector accounts for more than 60 per cent of the urban area, and in Lima, where the informal sector accounts for 70 per cent. In the majority of cities in Latin America, in fact, this percentage is high, varying from 30 to 50 per cent in the two largest countries of the subcontinent, Mexico and Brazil (see Brillembourg and Klumpner, this volume). Considering the fact that the development of a large informal sector is an urban reality in most Latin American cities, urban interventions ought to be aimed at creating integration between the separate parts of the city and should be stimulated by programmes which promote local development: the creation of a productive base capable of generating jobs and sustaining satisfactory levels of income. In this way, urban articulation – particularly in the form of urban policy – would contribute to improving the participation of all citizens.

We consider this crossing – this amalgamation of the physical, the economic, the cultural and the social – both as an intersection of the theoretical-practical fields and as systemic ordered practice. Thus, we advocate the need to approach urbanism, architecture and the social sciences in a democratic spirit, sensitive to dissonances and diversity and able to act in the complex ways necessary to respond to the realities of megacities. In this context, it is necessary to start from the multiple simultaneous conditions which already exist and continually emerge in the Latin American cityscape, conditions which hinder simplification and cannot be reduced to a single cause. These emerging conditions, the overlapping of multiple logics and uncertainties, must be considered at the same time. Thus, urban articulations must be able to function as modulators of interchange between each specific sector and the city as a whole, focusing on the importance of the relations between buildings, spaces and their established uses.

Figure 11.2 Night-time Perspective of Rocinha

Spaces of Flux and the Place of Spaces

The challenge found in the notion of urban articulation lies in the possibility to compose spaces of flux linked to worldwide networks while simultaneously consolidating existing centralities aimed at improving the performance of local urban structures. To create such spaces requires a search for differentiated levels of coherence which are singularised by their own intensities and yet are always interconnected. Hence the importance of establishing basic guidelines for each individual intervention, and of defining the 'connective' function of projected buildings and social spaces.

The urban dynamics of megacities are characterised by the condition of late capitalism. In this condition, each point of the territory is determined by overlapping logics whose appearance is aleatory – random and interconnected – but which need to be unmasked in order to address each individual case successfully. In other words, to be effective in this environment it is necessary to have the capacity to 'read', that is understand, the structure of each specific place. Here the main points of interest, much more than matters of scale or measure, are the type of relation that the different sectors maintain among themselves, as well as the conditions of centrality that will be modified by interventions. In this urban 'reading' what is especially important is the analysis of the conditions of the borders among the different recognised urban sectors; that is, the different directionalities, or the standards upon which certain zones are organised with higher intensity than others. These include the transitions – sometimes gradual or paused – from private to public spaces or the passages between public open spaces to semi-public closed spaces.

The urban system characterising contemporary Latin American megacities gives rise to conflicting forces of different origin and directionalities, sometimes antagonistic, sometimes intercepting each other, but where the balances are always unstable. This conflictive and unbalanced system defines an urban relational means that is required to intervene in the sensitive texture of relations characterised by movement and paths, hazard and apparent chaos. In this context, the global flux of capital, information and people produce strong local impacts where the traditional security structures upon which social life was based dissolve. Yet, while there are societies in which most members are connected, in other societies only a portion of the population has access to global networks. In fact, we almost always find a globalised sector in all large cities where directional functions are located (that is, the interconnected financial centres) coupled with extensive areas where most people live detached from global networks. What varies between cities, according to the context, is the ratio between its disconnected and connected parts.

An aerial vision of Rio de Janeiro, Caracas, São Paulo or Mexico City, and their areas of influence, would show us a great blotch where the urban fabric gradually disintegrates, spreading extensively and stopping only at exceptional places such as edges of rivers, lagoons or forests. In this scene, highways are like artificial rivers which join and separate, generating new services, both misguided and dispersed. Likewise, old local centres deteriorate or renew themselves, creating gaps in the urban fabric that result from a lack of industrial activity, in turn resulting from the arrival of new technological and productive systems and the modification of conditions of accessibility. Consequently, and because of their enormous size, these cities can be seen as systems in continual processes of transformation, which present formidable challenges to all those concerned with their development and those interested in extending the benefits of urban life to all citizens.

The aim of urban and social articulations is to attempt to reorganise and consolidate textures that facilitate new connections in order to provide informal areas with character and identity while strengthening – or creating – new centralities which do not exclude previous interventions. Considering that the interconnection of all aspects of the urban fabric and its established uses can only be considered from a multi-disciplinary perspective, urban articulations are also instrumental in the provision of public infrastructure and socio-political prestige. Although forced to act in accordance with market rules, the task that faces architects and urbanists is how to use urban strategies to generate quality spaces that do not erase the traces left by the development of territorial communities. To be responsible, an articulation must ask how we can point urban strategies in the right direction so as to articulate the city of fluxes with the city of places.

Conflicts and Coexistence

Amongst the many signs that inevitably coexist in megacities, three different types of urban space can be identified:

1. Spaces generated for traditional accumulation and substitution
There are places where certain architectural elements can be identified within an anonymous background, yet these places

constitute centralities when they reach a certain critical mass through the accumulation of functions and ways of life. Within these spaces the urban image is the result of community action interacting in a specific territory throughout a period of time as criteria and norms are permanently being customised, renegotiated or substituted. These urban sectors, identified as neighbourhoods (*bairros* in Portuguese, barrios in Spanish), offer features of structural stability that still define them as visual pictures belonging to the 'city'.

2. 'Authored' spaces

There are designed spaces in the city that are much in demand by powerful large corporations (national or multinational, public or private). These 'authored' spaces are generally based on special 'themes' and occupy strategic areas – such as entertainment parks, international exhibition complexes, historical centres (traditional quarters), recycled port areas, and so on. Authored spaces are usually disconnected (whether voluntarily or not) from the urban structure, constituting 'fantasy islands' in the archipelago of the city. In this type of space, images tend to become commodities, and the city becomes a series of franchise operations.

3. Spaces that escape public control

There are spaces with little or no public control that occupy great areas of the cities' peripheries and constitute archipelagos of exception with their own laws and social codes. In some cases, to act in this context would require planning to prevent disasters, what we could call the equivalent to 'war tactics'. In areas where the qualitative characteristics of space are low, urban design plays a key role in determining a new image. Urban design has much to contribute to the general resignifying of the system in order to improve the quality of life of those forced to live in such places because of a lack of alternatives. In these circumstances, urban design could function as a means to restore the qualitative dimensions of public space and to introduce urban legitimacy to places constituted without planning. In this sense, to urbanise the peripheries and the favelas requires approaching chaos with the intent to inscribe points of singularisation. These sectors of the urban network, which in many cases are not even acknowledged in city plans, constitute the 'noir' places of society – 'non-places', intervals in the experience of moving across the city. However, these spaces are also open to new possibilities for creativity, urban innovation, social experimentation and interaction. They constitute a source, the basic material to work with in order to articulate the broken city. Here, the singularised design (the building and its image) acquires maximum relevance and will lead to the constitution of an identity, enabling the galvanisation of the collective imagination in every intervention.

These three types of space tend to remain unarticulated, maintaining only relations of proximity; they do not make urban texture nor do they build a city. To think about these circumstances requires reflection on concepts such as 'urban edge' and public spaces, 'urban milieu' and public domain.

Figure 11.3 Before and After Intervention in Fubá

The Necessity of New Points of View

In a philosophical sense, the city can be understood as a series of fluxes of the most varied kind: music, painting, sculpture, architecture, information, movement and time. That is why Walter Benjamin (2002) maintained that cities are the plurality of humanity, an accumulation of existences and a multiplication of existence itself, a formidable past manufactured in assemblage. Understanding a city implies crossing the mysteries of its surface, and urban articulation must also, to a large extent, be formulated by keeping the eyes and feet as close as possible to the chosen site and the conditions under which we are requested to intervene. Thus, to absorb the spirit and circumstances of a city implies knowing how to follow and understand its traces, although these may be covered up by all sorts of tensions. For Benjamin, the contemporary city means the dissemination of 'all in the whole'; it has, at the same time, the joy of all and its own joy (Benjamin 2002). In the city, bodies, spirits and things are seductively mixed up, a seduction which is at the same time also utilitarian and aesthetic.

Therefore, despite everything, megacities still have in common with the original *polis* the fact that they constitute a fragmented totality which embodies a diversity that precedes the individual, thus constituting much more than the simple crowding together of people. In theory, it is possible to reach some degree of rationality in its structure. Its law is the accomplishment of a certain ratio between the cost of life and what it can provide – a certain contemporary way of living, a special life style – knowing that it always includes a degree of 'non-sense'. Within this ratio, it is necessary to experiment with new concepts and new forms to deal with the pre-existent, opening possibilities for the manifestation of social intelligence and thereby permitting free trajectories and modifications of spaces.

Today megacities constitute the 'local' of contemporary life which not only have the power to provoke distress and to create the possibility of evolution, but also to congregate, unify and make nexuses. These great cities, despite their drawbacks, provide the support of commonly determined values, the conscience of a destiny with others and, from this viewpoint, the citizen's ability to find a condition of accomplishment. In these conglomerates of artifice and nature, a multitude of human beings congregate by sharing (in spite of everything) a certain common understanding (the possessions they love, for instance, a tradition of hospitality, a landscape). For these reasons, urban and social articulation projects must be capable of structuring this condition of *locus*, acting as a bond between citizens.

Time and Space

Urban architectural projects always create a relation with space and time, and it involves a vision of the city as a broken totality. It implies a type of text ; it is an urban writing and, as such, it resembles a palimpsest that thinks and draws the city, thinking and drawing itself. In urban interventions, the notion of time is a variable that operates in an irreversible fashion. In the urban process, phenomena are observed in one continuum, for a specific duration of time without evidence of a beginning or a view of an end, in a state of permanent development and mutation. This resembles certain perceptions that could be associated with consecutiveness, ordinances, deduction, seriality. Space is a concept which implies a materiality, dimension, reality, pattern and structure. It is also associated with operations such as dissemination, splitting and induction. The processes that take place in space imply evolution or involution, the transformation of materiality. But space also presents us with uncertainty and is always a potential. Thus, it needs to be conquered.

Accordingly, the notion of urban articulation implies a type of planning which involves a structure or pattern – the special dispersal of its substance – according to the logic of the fragmented whole. To think about urban space, therefore, implies the intrinsic challenge of establishing an ordinance of ideas regarding its extension and duration. More precisely, in Latin America, urban articulations must act as activators which instigate, speculate and help to understand the need to create a spatial structure that can realise the potential of specific places and their surroundings.

In most of the large cities of Latin America, as indeed in most large cities everywhere, urban problems are always spatially characterised by the split between legal and illegal sectors. Such a split requires the production of non-exclusive centres of conviviality and the integration of abandoned and empty urban areas. To resolve these issues it is necessary to mobilise civil society and the government in order to carry out research at universities. It is also necessary to call for a renewed critical liaison with organisations in metropolitan centres and throughout the world, particularly Europe (as the origin of its historic urban models). Urban articulation, thus, involves a hybridisation between prospect and project; that is, between the use of formulas of a strategic and abstract nature, over a given period of time, and proposals of a tactical nature, expressed through concrete projects capable of gaining acceptability over the short term.

Urban and Social Articulation

In order to address the particularities of the Latin American context, urban and social articulation will have to focus on the following issues:

Figure 11.4 Before and After Intervention in Campinho

- To reflect on the new territorial phase of megacities by rethinking the relationship between and among the 'city within the city' and the 'diffuse city'; think about the notion of 'productive territories'
- To rethink new connectivities in the urban structure as a whole which generate new centralities and rearticulate existing ones
- To reflect on the subject of the 'edge', the limit. In other words, to refelect on the subject of 'margin' as a metaphorical theme in the contemporary city
- To create conditions of 'urban life' in areas excluded from the benefits of urbanity through the 'creation of the city', especially in informal areas
- To use interventions as a means of imprinting a cultural quality on a place; to use urban design itself as an occasion for cultural events
- To think about collective public spaces as offering not only the opportunity for social interaction but also as powerful infrastructural supports for information, communication and education
- To reinforce the collective character of space through the configuration of places where the diversity of functions and convivial activities guarantee attractiveness and potentiality
- To reflect on what would be a rich mode to inhabit urban space that involves incorporating 'affects', that is, the capacity to affect and to be affected by the space
- To introduce into the 'magma' of the contemporary metropolis an intermediate dimension implying a 'small city in the city', as a system of centralities of collective sites
- To listen to the demands of groups or individuals and then, helped by psychoanalytic methods of free association and fluctuating attention, translate these demands into 'sensitive aggregates' capable of representing various levels of 'consistency'
- To think about interventions from the perspective of urban renovation policy, including local development and infrastructure, which implies a hybridisation of space, landscape and infrastructure
- To articulate urban interventions with the protection, construction and reconstruction of the surrounding landscape substrata
- To consider landscape as infrastructure, as significant an element as transport and circulation. Both urban and landscape design demand reflection on the intervention of related disciplines (philosophy, urban anthropology, geography, art,

sociology, psychoanalysis, engineering) to extend our concepts of space and time through works, accomplishments, inquiries and speculations
• To think about urban questions as articulations within the realms of ethics, aesthetics and politics

Using urban and social articulation is important to battle against the following negative realities:

• The reduction of the public sphere
• The transformation of public space into merchandising domains
• The transformation of cities into ghettoes of consumption, entertainment and 'culture'
• The lack of quality in landscaping due to economic rather than spatial motivations
• The increasing costs of 'externalities' provoked by the process of globalisation, as evidenced in urban spaces through the increasing division between the included and the excluded, the increase in the disparity of investment in prestige facilities in different urban sectors, the abandonment or absence of public space and environmental disaggregation
• The continual growth in the 'deficit of the city' and the 'deficit of citizenship' in the enormous peripheral areas and shanty towns. The 'deficit of the city' and the 'deficit of citizenship' refer to the condition of physical fragmentation (created by investment in the privileged sectors of the city and the absence of investments in the rest of the urban grid) which determines the schizophrenic condition with self-excluded sectors (closed neighbourhoods) and excluded sectors (shanty towns), which results in an urbanity deficit, which means, in turn, the absence of places for the coexistence of differences.

As these two lists make clear, urban and social articulations in Latin America must be capable of working simultaneously at the pragmatic, the plastic and the conceptual levels. To do so involves the challenge of putting into practice the narrow link between so-called high culture and popular traditions, between the contribution and content of works at the worldwide level and the specificity of local circumstances. For this reason, it is a prerequisite of any urban project to know how to ask the right questions about the position and contextual specificities of the areas of intervention in terms of their history, economics, technical issues and the physical configuration process, as well as about social, cultural and productive relationships. Places should be thoroughly interrogated prior to, or as part of, every intervention. In addition, it is highly desirable to analyse the questions generated by the urban conditions of megacities from unusual perspectives and to search for a more efficient use and handling of materials as well as human resources. This would invert the current dominant logic and would give priority to quality solutions to the problem of the excluded majority, for they do not represent a peripheral problem, but one which affects the whole city due to its scale.

It is also necessary to approach cases of urban articulation from the point of view of creating the conditions for an effective and productive international contribution opposed to the globalisation of the economy (which has become a one-way path, a field of restrictions, predefined and mined). Rather than this one-way globalisation, we should strive towards a true globalisation or the universalisation of problems (conceived as a field of chances providing multiple options) capable of making possible a new description of ourselves and our urban structures. We advocate, in other words, participation in an extended globalised dialogue through partnerships, agreements, associations and contributions involving both public and private institutions and NGOs. The specific objective of such a global dialogue includes developing strategic alliances between the three sectors mentioned above in order to tackle more ambitious programmes (such as the Favela-Bairro project) and to contribute to the control of the public sphere by acting as the guarantor of appropriate use of investments. At stake here is the part that urban articulation can play in changing the current pattern of intervention by offering other alternatives to improve the day-to-day life of the city's permanent dwellers.

The Cartography of Subjectivity: Ethics, Aesthetics and Politics

Urban and social articulation operates as a multidimensional cartography of subjectivity production. In other words, because cities function as immense machines of subjectivity, not only individually but also collectively, what really matters is not infrastructure, communication or labour, but rather the capacity of redirecting our urban *devir* – a continuous process of urban becoming – through material or immaterial means. We know that buildings and spaces are capable of functioning as expressive machines, and that this unleashes affective and cognitive impulses; we know that all apprehensions of existence imply a recreation, a reinvention. Constructed spaces are essentially 'production sense machines' and thus make individual and collective subjectivity possible (Deleuze and Guattari 1994). Therefore it is necessary to rethink this complexity by considering simultaneously not only the technical, economic, ecological and abstract dimensions, but also the capacity of the city to produce subjectivity.

In order to think of the city as a producer of subjectivity, it is necessary to give priority to aesthetico-ethical components, even if we are acting in a continuum with every type of coercion (economic, political and social). To operate as fully as possible within the small margin left open for manoeuvring is the aesthetico-ethical responsibility of the architect-urbanist. For this very reason, it is important to consider the way in which psychoanalysis can alert us to the ethics involved in the economic, political, social and cultural determinations and limits of any urban articulation. In psychoanalytic terms, the 'projectional' act (Lacan 1996) implies an ethical position that, in general terms, can be summarised as doing what it is necessary to do, knowing that this duty is not a moral or straightforward order. It is a duty which permanently puts into play what is 'beyond demand', that is, the desire in the projectional act (Lacan 1986; 1996). It is not about trying to please any one as a form of seduction or harmony. Rather, it is about an architecture made not to please the client, but because it is necessary from an aesthetic or any other point of view. Through urban and social articulations, and, more generally, with the input of the multiple disciplines which involve the formalisation of urban space, the architect-urbanist must focus on the decisive bifurcations of the city in order to develop their design and its intentions. He or she must be capable of establishing the interrelationship between ethics (which involves principles), politics (which involves necessary complex actions for materialising principles) and aesthetics (which always implies a certain degree of defiance in order to introduce new alternatives). Interventions in the broken city must, therefore, be conceived as a strategy of singularisation, as the result of the crossing between individual creativity supported by multidisciplinary interaction and the multiple material and social coercions it must navigate.

The City of Flows and the City of Places: The Linkage of the Symbolic, the Imaginary and the Real

The magnitude of Latin American metropolises complicates the function of the city as a theatre of social relations: random, anonymous and cosmopolitan. The circuits of displacement create urban cartographies based on the criteria of mobility where each citizen creates their own mental map formed by the succession of fragmented landscapes whose conductive thread is the routine of travel. This obliges us to direct our attention toward the places and the ways in which social relations are produced in everyday life. The city constitutes a kind of landscape built of fragments, among which are the empty territories of urban amnesia. The search for 'units of environment' – or those places where social relations are produced in everyday life – attempts to offer aesthetico-cultural alternatives to both the bureaucratic impositions and the mercantile offer which is capable of reformulating the established social control imposed by official governmental plans and public politics.

The notion of 'smooth' and 'striated' space – terms borrowed from Deleuze and Guattari (1994) – can help us understand and represent the different types of space characterising Latin American cities. Smooth space is derived from individual itineraries that favour unpredictable relations, while striated space could be linked with static or less dynamic formations. These notions of space can be used to explain the difference between the formal and the informal city: in striated space (the formal city), the lines or journeys are subordinate to points of reference while in smooth space (the informal city) the points are subordinated to the journey's random displacement, which Deleuze and Guattari (1994) link to nomad space. In the large Latin American metropolis, we inhabit both the striated spaces of the formal city, where we live and through which we cross, and the smooth spaces of the informal city that, sometimes, act as limits and hardly accessible spaces.

To imagine, formalise and materialise the points of contact and the passages between both types of space entails connecting two types of society: the included and the excluded. Both smooth and striated, formal and informal are projecting spaces that concentrate a sufficient critical mass capable of working as attractors of urbanity, allowing and inducing a praxis of the urban as a type of sociability capable of radicalising and generalising democratic life, teaching us to coexist *in* difference.

Let us now discuss another aspect which stems from this discussion and refers to the complexities of this complex kind of urban praxis, that is, the need to articulate three dimensions of the social sphere: the symbolic with the imaginary and the real. At this point, I would like to propose that the *symbolic* makes what is specific to a culture: the meaningful marks and rules of engagement in each culture. Sometimes the symbolic is absent, which in turn generates the imaginary. Also, contrary to many critics – who argue that the imaginary is produced by daily life experience – I sustain that the *imaginary* is what produces the experience of daily life and, hence, it is always being reconfigured, always restructuring itself. It includes the rivalries, the feelings of identification or rejection, of non-identification or belonging. It might also include the ambiguity of both feelings: the sensation of belonging and rejection. The imaginary is what takes place as a result of the interaction between individual and collective life. *The real*, thus, can be defined as an amalgam between the symbolic and the imaginary: those objects and spaces that we construct through modifications of the existing environment; physical or otherwise.

It is precisely here, at the point of conflict between the symbolic, the imaginary and the real – or the conflict between meaning, perception and existence – that we need to attempt to introduce the objects which permit new connections to be established. For this reason, urban articulations respond to specific situations by proposing one or multiple alternative situations. Urban articulations seek to transform one situation into another , they do not attempt to transform reality but to commit it to what it could be. With a neverending present and a field of significances that is not realised, we, architect-urbanists, look at the world in suspended expectation for new senses to emerge. We attempt to interpret what the place 'wants to be' (to paraphrase Kahn's famous lecture on materiality) and 'read' the existing relations between events and objects. The project does not aim to confirm what already exists, but rather to 'make visible the invisible', to form a new possibility by means of the interaction between the symbolic, the imaginary and the real, helping to materialise what we wish but did not know. This is why the experience of a place is to do with much more than the physical dimensions it consists of. Place is not composed, but is an experience of the senses, of integral perceptions that do not disintegrate into information. Place is the space of interaction of significances and, hence, of movements, contextual flows and ebbs.

References

Benjamin, W. 2002. *The Arcades Project*. Cambridge, MA: Harvard University Press.
Deleuze, G. and F. Guattari. 1994. *Rizoma*. Mexico City: Ediciones Coyoacán.
Lacan, J. 1986. *Le Seminaire, livre VII: L'Ethique de la Psychanalyse, 1959–1960*. Paris: Seuil.
——— 1996. *Écrits*. Paris: Seuil.

Chapter 12

Public-City in Manifesto: The Formal City In-formed by Public Interest

Claudio Vekstein

Public Formal Excuse

This chapter exercises a formal structuring of rather conventional definitions and principles in a non-prescribed (informal), sometimes misaligned sequence. The construct could be seen as an abrupt manifestation of directives in order more promptly to arrive at the disciplinary knowledge necessary to outline an unpredictable, provocative, perhaps even at moments irresponsible, course of action. Because of this embedded formal–informal approach, and depending on the reader's academic position, some might feel slightly uncomfortable, sometimes disrupted, or even offended. While these apparently isolated or underarticulated formal propositions are informed by an undisciplined, perhaps inelegant, series of topical anchors and accelerated proliferations, what follows emerges with the shape of a sudden manifesto or a programme for an urgent course of action representing the position of the author and his committed fellows.[1] The illustrations demonstrate, without a necessarily direct correlation to the text, part of his work and specific expertise as a public architect and activist.

Terminology: Public-ness

Public. This term refers to the people, pertaining to the people, belonging to the people. The changing social body of desire, it must seek new channels and different combinations, reforming itself at every instance, in order to manifest itself.

Public rights. This term refers to the concept of the public having access to a universal status, regardless of their economic and political standing or their social and racial identity, in order to safeguard the individual against arbitrary uses of power by the government.

As a term, *public rights* also signifies a small subset of values that should be available for implementation by an individual or government. These rights commonly include the right to life, the right to an adequate standard of living, the right to self-determination, the right to education, the right to participation in cultural and political life regarding the well-being of individuals, freedom from mistreatment, freedom of religion, freedom of expression, freedom of movement, freedom of individuals and, finally, representation of the human interest in government.

Public interest. This term describes the common well-being of a society. It is central to the nature of government itself. While nearly everyone claims that aiding the common well-being or general welfare is positive, there is little, if any, consensus on what exactly constitutes the public interest.

There are different views on how many members of the public must benefit from an action before it can be declared to be in the public interest. At one extreme, an action has to benefit every single member of society in order to be truly in the public interest. At the other extreme, any action can be in the public interest if it benefits some members of the population as long as it does not harm the others. We are all a minority in some capacity; thus, safeguarding and promoting minority rights becomes an essential aspect of the public interest. But the public interest is often contrasted with private or individual interests, under the assumption that what is good for society may not be good for a given individual and vice versa.

Public space. This term refers to a place to which everyone has the right of access and from which no one is excluded or discriminated against on economic, social, political or racial grounds. It is a place intended to have democratic constraints and is provided by a depersonalised state authority. Activities and dependencies from the personal-private sphere emerge into the public sphere through public space; all elements of the private sphere have the features necessary to become publicly relevant. Public space is the primary spatial manifestation of public rights. Its existence is normally the realisation of public interest.

Figure 12.1 River Coast Park, Monument and Amphitheatre (1999–2001), Vicente López, Buenos Aires Province, Argentina. Designed by Claudio Vekstein (photographs Sergio Esmoris)

Activating the Public: Further Concepts

Public politics. This is a decision-making process dealing with issues that must involve more than one single individual since the issues concern and affect many individuals in a group; it is provoked by the sense of progress, well-being and liveability in the community. Common political issues include poverty, violence, justice, human rights, equality, crime and the environment. Public politics usually focus on the reconciliation of conflicting perspectives or interests. When the desire of politics is to activate the public, it is commonly pursued through public works.

Public works. This refers to activities, like an internal improvement, which result in some constructed object by which the people (represented by their government) improve its urban infrastructure in order to enhance public rights in support of the public interest. Examples of common internal improvements are: airports, canals, dams, dykes, pipelines, railroads, roads, tunnels, harbours. 'Public works' is a broader term, it can include things such as: mines, water purification and sewage treatment centres, schools, hospitals and recreation facilities. Public works require major political agreements, but do not necessarily require majority consensus.

Figure 12.2 Municipal Institute for the Rehabilitation of the Disabled (2001–2004), Vicente López, Buenos Aires Province, Argentina. Designed by Claudio Vekstein and Marta Tello (photograph by Sergio Esmoris)

Public Opinion and the Formal

Public opinion is the aggregate of individual attitudes held by the population. It developed as a concept through urbanisation along with the rise of 'the public', the moment when people's opinions became an important measure of political contention. However, the term public opinion implies that there are many publics, not just one. Each of these publics comes into being when an issue arises and ceases to exist when the issue is resolved. Public opinion polling cannot measure the public; the mass is a form of collective behaviour different from the public.

Thus, public opinion provides the required or expected mandate for the city to operate. In order to maintain the image of the political agenda, public opinion provides a sample reaction to the selected set of circumstances it is seen to address. The discrete set of circumstances that it chooses to frame acts as a module, and the sequencing of these modules contributes to the construction of the 'aura' of power.

In its attempt to provide the instructions and constructions deemed necessary to generate fullness, public opinion risks becoming cancerous and empty. This is due to its systematically regulatory and, therefore, repetitive nature. The principles of human nature, on the other hand, impose constantly shifting rules on this formal organism; passage, transition and inference are among the demands put on the artifice that is the city. These demands carve niches in the smooth, concrete aura of the formal organism and thereby create the necessary cracks in the polished, representational image of publicity to provide a balanced continuity between the abstract and the actual. In its attempt forcefully to create unity, it only creates the illusion of a need for unity. Public opinion is a desperate principle, a consequence.

Public Interest and the Informal

Starting off as the symbiotic tissue that informs the formal urban condition, public interest manifests itself, necessarily and actively, in the informal layers of the city structure. The formal cannot survive without the informal. Thus, in principle, public interests appear informally at all times in the interstices of the formal system, potentially providing the glue that unites the various parts of the city. In spite of appearing to attain complete autonomy, the informal rarely reaches this position because its role is to link together formal units and, consequently, it occupies a dependent position in the structure of the formal system.

The informal emerges in order to fill a gap caused by the inadequacies of the formal system: its inability to meet the meticulous particularities of public interest. The needs created in the formal are fulfilled in the informal system as a basic negative dialectic movement that allows recuperation of alienated properties, helping to smooth the functioning of the whole. While the informal advocates solutions to unmet needs and alienated conditions, it paradoxically allows participants the opportunity to continue to function in the formal system by responding to the genuine desire of individuals to band together to accomplish their goals without the prohibitions of formal restrictions.

Invisible social needs and demands rise to the surface as an informal reaction to the abstract machinery and institutions of the formal city. But the informal tends to become trapped by the formal because of its reactive nature. Emulating the procedure of an abstract machine, the informal surrounds itself with so much data and accumulated information that it can no longer be disputed but must instead simply be accepted and 'formalised'; eventually, it emerges as a new abstract machine. Thus the informal can be seen as the paradoxical formalisation of the abstract machine.

By supporting the allegedly real world, the formal in itself is apologetic for it reproduces the strategy of the informal by reinforcing its consistencies. But, the informal is not so different insofar as it is a celebration of the asymmetrical consistencies that it is capable of providing. The informal alone is, in this respect, a sort of celebration of the formal in its dysfunctional mode. It is not effective; its contradictory discourse in defence, or in negative praise of mere chaos, simply neglects to support the argument that it is trying to deny.

Public Sentencing of the City

With the public sentencing of the formal–informal city, the uninspired, unnoticed, empty layers of information passing on top of one another emerge not as an absurd but as a symbiotic structure of action from which to render the drama of public space. Sentencing activates public-ness up to the birth of delirium, fusing differences into a situational, structural, phenomenal artifice. These artifices refract rays of immanence back into its soul; more specifically, back into its people. Revealing the invisible, hidden, enigmatically complex dimension of the public, it results in an intensive form of expression of collective human affect and public demonstration.

By sentencing, the art of public demonstration – that symbiotic act of making real the positions of the affected through the activation of the cityscape – gains a musculo-skeletal body which is embedded in the city streets. Mapping itself sinuously onto the public organ, the demonstration follows a balancing path, interlacing the most exalted states of being with menacing feelings; floors, walls, plazas and roofs frame skies heavy with constellations. These demonstrations are essential elements of the charged public atmosphere; standing to empower the voiceless, struggling to liberate the unseen, constantly seeking the next unknown balance, demonstrating the remarkable human spirit for all to witness.

Public Display of Affection

Public display of affection is an informal act or manifestation of physically demonstrated affection for another person (or group of people) in the clear view of others within a formal setting or in a public space. It is an honest communication of intention. Frequently, this sudden, unexpected behaviour is considered to be in bad taste or to be an unacceptable act, an act of public nuisance, and in some places it is even considered criminal.

The familiar (*heimlich*), friendly, comfortable, expected fabric of the common imagination is interrupted by that which should be kept secret, that which is considered an act of deceit, the concealed, the secretive ... suddenly changing the familiar into the unfamiliar (*unheimlich*), the unaccustomed, the weird, that which should have been kept secret but has been revealed, becoming the uncanny. Public displays of affection violate established customs and norms by making certain what is more comfortable when left uncertain; in other words, by making clear what might otherwise be left ambiguous. These acts of humanity are revolving migrations of the unspoken rules of society.

Individual public displays of affection, even though casual, are considered to be impolite, an exaggerated form of personal expression in disregard of public opinion. But when turned into public manifestations, into demonstrations, they tend to be accepted as a massive form of political expression, social content or collective satisfaction, transformation and celebration: these are the potential acts of public architecture.

Figure 12.3 Emergency Room for Municipal Hospital (2004/5), Vicente López, Buenos Aires Province, Argentina. Designed by Claudio Vekstein and Marta Tello (photograph by Sergio Esmoris)

The Public-City

Public Healing through Contagion in the City

The city gets healthy by becoming contagious. The autonomy of the infection slowly emerges, forming a new kind of organism that has its own transformative potential. When coming in contact with an infected carrier, new areas of the city and its public catch this contagion. Reformulating the physical/metaphysical engagement and nature of the public – as a germ that could (be)come materially in a building or in the city – leads to a fundamental definition of 'public-ness' as a whole possible territory for informing/infecting architecture. These complex territories of public-ness are formed/informed, then, by a multiplicity of forces that are always embedded and refractive of the dynamic conflict of different localised interests in the urban public arena. This is the abstract machine when in collision with the impulsive realities inherent in the process of realising public architecture.

Designing the architecture of public works implies serious challenges both in developed and developing countries, as it does in the case of Latin America. But specialists in the latter case must pursue aspirations in excess of or in addition to purely functional endeavours: design should not only be affordable and sustainable in terms of durability and economic and physical means, but should also become an instrument for transforming individuals into a strong social community. Addressing the individual's current needs, design should provide a sustainable and meaningful sense of healing.

Physical and social healing starts with the public having access to its rights to a universal status, regardless of economic, social, political or racial categories. People are healed not only by technology but also by individuals – socio-political leaders, professionals and so on – who are, in turn, members of larger groups. In this way, the public-city extends, not through sympathy but through generosity, a sense of belonging, of mutual placed-ness. The edifices become public, part of the people; they pertain to the people, belong to the people and reactivate local idiosyncrasies and the relevance of the social bond, thus cultivating civic citizenship.

Public Acts of Architecture or Public-City Works

From a building to an infrastructural project or a city fragment, public acts of architecture provide real, comprehensive constructs to help localised urban constrictions meet occasional social emergences (public interest).

Public acts of architecture offer an embedded (reactive), but at the same time, expansive (active, autonomous) fertile architectural and urban realisation, a rich fabric of complex textures able to reconcile and surpass the simplistic formal–informal contradiction. When architecture operates not only in materially confined ways, but also in metaphysical, psychological, socio-cultural and political dimensions at the same time, it inexorably immerses itself in the real grounds of the urban complex while trying to become a powerful tool for the public enhancement of the city.

Public architecture operates also as an active messenger, migrating context and content from place to place. While we as individuals carry (social, cultural, personal) messages, our architecture, even though always trying to be local, carries messages in the form of silent but massive migrations of distant social or geographical landscapes that will disappear and reappear intermittently in the work, constantly flashing from one spot to another. Mapping and scratching out these migratory territories of public-ness at all possible scales is what turns urban constrictions into public releases for the city.

The public-city will thus perform and demonstrate in its urban design the meaningful essence of healed public spaces by persistently and precisely articulating the formal (institutional) with the informal and intense public life of the people. Social invisibilities, local lore, that which has been (nearly) forgotten, that which has managed to survive, the marginalised, the alienated, the denied, those not officially recognised, or those confronted by homogenisation as a condition for their integration, can appear in the design as particular and patient counterpoints to the abstract mechanisms of the city, uniting members in a dynamic, common, renewed health. Public architecture as 'healing works', in this respect, is a sort of contagious cure that reunites the community. The public-city is one that initiates the transformation of sick individuals into a stronger, healed community through a chain reaction, an epidemic that spreads the public healing process throughout the whole of the city. Each member heals another one, reverting and thus transforming social disappearances into a manifestation of all the people, the public. As a construction and built demonstration of dignity towards inclusion, the architecture of public works becomes a social celebration, a public display of affection from the city to the people for collective engagement, communal conquest and mutual realisation.

The intensification of urban relationships in the form of constructing fragmentary figural constellations makes its dance of repair in an almost digital stimulation: the formal–informal city, and its associated socio-cultural uncanny, are immutably transfigured into public illumination.

Emerging suddenly from its interior like a photographic image in a dark room, a calm reappearance of the ordinary turned extraordinary, public architecture acting for social transformation operates as an enigmatic, open manifestation of the 'Hand of God' right before everyone's eyes.

Figure 12.4 Emergency Room for Municipal Hospital (2004/5), Vicente López, Buenos Aires Province, Argentina. Designed by Claudio Vekstein and Marta Tello (photograph by Sergio Esmoris)

Notes

1. This chapter was written with contributions from Colin Billings and draws on a number of contemporary thinkers whose work has influenced our scholarly work, as well as our professional practice. Although the works are not cited directly in the main text, their contribution is acknowledged in the list of references.

References

Adorno, T. 1991. *Culture Industry*. New York: Routledge.
Derrida, J. 1976. *Of Grammatology*. Baltimore, MD: Johns Hopkins University Press.
Deleuze, G. 2001. *Pure Immanence: Essays on A Life*. New York: Zone Books.

Habermas, J. 1989. *The Structural Transformation of the Public Sphere*. Cambridge, MA: MIT Press.

Lacan, J. 1981. *The Four Fundamental Concepts of Psychoanalysis*. New York: Norton.

Laguerre, M. 1994. *The Informal City*. Basingstoke: Palgrave Macmillan.

Zepke S. 2004. *Art as Abstract Machine: Ontology and Aesthetics in Deleuze and Guattari*. New York: Routledge.

Notes on Contributors

Lea Knudsen Allen received her Ph.D. from the Department of English Literatures and Cultures at Brown University. She has worked extensively on issues to do with travel narratives, transmigration and cultural representation which are also the topic of her thesis, 'Cosmopolite Subjectivities and the Mediterranean in Early Modern England'. In her dissertation Lea argues that representations of the Mediterranean provided early modern English poets, playwrights and travellers with the means to imagine a metropolitan identity. In addition, Lea Allen has an interest in architecture and spatial representation, and has collaborated in various publications about architecture in the Americas.

Jose (Zeca) Brandão graduated from the Faculdade Integradas Bennett (Rio de Janeiro, Brazil) in 1979 and is a practising architect. In 1985 he undertook postgraduate studies in urban development planning at Universidade Catolica de Pernambuco (Recife, Brazil). He later followed this with an M.A. in Housing Studies and Energy and Environmental Technology from the Architectural Association (London), from where he also received his Ph.D. in Urban Design in 2004. Zeca is currently associate professor of architectural and urban design at the Universidade Federal de Pernambuco where he is a member of the Urban Development Graduate Programme and Director of the Architectural and Urban Design Laboratory (LADU). In addition, Zeca is currently the Executive Secretary of Urban Design for the city of Pernambuco. Zeca's professional practice has won awards at the second and third Bienal Internacional de Arquitetura do Brasil in 1994 and 1996, and at the tenth Bienal Internacional de Arquitetura de Quito (Equador) as well as at the second Premio Jovens Arquitetos do Brasil (São Paulo, Brasil).

Alfredo Brillembourg was born in New York in 1961. He received a
B.A. in Architecture in 1984 and an M.Sc. in Architectural Design in 1986
from Columbia University. In 1992 he received a second architecture
degree from the Central University of Venezuela and began his
independent practice in architecture. In 1993 he founded U-TT in Caracas,
Venezuela. Since 1994 he has been a member of the Venezuelan
Architects and Engineers Association and has been a guest professor at the
University José Maria Vargas, the University Simon Bolívar and the
Central University of Venezuela. As principal design partner at U-TT, he
has overseen the design and construction of a wide variety of building
types, including: master plans, commercial offices, corporate
headquarters, hotels, department stores, shopping centers, higher
educational facilities, community centres, public plazas, memorials and
residences. Since 2000, he has been a regular guest at studio juries in the
Graduate School of Architecture and Planning, Columbia University and
the Cooper Union School for the Advancement of Science and Art. He has
given papers on architecture at conferences in both Europe and America.

Jorge Fiori is a sociologist and urban planner. He teaches in the
Development Planning Unit, University College London, where he is a
senior lecturer, and at the Architectural Association Graduate School,
where he is Chair of the Graduate Management Committee and Director
of the Housing and Urbanism Graduate Programme. He has been a
visiting lecturer at several Latin American and European universities. In
addition to his academic work, he is consultant to various international
urban development agencies on urban planning and housing policy. His
research and publications focus mainly on issues of housing and urban
development policy. Currently, he is researching and working on the
subject of spatial strategies and urban social policy, with particular
reference to the role of urbanism and design in slum upgrading and
poverty reduction in the cities of the developing world.

Margarita Greene is a qualified architect (1973); she holds an M.A. in
Sociology (1988) from the Pontificia Universidad Católica de Chile
(1973) and a Ph.D. (2002) from University College London. She started
her professional work as an architect in Leeds, England, and had a
professional practice until the end of the 1980s. From 1988 to 1989 she
was a research fellow at the Unit of Advanced Architectural Studies,
University College London; she was also consultant to the Ministry of
Housing and Urbanism (MINVU) in Santiago de Chile (1990–1991) and
since 1992 she has taught full time at the School of Architecture,

Pontificia Universidad de Chile (PUC), where she leads multidisciplinary research teams. She has been consultant to the Chilean Government (Ministry of the Interior, Ministry of Housing and Urbanism, and the Treasury), and to several international agencies (GTZ, SIDA, ILPES, ECLA, PNUD, WB, IDB, LILP) and non-governmental organisations in Chile and Latin America (Argentina, Bolivia, Colombia, Uruguay). At present she is Director of Research and Graduate Studies at the Faculty of Architecture, Design and Urban Studies, PUC.

Felipe Hernández is an architect and lecturer in Architectural Design, History and Theory at the University of Cambridge. He has an M.A. in Architecture and Critical Theory and received his Ph.D. from the University of Nottingham. He has taught at the Bartlett School of Architecture (University College London), and at the universities of Liverpool, Nottingham, Sheffield and East London as well as in the School of Art and Design at Nottingham Trent University. He has published extensively on contemporary Latin American cities focusing on the multiplicity of architectural practices that operate simultaneously in the constant reshaping of the continent's cities. He is the author of *Beyond Modernist Masters: Contemporary Architecture in Latin America* (Birkhäuser 2010) and *Bhabha for Architects* (Routledge 2009). He is also co-editor of *Transculturation: Cities, Space and Architecture in Latin America* (2005).

Jorge Mário Jáuregui is an architect-urbanist based in Rio de Janeiro, working with public and private clients on projects of public interest, in both the formal and informal areas of the city. As a consequence, his professional practice has developed critical-theoretical thinking in relation to contemporary architectural and urban issues through regular publications in specialised media. He is also coordinator of the Architectural and Urban Studies Centre of Rio de Janeiro, associate researcher with the Laboratory of Morphology, Buenos Aires (SICyT-FADU/UBA), and a member of the 'Art and Psychoanalysis Cartel' of the psychoanalytic institution Letra Freudiana in Rio.

Jorge Mário Jáuregui was recipient of the Veronica Rudge Green Prize in Urban Design, from Harvard University, Graduate School of Design in 2000 and the Grande Prêmio of the Bienal de São Paulo in 1999. His current projects focus on the expandable house; the question of transdisciplinarity; the connection between strategic planning, urban genetic, sustainable development and prospects; and the tension between the 'formal' and the 'informal' in the broken city.

Paola Jirón is an academic at the Institute of Housing, Faculty of Architecture and Urbanism at the University of Chile, where she was director from 2000 to 2003. She has carried out extensive research, teaching and consultancy work in the areas of housing policy, urban quality of life, mobility, residential satisfaction and gender in human settlements. She is currently Vice-Chair of the Advisory Board of the Human Settlement Network organised by the United Nations Habitat Programme. She holds a bachelors degree from Concordia University, Canada and an M.Sc. from University College London. She recently completed a Ph.D. in Urban and Regional Planning at the London School of Economics and Political Science.

Peter Kellett is senior lecturer in the School of Architecture, Planning and Landscape at the University of Newcastle upon Tyne. He is a qualified architect with an M.A. in Social Anthropology and has worked and researched in Latin America for many years. His Ph.D. is an ethnographic study of informal housing processes in northern Colombia, and his research continues to focus largely on housing, particularly on understanding how disadvantaged households create, use and value dwelling environments in cities in the developing world. He has lectured and published widely, and in addition to his work in Latin America he has worked on large comparative research projects in Asia and Africa, as well as in the U.K.

Hubert Klumpner graduated from the University of Applied Arts in Vienna, in the master class of Professor Hans Hollein. He received an M.Sc. in Architecture and Urban Design from Columbia University. Since 1997, he has been a member of the German Chamber of Architects. He has lectured at institutions in Europe and North and South America, has taught at the Academy of Applied Arts in Vienna, the International Summer Academy in Salzburg, and has been a visiting professor at the Central University of Venezuela. Since 2001 he has been the urbanism consultant of the International Program for Social and Cultural Development in Latin America (OAE and UNESCO). In 1998 he joined Alfredo Brillembourg as Director of U-TT in Caracas.

Fernando Luiz Lara is an assistant professor at the Taubman College of Architecture and Urban Planning, University of Michigan. A native of Brazil, Lara has taught at both the Catholic University and the Federal University of Minas Gerais, as well as at Lawrence Technological University, before joining Michigan in 2004. With many articles in academic and professional journals in Brazil and the U.S., Lara has lectured on Brazilian architecture in Belgium, Canada, Guatemala, India, Mexico and Korea in the last couple of years. Professor Lara's teaching and research interests are in the areas of housing, modernist spatiality and architectural design methods. His current research includes a comparative analysis of contemporary housing solutions in Brazil, Russia, Korea and India, with emphasis on the permanence of modernist spatiality. He currently teaches courses in housing design (formal and informal), peripheral modernisms, and leads a design studio. Fernando Lara is also a registered architect practising in Brazil, where he regularly enters competitions. In 2005 his partnership with Humberto Hermeto won first prize in the competition for the headquarters of the State Orchestra of Minas Gerais, Brazil.

Zeuler R.M.A. Lima is an architect and assistant professor at the School of Architecture at Washington University. He also taught at the University of São Paulo (1988–1996) and at the University of Michigan (1997–1999). He received his Ph.D. from the University of São Paulo with a dissertation titled 'City as Spectacle' and was the 2001/2002 Mellon Postdoctoral Fellow at the Heyman Center for the Humanities at Columbia University, co-teaching graduate seminars with Professor Andreas Huyssen. Dr Lima has written extensively on architecture and urbanism in the second part of the twentieth century and is currently preparing a book on modernism and the work of the Italian-Brazilian architect Lina Bo Bardi. He is the recipient of the 2007 International Bruno Zevi Prize for architectural criticism.

Rahul Mehrotra is an Indian architect and urban designer trained at the School of Architecture, Ahmedabad and the Graduate School of Design at Harvard University. He has been in private practice since 1990, and works on architecture, urban design and conservation projects. He has built extensively in India, and besides several single family houses, his projects include the Laxmi Machine Works Corporate Office in Coimbatore, an Extension to the Prince of Wales Museum in Bombay, an Institute for Rural development in Tulzapur, the restoration of the Chowmahalla Palace in Hyderabad. He also developed (with the Taj Mahal Conservation Collaborative) the master plan for the Taj Mahal and its surroundings. From 1994 to 2006, Professor Mehrotra was the Executive Director of the Urban Design Research Institute, which promotes awareness and research on the city of Bombay, and he is now a Trustee of the Institute. He has written several books on Bombay, including *Bombay, the Cities Within*, and has lectured extensively on urban design, conservation and architecture in India. He also serves on several government committees that are responsible for historic preservation and the conservation as well as creation of public spaces in Bombay. He currently teaches at the Massachusetts Institute of Technology, where he is an associate professor.

Vera M. Pallamin is an associate professor at the Faculdade de Arquitetura e Urbanismo of the University of São Paulo, and holds degrees in architecture and philosophy. She has extensively researched twentieth-century aesthetics and architectural theory, and received her Ph.D. from the University of São Paulo on the work of philosopher Maurice Merleau-Ponty. She has undertaken post-doctoral research on art and the public sphere at the University of California, Berkeley and the Istituto Politecnico di Firenze, Italy. She was editor-in-chief of the graduate *Journal Faculdade de Arquitetura e Urbanismo* at the University of São Paulo (2001–2004) and has organised several colloquia and conferences on urban space, culture and the public sphere. She has written extensively on public art, politics and aesthetics and has also undertaken public art works in São Paulo.

Ronaldo Ramírez graduated in 1962 from the Faculty of Architecture and Urban Studies, Universidad de Chile, were he taught Urban Sociology until 1974. He moved to England in that year to work at the Development Planning Unit (DPU) of University College London, where he remained as a senior academic until 2006. His teaching, research and consultancy work has mainly been focused on theories and practices of urban social issues in the Third World, particularly development processes, social housing and urban poverty. His research includes poor human settlements in Chile, Venezuela, Brazil and Cuba, and he has been consultant on similar topics for UN-Habitat (e.g., Senegal, Ivory Coast, India), the World Bank (Indonesia), USAID (Jordan), Unicef (Egypt), UNDP (Costa Rica), and ODA (e.g., India, Sri Lanka, Mexico), and others.

He designed and directed the master courses in Urban Development Planning and in International Housing Studies offered by DPU, and has given lectures and seminars in other universities in the U.K. (Cardiff, LSE, AA), Europe (Venice, Madrid, Darmstadt) and the Americas (Berkeley, Argentina). Recent publications include: 'State and Civil Society in the *Barrios* of Havana, Cuba' (*Environment and Urbanization*, 2005); 'Urban Poverty Reduction and Urban Security

Consolidation: A New Paradigm at Work?' (UN-Habitat UMP Paper Series, no.20, 2002); and *'Favela Bairro* and a New Generation of Housing Programmes for the Urban Poor' (with L.Riley and J.Fiori, *Geoforum* 32, 2001).

Eduardo Rojas is principal specialist in Urban Development with the Inter-American Development Bank (IDB). His current responsibilities comprise policy and strategy formulation and best-practice research and dissemination in the urban sector. His main areas of work include urban heritage preservation, integrated urban development and housing sector reform. He also serves as team leader and advisor of project teams in the assessment of innovative urban development, municipal finance, housing, and urban heritage preservation loans. Prior to joining IDB, he worked with the Regional Development Department of the Organization of American States and as Assistant Professor of Urban Planning for the Masters Degree Program in Urban Studies at the Catholic University of Chile.

He is the author of several books, a regular contributor to technical journals, and guest lecturer at European and American universities. He holds a degree in architecture from the Catholic University of Chile, an M.Phil. in Urban and Regional Planning from the University of Edinburgh, an M.B.A. with a concentration on finance from Johns Hopkins University, and a Diploma in Environmental Management from the Centre d'Etudes Industrielles in Geneva, Switzerland.

Roberto Segre was born in Italy in 1934 and left the country for Argentina in 1939. After graduating in architecture from the University of Buenos Aires in 1960, he was invited in 1963 by the revolutionary government of Cuba to teach at the School of Architecture in Havana, where he became Emeritus Professor (2006). In 1994 he was invited to teach for the postgraduate Course in Urbanism at the School of Architecture and Urbanism of the Federal University of Rio de Janeiro, Brazil, where he still works. In 2007, he became Coordinator of DOCOMOMO-Rio. He obtained a Doctorate in Sciences of Art in Cuba, and another in Urban and Regional Planning in Brazil. He has published more than 35 books and 400 essays on Latin American and Caribbean Architecture. With a Guggenheim Fellowship (1985), he carried out research in the Antillean Islands, and in 2003 published the book *Arquitectura Antillana del Siglo XX* (Bogotá, Havana) which won first prize at the fourth Iberoamerican Biennale of Architecture in Lima, Peru.

Annalisa Spencer received her degree in architecture (M.Arch.) from the School of Architecture at the University of Liverpool in 2006. Her dissertation, 'The Informal Architecture of Brasilia: An Analysis of the Contemporary Urban Role of the Satellite Settlements', received the school's award for the best piece of theoretical work and was nominated for the RIBA President's Medals Awards. She is currently completing her RIBA Part 3 in order to register as an architect in the United Kingdom.

Claudio Vekstein is Professor in the Masters of Architecture Program, Arizona State University, U.S.A. He also runs a practice specialising in the architecture of public works, both in Buenos Aires, Argentina (since 1996) and in Phoenix, Arizona (since 2002). His built works include the Extension for the Fine Arts School and Museum, the Monument to Amancio Williams, River Coast Park and Amphitheater, Institute for the Disabled, Vicente López Emergency Room, all of them in Buenos Aires; other projects are underway in Arizona. His work has been published and exhibited in Argentina, Brazil, Mexico, U.S.A., Spain, Germany, Holland and Austria, and several projects have received awards from the Buenos Aires Architects Association (2001), the National Fine Arts Museum, Buenos Aires (2002) and the Association of Collegiate Schools of Architecture, U.S.A. (2003). Born in 1965 in Argentina, he studied at the School of Architecture and Urbanism, Buenos Aires University, became a disciple of South American master architect Amancio Williams and completed a masters degree at the Staedelschule Frankfurt Art Academy under Professors Enric Miralles and Peter Cook.

Index

Lightning Source UK Ltd.
Milton Keynes UK
UKOW051427120413

209133UK00003B/42/P